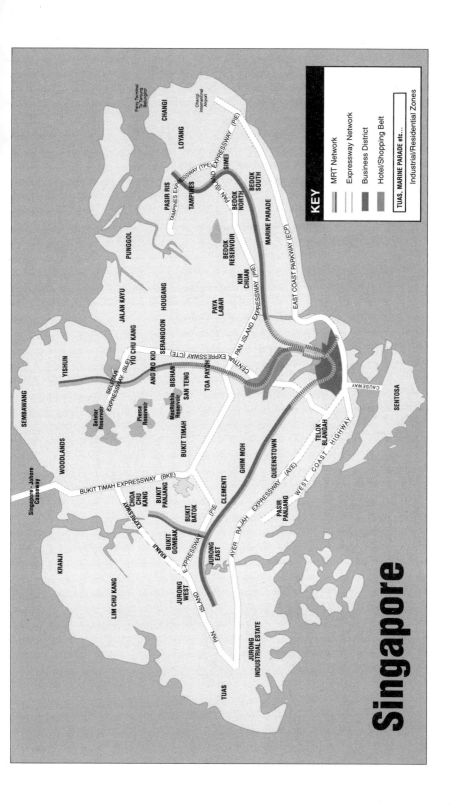

Singapore

SINGAPORE: THE GLOBAL CITY-STATE

Also by Geoffrey Murray

THE RAMPANT DRAGON
SYNERGY: JAPANESE COMPANIES IN BRITAIN
CHINA: THE LAST GREAT MARKET

Singapore

The Global City-State

Geoffrey Murray & Audrey Perera

ST. MARTIN'S PRESS

SINGAPORE: The Global City-State

St. Martin's Press, Scholarly and Reference Division, 175 Fifth Avenue, New York, N.Y. 10010

First published in the United States of America in 1996

Printed in England

ISBN: 0–312–12958–0 (Cloth)
ISBN: 0–312–12959–9 (Paper)

Library of Congress Cataloging-in-Publication Data

Murray, Geoffrey, 1942–
    Singapore : the global city-state / by Geoffrey Murray and Audrey Perera.
        p.   cm. - - (Pacific rim business series)
        Includes bibliographical references and index.
        ISBN 0–312–12958–0 (cloth). - - ISBN 0–312–12959–9 (pbk.)
      1. Singapore- -Commerce. 2. Investments, Foreign- -Singapore.
   3. Singapore- -Economic conditions. I. Perera, Audrey. II. Title.
III. Series.
HF3800.67.M87 1996
658'.049'095957- -dc20   95–31701
                                                           CIP

CONTENTS

NOTE: All $ references should be taken as the Singapore dollar unless otherwise specified

Foreword

SINGAPORE has a special place in my life. It was on the lawn at Raffles Hotel – eating dinner under the stars in April 1966 en route from Australia as a foreign correspondent to cover the developing war in South Vietnam – that I began a love affair with Asia which continues to this day. The journey then proceeded via India, Iran and Japan (with numerous side trips to South Korea, the Philippines and Taiwan), before finally in 1984 I was able to return to spend five years in the republic working first as a journalist and then as a journalism teacher. Five years on again, I was able to return to conduct research on this book with my co-author Audrey Perera.

Not unexpectedly, the thirty-year gap has witnessed enormous change. Beach Road fronting Raffles no longer lives up to its name as land reclamation has clawed a few more acres of precious land from the sea. Raffles itself has undergone renovation, 'refurbished' in marble for Japanese tourists, and in the process losing that special ambience redolent of a more genteel era which captured the affection of many international travellers over the years. But at least the Tiffin Room still serves an outstanding curry! Bugis Street, the seedy haunt of gorgeously-dressed transvestites which had fallen on hard times, has reopened but as a pale imitation, with none of the old rakish garishness that made it a tourist must.

One could easily go on listing the physical transformation that Singapore has undergone – and argue the merits of whether the disappearance, or artificial preservation, of so many old familiar landmarks in colourful areas like Chinatown and Little India is for better or for worse. The bumboats that crowded the Singapore River, for example, are gone, and one can breathe easier as a result. The functionally unglamorous riverside warehouses, once crammed with rubber, spices and other commodities from the region, have also gone, replaced by restaurants offering a culinary tour of the world and glittering fashion boutiques that have brought an exciting new vibrancy to a decaying area. The old entrepot port is now the world's second busiest container transhipment centre, with forklift trucks replacing human muscle, while the skyline of the adjacent central business and financial district is a mini version of Manhattan with only a few overshadowed remnants of the colonial era.

The inhabitants of decaying inner-city slums were long ago moved out to suburban Housing Development Board (HDB) estates – endless state-provided, functional apartment blocks distinguished from one another by little more than a number. From there, many of them, or at least their upwardly-mobile children, have now moved on to the privately-built, Mediterranean-style condominiums with exotic names, from which, they emerge, mobile telephone always to hand, to take their Japanese or German luxury car into town to browse in the chandelier-lit retail palaces of Orchard Road.

Attitudes have changed. Manual jobs that would have been grabbed with relief and even delight by the coolie immigrant generation are now looked on with disdain by anyone with an education; today, such jobs have to be filled by unskilled and semi-skilled labour imported from developing countries of the surrounding region.

Amidst all this, the one thing that has not changed is the Singaporean determination to survive, inherited from those poor immigrants who flocked to the newly-established British colony in the nineteenth century and sweated to make a little money for a better life.

When Singapore in the mid-1960s was suddenly divorced from neighbouring Malaysia and forced to fend for itself, there were more than a few pundits then who did not give the puny infant much chance of survival. Yet 30 years on, the supposed 'basket case' has matured into one of the strongest economies in the world, with financial and political clout far beyond what is essentially nothing more than a medium-sized city.

This book sets out to examine how Singapore was able to achieve this so-called 'economic miracle'. (Although a much overused phrase it actually has some meaning in this case.) It will chart the tiny island's development over the past 30 years, surviving several crises along the way and emerging stronger from each. The key elements that have enabled Singapore to survive – strong government, an emphasis on educational excellence and imaginative and pragmatic policies to attract and keep foreign investment, for example – will be examined, before moving on to look at where this nation of only three million or so people stands today, and its prospects for the future.

The sub-title 'The Global City-State' reflects Singapore's ambitions. It has no resources other than the hard work and brains of its citizens, and the farsighted vision of its political leaders. It has a limited amount of labour and even more limited land. Singapore's economic well-being is predicated on its ability to stay one step ahead of the competition and reach out to create a vast hinterland beyond its borders in which its entrepreneurs, with government assistance, can operate and flourish.

The first stage of this was the creation of the 'Growth Triangle', involving cooperation with its neighbours Indonesia and Malaysia, with Singapore providing the support facilities – administration, banking, research and development etc. – for manufacturing operations moved out of an overcrowded island to nearby areas able to offer cheap labour and land. This concept is explained and analyzed in Chapter Three.

But even as the Growth Triangle is still at a relative formative stage, Singapore has raised its sights to much more ambitious goals. Now, the emphasis is on the concept of 'Singapore Inc.' a partnership between government and the private sector to forge trade and investment links with countries with which there are important ethnic links, such as China and India, as well as some of the emerging economies of Southeast Asia such as Myanmar and Vietnam.

But the new regionalization policy does not stop there. Singapore's leaders are thinking globally. Taking advantage of a geographically advantageous position that first attracted its founder Stamford Raffles, Singapore sees itself playing a role on the global stage as a 'business broker' through a partnership between local companies and those of the developed world, including the giant multinational corporations, to invest in those neighbouring countries already referred to.

The men who are developing this new policy are very matter-of-fact. Yes, maybe in a few years, these same companies and countries will decide they do not need a broker and can deal direct. Well, never mind, Singapore will have had a few good years out of the idea, and then it will have to think of something new – just as it has done so many times in the past.

How will it work? Why Singapore? And what opportunities will it open up for Western companies in Asia? Chapter Four examines this question and attempts to come to some tentative conclusions – inevitably tentative because the concept is still so new.

Singapore: The Global City-State, however, is also intended as a practical primer for doing business in, and with Singapore. Subsequent chapters analyze first the country's emerging industrial profile, and then concentrate on two of the most important high-tech growth areas – electronics and information technology.

Information is provided on the regulations covering the establishment of businesses in Singapore – and Indonesia and Malaysia, in regard to their involvement in the Growth Triangle – the taxation systems, and the various incentives offered to foreign businesses to invest and the relevant labour laws of the three countries. Finally, there is a brief introduction to living in Singapore from a foreigner's point of view, as well as a look inside the mind of the average Singaporean.

Each chapter begins with a list of key points and subjects are then dealt with under separate sub-headings. This has been done to enable the business reader to dip in and out of the book if so desired, using it as a handy reference on specific subjects as required.

The discerning reader might note that while I conducted a number of interviews during my research in Singapore, none of these was with senior government officials. Interviews were certainly sought with several of the key players, but all declined for the same reason – that this could be seen as an endorsement for this book. As a result, I have had to rely on public speeches and other published material for an insight into the thinking of the Singapore Government.

Singapore: The Global City-State is the second in a Pacific Rim business series which was launched in 1994 with the appearance of *China: The Last Great Market* published by China Library. The purpose of the series is to examine the key economies of the region and the business opportunities that they offer the international businessman, as well as providing essential background information for the student concerned with regional politics and economics. The next volume in the series will cover Vietnam, and, under the existing plan, others are scheduled to follow on Indonesia, Malaysia and Taiwan.

Inevitably – and particularly in the case of Singapore – there will be some overlap, because of the growing interdependence of the various countries involved. Together, it is envisaged the series will provide a detailed look at an area that is expected to be a vital engine of growth for the global economy in the opening years of the twenty-first century. And if there is one country in Asia that epitomizes this drive it must surely be Singapore.

GEOFFREY MURRAY
Series Consulting Editor
June 1995

1 Singapore – the business climate of the 1990s

KEY POINTS

- Turning vulnerability into virtue
- Why Singapore prospered
- Efforts to stay competitive
- What can go wrong and why
- The 'can do' attitude of the Economic Development Board
- Place in the top 10 of 'rich' nations
- Rapid growth in foreign investment
- Priority objectives for the mid-1990s and beyond
- Concept of Singapore Unlimited

GOVERNMENT LEADS

SINGAPORE'S STORY as an independent nation is one of continuous effort to carve out a secure niche for a tiny, highly vulnerable country in a rapidly changing and very competitive world. Because of its size – a drive from coast to coast takes only half an hour in the right traffic conditions – and small population – at just over three million no bigger than a medium-sized city in many countries – Singapore is always exposed to changes in the global economy.

Yet it is a fact that this small island today has a higher standard of living than Britain. It is not the first former colony to show a clean pair of economic heels to the motherland – the United States achieved that a long time ago – but it should be the one that perhaps gives most pause for thought.

Singapore has been able to turn its supposed limitations into a strength through an acquired ability to change pace and adapt quickly to changing circumstances, both nationally and internationally. The political and economic agenda has been very clearly articulated over the years by the PAP [People's Action Party] Government, which no longer has to spend a great deal of time trying to win a consensus in favour of a switch in direction.

The government has a considerable stake in the economy. Whereas in most countries, the State-owned sector is ailing, most of the government-led companies in Singapore have prospered under the leadership of a pool of talented men who combine business and political acumen, able to move from running a ministry to running a large commercial enterprise and back again with consummate ease.

The government has made, and continues to make, efforts to lessen its business involvement through privitization. Nevertheless, the new economic stratagems – such as the regionalization drive to be discussed later – require a continued strong government presence to create the right environment for investment and show the way through the creation of consortia that bring together the public and private sectors. Many governments have sought to control the direction of national economic development, with varying levels of success. But, it is hoped to demonstrate in this book that no country has been able to do this as imaginatively and successfully as Singapore.

Yet, nothing can be taken for granted. '[D]espite Singapore's achievements, there is a heavy sense of insecurity, bordering on paranoia. Government officials say that the country, although it is wealthy, is economically fragile. It is vulnerable. It needs protecting at all times. Singaporeans are constantly warned of the dangers of complacency, of becoming flabby, of losing their competitive edge. The government says there can be no rest if Singapore is to achieve its goal of joining the "premier league" of nations.[1]

'We are doing well, but like a sports champion, our position is never secure,' Deputy Prime Minister Lee Hsien Loong told a group of students in early 1995. 'After winning one tournament, the champion must immediately start training for the next one. He stays on top only so long as he fights to maintain this leading position. Likewise Singapore. . .we must always stay ahead. We have become so used to 25 years of apparently effortless success that we may find it difficult to imagine that [it is possible to fall behind]. But in fact it can happen easily. External factors totally beyond our control may overwhelm us, despite all that we do. A global economic crisis may cause the world trading system to break down into protectionist blocs, and deprive us of export markets, without which our industries cannot survive.'[2]

Much of the effort to stay ahead is channelled through the Economic Development Board, whose chairman, Philip Yeo sums up its role as always being 'entrepreneurial, lean and agile. We must move fast [harnessing] the energy of our best and brightest people.' The most important attributes for an EDB officer, he says, are a 'can do' attitude and an energy to make things happen.

'It was [this] attitude that brought Singapore from what it was 33 years ago, an undeveloped young nation with severe unemployment, to what it is today, a successful developing nation with full employment. [Our] mission must be translated into a conviction that Singapore will continue to be successful. From this conviction, our officers can derive the determination to see that Singapore succeeds in whatever it undertakes – whether for itself or for our investors and partners in economic development.'[3]

What Singapore has managed to master so well is a concept given the title of 'strategic pragmatism' by American corporate culture guru Professor Edgar Schlein. According to Mr Yeo, 'the "strategic" dimension comes from the recognition of our own development strategies and priorities, placed alongside the investors' corporate and business strategies. The "pragmatism" indicates our understanding of international business needs, organizational structures, investor psychology and decision-making processes. Our ability to mesh all these together for a win-win situation [has become] EDB's proprietory software.'[4]

This theme is picked up by Mrs Lee Ju Song, Deputy Executive Director of the Singapore International Chamber of Commerce (SICC), who says: 'Because Singapore is very small we have to look beyond the horizon and develop an external economy. In wanting to do so, we have to be able to identify niches. Speed is definitely going to be the key to success. It's not like in the past when you were talking about economies of scales to be successful. I think now that we are talking about the economics of scopes. We are setting up a set of international networks of satellite economic alliances to be successful. We have to be very boutique-like in our approach to business.

'We must have effective market flexibility and speed in order to succeed and we are trying to use this strength that we have in tying up with our business partners outside the region for a joint presence in countries such as China, Vietnam and India, as well as in ASEAN (Association of Southeast Asian Nations). The success of Singapore is going to be dependent on the successes of our trade partners, our major business partners. Because the bigger the economic cake, the more to share between the major participants and the more Singapore is likely to benefit.'[5]

Singapore's neighbours are not sitting back and letting it run away with all the riches. Indonesia is deregulating its economy, promoting freer trade, and trying to attract substantial amounts of foreign investments. Long dependent on the revenues from its massive oil and gas reserves, it now earns more from the export of manufactured goods. Malaysia is promoting a Vision 2020, to become a developed country in all respects by that year. Between 1989 and 1994, Malaysia actually achieved a higher growth rate than Singapore, although admittedly from a lower base.

Faced with this challenge, Lee Hsien Loong, in the speech referred to earlier, insisted that the only answer for Singapore was to become like Switzerland. '[It] is surrounded by the developed countries of Europe, yet it still prospers, and sustains a standard of living higher than its neighbours. It prospers not by having lower wages than its neighbours or because its neighbours are weak. It prospers because the Swiss have the skills and training to justify their higher wages, their banks enjoy a worldwide reputation for prudence and discretion, and their companies are developing opportunities and businesses all over the world. [And] unless we strive to do our utmost to achieve what Switzerland has done, we are in serious trouble.'[6]

STAYING COMPETITIVE

One British writer visiting Singapore in 1994 wrote: '[T]here is no denying the vibes from an omnipresent economic energy. This can be felt even on the Mass Transit System. As my train approached Raffles Place Station one day there was a woman on my left in her early twenties deep into an article headlined "A Tale Of Two

Contrasting Bourses". In front, a man was wading through chapter seven of *Designing A Database* and, on my left, another young man was loudly telling a colleague that selling 49 per cent of his company was 'the most logical thing to do'.

'Elsewhere, in the Orchard Road shopping centre, a student on the bus, with an electronic pager, meekly accepted political restrictions as part of a code of conduct drawn up by his elders. All he wanted to do was to make some money and be a successful engineer, the most prestigious job he said a student could aspire to. These are Singapore's wannabees staking their claim to the knowledge nirvana that beckons. They learn the three Rs to qualify for the four Cs – Cash, Credit Card, Car and Condominiums.'[7]

There is no doubt that the international business community mostly likes what it sees. In the World Competitiveness Report produced annually by the Swiss-based World Economic Forum and International Institute for Management Development, for example, Singapore was first in 1993 for the fifth year running among New Industrializing Economies, ahead of Hong Kong and Taiwan. The report uses 371 criteria divided into eight factors of competitiveness: domestic economy, internationalization government, finance, infrastructure, management, science and technology, and people. Two-thirds of the assessment is based on economy data and the remainder on an Executive Opinion Survey with 2,160 respondents worldwide.

In the annual Business Environment Risks Intelligence (BERI) report for 1994, Singapore was rated joint third with Taiwan behind Switzerland and Japan regarding the investment climate. The ratings are based on three factors: operations risk, political risk and remittance and repatriation. In operations risk, which takes into account factors such as policy continuity, economic growth, monetary policy and labour productivity, Singapore was second to Switzerland, and the same order was preserved for political stability; in remittance and repatriation, Singapore was fifth behind Japan, Switzerland, Taiwan and the Netherlands. In the 1995 BERI report, Singapore had moved ahead of Japan into second place overall behind Switzerland, while sharing top spot in Asia with Taiwan.[8]

Singapore has joined a select group of industrialized nations as a holder of Standard and Poors AAA credit rating on its long-term government debt. The rating agency said the decision to upgrade

Singapore from AA-plus reflected a continued improvement in its already robust public finances and external financial position. The country had become '. . .a well diversified service and manufacturing-based export economy and a regional centre for trade arrayed with top-notch transportation, communication and banking facilities'. Japan is the only other sovereign borrower in the East Asia region to be awarded the much-coveted AAA rating by the New York-based agency. The rival agency Moody's accords Singapore Aa2, its third highest rating.[9]

According to the World Bank Atlas, in 1994 Singapore was the 18th richest country in the world. With a Gross National Product per capita of US$19,310, it was placed ahead of several developed countries such as Britain and Australia – the first year that it had moved ahead of its former colonial master. As recently as 1988, the island seemed a long way off with GNP per head of just $9,050, which put it in 26th place.

But Singapore's results are even more impressive when countries are ranked on the 'real' values of the incomes they enjoy, known as 'purchasing power parity' reflecting the purchasing power of a person in a country after adjusting for different price levels in various countries. On this basis, Singapore is ranked ninth with $20,470, only $510 behind Germany in eighth place. The only countries of comparative size ahead of it are the oil-rich Gulf states of Qatar and United Arab Emirates.

With inflation being lower than most countries, and the economy growing so rapidly, it is likely Singapore will be placed even higher in the 1995 ratings. And assuming it keeps up its rapid growth and economic competitiveness, some economists speculate it could well rise to the top spot in the PPP table by the end of the century. There are certain complications with these figures. Some economists argue that it is also wrong to compare a city-state with large countries, where national figures might be held down by urban-rural disparities. A more accurate comparison might be to put Singapore against world cities like London, New York or Tokyo. But even if the calculation is somewhat flawed, it still demonstrates just how far Singapore has come in a short time.

It rates even better in a ranking done by global strategist David Roche, President of Independent Strategy in London, who studied all the 'emerging markets' in the developing world and constructed an index to measure the key social, economic, political and cultural success factors in economic development. Singapore was top, ahead of Hong Kong.

He describes the common features of successful emerging economies thus:

'First, they have homogenous societies that focus on getting rich and have legal systems to match that ambition. Second, they finance over 95 per cent of their development needs out of their own pockets and limit expenditure on external finance to long-term money inflows not exceeding five to six per cent of gross domestic product. Third, their governments boost domestic national savings rates by running budget surpluses (or at least balanced budgets), and focus resources on education, health and industrialization. And fourth, their economies are wide open to international trade and run current account deficits no greater than three to four per cent of GDP.'

Mr Roche cites Singapore as a prime example of how successful economies manage capital inflows by letting their exchange rates appreciate. 'A rising currency gives a market signal to domestic producers: move your product upmarket and boost productivity, or else lose competitiveness in domestic and export markets. Singapore has been producing ever-more sophisticated goods for years, while letting the currency appreciate. The rest of Southeast Asia will have to follow.'[10]

Singapore is sitting on a mountain of savings to fulfill its ambitions. It has foreign exchange reserves of about US$60 billion, making Singaporeans the new rich of Asia. 'In Perth [a popular place for migrants and tourist visitors from the city state] Singaporeans are called birds,' says Prime Minister Goh Chok Tong. 'When they go into shops they go: "Cheap, cheap".'[11]

Apart from the recessionary glitch in the mid-1980s, Singapore has continued to grow and prosper at a rapid rate. In 1992, the economy grew six per cent, rising to 9.9 per cent in 1993 and 10.1 per cent in 1994. Another double-digit performance was expected in 1995. These are outstanding growth rates by anyone's standard, made all the more impressive by the fact that the government has managed to avoid the roller-coaster economic ride endured by most of the developed economies in the West.

Equally impressive are the figures for foreign investment. International business shows little sign of turning away from the city-state, even if the nature of its commitment is changing. The big three – the United States, Japan and Europe – continue to pour money into Singapore in record amounts. In 1994, for example, the United States committed $2.45 billion (compared to $1.45 billion in 1993), Japan contributed $913.8 million ($779.4 million) and Europe $907 million ($857.2 million).[11] Much of the investment was in the high value-added chemicals and electronics sectors. Singapore is the world's leading producer of computer disk drives. It is an important centre of the petrochemical and pharmaceutical industries. It is the world's third biggest oil refining centre. Its financial services sector rivals Tokyo and Hong Kong in many areas.[12]

This has been achieved, Deputy Prime Minister Lee Hsien Loong insisted, '. . .by getting our overall policies right – maintaining high savings rates, emphasising education and training, investing in infrastructure, avoiding handouts and state welfare. Foreign investors and the financial markets know this. [They] have confidence in the political stability, the soundness of the system, the prudence of our policies and our exchange rate'.

But beyond this, there is the people factor. According to Mr Lee, one of Singapore's major strengths has been '. . .our cohesive society. We have shown unity of purpose and a consensus on national goals. We are prepared to put aside individual interests to achieve these goals, confident that while not everyone will benefit from every measure or policy, in the long run all will benefit from Singapore's progress. This social cohesion has been a vital competitive advantage, which has compensated for our small size and other limitations. It has helped us to develop a sense of common nationhood, of belonging together and owing responsibility towards one another, without which no amount of creative policy-making by the Government could have succeeded.'

This social cohesion has arisen out of the shared experience of the difficult years of independence, strong government leadership and the rapid economic growth which has improved the lives of all Singaporeans and given most of them a stake in the country's continued success. What worries government leaders – and provokes continuing exhortations to the citizenry from men like Mr Lee – is that with fading memories of the years of struggle, when everyone had to pull together for sheer survival, a new generation will want to 'widen the limits of what is permissible and move the out-of-bounds markers'. Secondly, success might breed complacency. But on the other hand, there is also a need to avoid crying wolf too often so that the message becomes dulled through familiarity.

To stay ahead, Mr Lee stressed, required a sustained performance, both as individuals and as a country. Singapore was involved in a marathon and its citizens had to run fast and run without end. But how to do this without slackening, without getting tired?

'We have inculcated in the population the need always to be outstanding, because otherwise we lose our reason for existence. Never settle for second best. But how can we be sure that after some time, someone might chirp up and say: "Why must we be best in everything we do? Can't we take things a little easier? So much stress and strain; won't it be good enough if we are just No.2 once in a while?"

'Societies which are put under severe long-term stress eventually become exhausted. Even Israel, with several thousand years of Jewish history and religion to bind the citizens together, found the decades of war with the Arab countries overwhelming. In a purely military sense, Israel won all the wars it fought, but the strain on the society was enormous. [. . .]On the other hand, societies under no stress at all get slack and flabby. The Gurkhas come from Nepal, on the rugged foothills of the Himalayas, not from any South Sea island. Singapore is not a South Sea island. No breadfruit trees grow naturally to provide for our needs. We face major challenges ahead. But because we have done so well, and the potential problems seem so remote, we risk lulling ourselves into complacency. We must never discourage or demoralize Singaporeans by exaggerating the difficulty of the task ahead. Whatever problems may lie ahead, they are far less daunting than the dangers Singapore faced, and surmounted, when we became independent, and when we were far less equipped to deal with them. At the same time, we must get Singaporeans to understand the unique circumstances we live under, and to strive harder to do well despite the constraints. This is a fine balance to maintain.'[13]

POLICY OBJECTIVES

Explaining exactly what the government has in mind, as outlined above by Lee Hsieng Loong, will be the purpose of the rest of this book. For the moment, it will perhaps suffice to look briefly at the goals the EDB set itself at the beginning of 1995 to keep the economic success story on track.

There would be, it said, a continuing effort to encourage local companies to upgrade their business and manufacturing capabilities, ensuring that the manufacturing sector remained strong, competitive and a core engine of economic growth. With a strong domestic base, Singapore would then be able to strengthen its linkages with the regional economies and take full advantage of the vibrant growth in the Asia-Pacific region.

It identified four key thrusts for the year ahead:

■**Manufacturing 2000**, designed to strengthen the manu-facturing clusters now being created by identifying gaps and promoting investment to fill those gaps in the industrial sector. The EDB pledged to work with the National Productivity Board to upgrade skills and encourage reskilling of the workforce, and with the National Science and Technology Board to provide more incentives for companies to carry out more research and innovation as well as focus on application development, process engineering and product design.

■**International Business Hub 2000**, designed to strengthen Singapore's position as an international business hub supporting its manufacturing and regionalization thrusts. The EDB and other agencies will encourage workers in the services sector to acquire new skills 'which are necessary if Singapore is to become a gateway to the region for the movement of goods and services, as well as information, capital and knowledge'. A multi-agency approach will be stepped up to encourage companies to use Singapore as a home base for trade, investment and business development for the region.

■**Local Enterprise 2000**, under which the EDB will continue to promote the general upgrading of small and medium enterprises, encouraging them to seek the status of Promising Local Enterprises capable of becoming major players in key clusters as well as expanding their capabilities to participate in regional growth. Linkages creating mutually beneficial synergy will be created between these local enterprises and MNCs.

■**Regionalization 2000**, which aims to create an external economy that will enhance the domestic economy (i.e. creating a strong GDP and expanded GNP). The EDB will continue to strengthen the economic linkages with the surrounding region. Much effort will go into ensuring the success of so-called 'flagship projects', major investments in places like China and India, led by government but in which the private sector will play an increasing role. Partnerships will be promoted with MNCs by co-investing with them in Singapore and the region.

All this is part of a general concept known as **Singapore Unlimited** or **Singapore Inc.**, stressing partnership with other government agencies in Singapore, international partners and corporate allies. This is summed up by the EDB in the following way:

'The EDB will continue to strengthen Singapore's GDP by drawing on the technology and skills of the world. In other words, bringing the world to Singapore in an unlimited manner to complement Singapore's resources and assets. Singapore Unlimited seeks to borrow economic space and resources to help grow our GNP. [The] economic activities [should be] relevant to the region and to our customer base so as to sustain optimal economic growth.'[15]

In conclusion, therefore, Singapore is now moving onto a higher plateau than before, where the competition will be tougher than ever before. According to Goh Chok Tong: 'Competing as an NIE (newly industrializing economy) is like competing in the Malaysia Cup. Winning it does not make us the regional champion and certainly not the world champions. But it should make us more seasoned for bigger tournaments. Unfortunately, economic competition is tougher than that. Now that Singapore is a near developed country, the competition will be even tougher. It's like being catapulted to play in the World Cup finals.'[16]

This chapter has concentrated on the economic performance of Singapore in the mid-1990s. But this also has to be considered against the wider backdrop of the country's short history. Before proceeding further to examine the future, therefore, it will be helpful to move the story back to the time when Singapore was first placed on the trading map.

CHAPTER NOTES

1. 'The champion must fight to stay on top'. *Financial Times* Survey, 24/2/95.
2. Speech at Nanyang Technological University 10/2/95. Text carried in full by *Straits Times* 13-14/2/95
3. Economic Development Board Yearbook 1994, p4
4. Ibid., p8
5. Interview in Singapore 7/1/95
6. See note 2.
7. 'The Colony strikes back', by Victor Keegan. *The Guardian* 12/12/1994.
8. *Straits Times* 23/1/95.
9. 'Singapore wins S & P's triple A credit rating', *Financial Times* 5/3/95.
10. 'Other Mexicos in the developing world,' *Asian Wall Street Journal* 6/2/95.
11. FT survey, as note 1.
12. EDB press briefing 27/1/95.
13. See note 2.
14. An explanation of the work of these and other government agencies is contained in the appendices.
15. EDB press release 29/1/95.
16. 'Teamwork needed to beat tougher competition: PM.' *Straits Times*, p.1, 29/6/95.

2 From trading-post to nationhood

KEY POINTS

- How a small trading post became a regional hub
- The creation of a multi-ethnic society
- The transient nature of the population under British colonial rule
- How Japanese occupation helped create an identification with Singapore
- Membership of the Malaysian Federation in the 1960s, and shock expulsion
- How Lee Kuan Yew set about overcoming economic vulner-ability through a combination of tight political controls and economic pragmatism
- The key programmes to carry Singapore into the next century as a 'centre of excellence' in manufacturing, technology and services

MODEST BEGINNINGS

MODERN SINGAPORE was founded in 1819 by Sir Stamford Raffles as a trading post for the East India Company, and quickly became the hub of British enterprise in Southeast Asia. In 1820, Raffles wrote to a cousin in England, noting: 'My settlement continues to thrive most wonderfully; it is all and everything I could wish and if no untimely fate awaits it, promises to become the emporium and pride of the East.'[1] Today, he would have reason to be very happy with how his protégé developed.

Subsequent history can be sketched very briefly. In 1867 the

Straits Settlements of Singapore, Penang and Malacca became British colonies, and in 1946 Singapore was made a separate crown colony of the United Kingdom. Internal self-government with a fully elected government came in 1959 and four years later Singapore joined Malaya as one of the constituent states of the new federation of Malaysia, with virtual freedom from colonial rule. The marriage with Malaysia, however, foundered on Chinese and Malay antipathy towards each other, and on 9 August 1965 Singapore separated by mutual agreement to become an independent republic.

Singapore consists of a main island 42 km by 23 kilometres, with 48 offshore islets, about half of them inhabited. Land reclamation, however, has given Singapore considerable additional territory from that known to Raffles.

He took over a derelict trading town and obscure fishing village surrounded by swamp. Because the island was sparsely populated – containing a total of some 120 Malays and 30 Chinese when he landed[2] – he threw it wide open to immigration. Had he not made this decision, Singapore's history might have been entirely different. As it was, the open door drew immigrants, first by the hundreds and then thousands, from over-populated India and China and to a lesser extent Indonesia. Some came in expectations of making vast fortunes quickly; others to escape grinding poverty and intimidating turmoil in their homeland; others because they fell for the smooth sales-talk of labour contractors.

Whatever the reasons, the immigrants came not to settle but to earn a living prior to retirement in their homeland. There was no attachment to the country they worked in. It was a work-place, an office and nothing else. They did not see themselves as makers of a Singapore history, as settlers shaping a future for themselves and their children in Singapore. According to Lee Kuan Yew: 'Singapore used to be a conglomeration of migrants, each man for himself. If he cared for anybody else at all, it was his own immediate family.'[3]

By 1836, the Chinese population had grown to 13,700 and outnumbered the Malay population of 12,500. (The gap continued to widen thereafter so that, by the end of the 1980s, the population of 2.7 million consisted of 76 per cent Chinese, 15 per cent Malay, and 6 .5 per cent Indian.) Without a police force or army and fearing racial conflicts, Raffles segregated the various ethnic groups, assigning the jetty and Singapore River areas to the Hokkien Chinese (especially traders from Malacca) and the British so as to facilitate their business.

'This policy led eventually to the formation of ethnic and sub-ethnic enclaves. It made mutual understanding impossible and misunderstanding in turn bred much prejudice and stereotyping. The early settlers in Singapore, whether Chinese, Malay or Indian, were predominantly illiterate or semi-literate and poor. On the other hand, the British and other European traders and colonial administrators were wealthy and powerful. The British aim was single-mindedly to make money by exploiting every opportunity available in Singapore and the region. The Chinese and Indian immigrants were similarly motivated.

'There were then many opportunities to create wealth in the new country created especially to promote trade. This rapidly gave rise to occupational and trade specialization by various ethnic and sub-ethnic groups. The British and other European and Hokkien merchants dominated international trade, the British and Indians were prominent in colonial administration and public works, the Cantonese and Hakkas specialized in building and construction, and the Hainanese in food retail.

'Gradually disparity in income and wealth appeared and widened among individuals and ethnic groups as some trades and occupations offered more than others. Thus slowly a plural society evolved with closely bonded ethnic groups divided by culture, religion, language and social class. These ethnic groups were also segregated geographically and socially as differences in language, religion, and trade pulled them apart. Thus the colony of Singapore was culturally, demographically and politically an extension of Britain, Malaya, Indonesia, China and India.'[4]

According to one authority, '. . .the identification of the local population with Singapore was essentially a post-World War 2 phenomenon'.[5] There was virtually no political interest or activity in Singapore until the turn of the twentieth century. It was not until the 1930s that Singapore had a less transient population, when the British actively encouraged female immigration for a more settled society. Those without strong ties in Singapore departed for their homelands during the Great Depression of the Thirties. 'The fall of the "impregnable" British fortress of Singapore in February 1942, leading to three-and-a-half-years of Japanese occupation, with the total eclipse of the vaunted European supremacy over Southeast Asia, further severed the links with ancestral homelands while creating in the various races an emotional attachment to Singapore as they suffered together. For the vast majority of the Chinese in particular, with a communist insurgency at hand in the Malay Peninsula and Singapore, when China turned communist in 1949, that door was effectively shut and remained so for two decades.'[6]

But those who decided their future lay in Singapore must have wondered for a while if they had made the right decision. 'Singapore was a "basket case" in 1959 and most problems of the time were inherited by the post-independence government in 1965. The country was wracked by strikes, lockouts, racial and religious conflicts and riots.'[7] And if the Japanese occupation was a traumatic moment in moulding the distinctive Singaporean character, the abrupt separation from the Malaysian Federation was no less so. Combined with the military threat posed by Indonesia's 'Konfrontasi' policy, and an extremely fragile economy, there were many who did not hold out much hope for Singapore's long-term survival as an independent state.

Lee Kuan Yew had no doubts that the main answer lay in hard work, for '. . .the world did not owe them [Singaporeans] a living'.[8] That message became even more urgent when, in 1968, the British Government suddenly decided to accelerate the withdrawal of its military presence east of Suez – which effectively meant Singapore – within three years. An estimated one-fifth of the island's national income and 40,000 jobs were generated by the British bases.

Former President C.V.Devan Nair (at the time Secretary-General of the National Trades Union Congress) recalled in the early 1970s that 'Little more than a dozen years ago, Singapore was just like any other developing country. We were notorious for our depleted treasury, growing unemployment, slogan-shouting and strike-happy trade unions, riot-prone students and wide-spread social indiscipline. In fact, Singapore was then regarded as one of the riskiest places in the world for investment. The experts, both local and foreign, predicted all kinds of calamities for us, like growing social unrest, and, at worst, a communist take-over. Then, in the wake of political turbulence, there was the short-lived merger with Malaysia, followed by eviction from the federation. A punch-drunk Singapore then reeled under the announcement of impending British withdrawal and the threat of massive unemployment.'[9]

Unlike most developing countries, Singapore had no agricultural base to build on, no natural resources it could tap to generate instant wealth. As a compact urban society, the compulsions on Singapore for rapid industrial development were, therefore, perhaps even greater than most other countries. These compulsions became especially acute after the eviction from Malaysia. 'The gist of the Singapore solution was plain and straightforward – Industrialize or Bust! Most people thought Singapore would bust. We did not. And thereby hangs the tale of a many-sided and multi-pronged social, educational, economic and cultural effort, which inspired the confidence and the disciplined response of a hard-working people.'[10]

Singapore succeeded, in Devan Nair's estimation, through several factors, including an incorruptible political leadership which adopted a '. . .hard-headed, pragmatic and no-nonsense approach' to settling the political, economic, social and educational priorities, a multi-racial approach to the problems of nation-building in a heterogeneous society, a population of immigrant stock, 'unhampered by religious and cultural taboos and shibboleths which inhibit the social and technological innovations necessary for modernization and economic growth, and a work-force willing to respond to the call for hard work and social discipline'.[11]

A HUB FOR OCEAN TRADE

The main, if not sole reason for Singapore's original growth had been its geographical position and excellent harbour, which, combined with the energy and enterprise of the early immigrants, had enabled it to emerge as a flourishing centre for ocean-borne entrepot trade. The early monopoly of the China trade by the British East India Company and the commercial exploitation of the region by the Dutch (based next door in what was to become Indonesia), helped establish this position. This trade gave way to a new pattern towards the end of the nineteenth century with the emergence of the region's tin and rubber. As early as 1918, Singapore became the world's principal rubber exporting centre.

Its position had already been enhanced, and its entrepot trade given further impetus, with the opening of the Suez Canal in 1869, the advent of the steamship and the beginning of the international telegraph in the 1870s. These coupled with the supply of raw materials and foodstuffs for the industrialization in Europe, and the securing of markets for their goods greatly expanded trade and commercial activities. As a result, with the exception of the depression period following World War 1, Singapore enjoyed a century of uninterrupted growth.

This entrepot trade continued to grow into the 1950s, exporting the region's natural produce and serving as a centre for the collection of tropical produce for export and distribution of manufactured goods from Europe. But there was a growing realization within the government that this could not last. Increasingly, neighbouring countries would want to handle their own commodity trade with the rest of the world rather than continue to allow Singapore to take all the profits. 'Malaysia and Indonesia [. . .] had taken up the processing of their rubber for direct export, and tendency to bypass Singapore also applied to other basic commodities.'[12]

It was then that the foundations were laid for an industrial policy that would quickly lead to the emergence of a global city-state with a world-wide market.

INDUSTRIAL POLICY

Singapore was built on a five-pronged policy – free trade, high savings, full employment and an equitable wage policy, a foreign investment-friendly environment and a development-oriented government. Free trade was considered the correct policy for a small nation to pursue: buying from the cheapest sources and selling in the dearest markets; and unless prohibited by the United Nations, trading with any nation willing to trade with it. Singapore had a gross domestic savings to GDP ratio of 10 per cent in 1965, but this had risen to 42 per cent in 1985 – well in excess of Japan (32 per cent) whose post-war industrial success was built on the savings of its citizens. The high rate enabled Singapore to finance its development without having to rely on inflationary finance, external aid and foreign borrowing.

A welcoming environment for foreign investment could only be achieved with labour harmony, through a careful process of consultation and cooperation between government, management and labour. 'Full employment and equitable wage policy: the creation and enlargement of the national cake is a very important facet of economic development, as is the equitable sharing of the cake. Growth must benefit and be seen to benefit the vast majority, if not the entire population. With more than 80 per cent of the labour force being employees, much of the sharing process falters unless an equitable wage policy is pursued. The symbiotic relationship between the government and the unions cannot be maintained if workers feel unfairly and unjustly treated.'[13]

Mr Goh Chok Tong, who succeeded Lee Kuan Yew as prime minister in 1989, took up this theme when, during an official visit to India in January 1995, he was asked by a businesswoman how Singapore had managed to transform itself from a 'problem-ridden city to the role model of today'. There were, he replied, five factors: a free-market economy, prudent budgeting, high savings, sound social policies and strong leadership.

Singapore was lucky in having chosen the free market as its economic model (which was not a foregone conclusion because for a time in the 1950s and 1960s it had been considered ripe for communist take-over). It had also embarked on certain correct socio-economic policies. Prudent budgetary practice meant that there was a budget surplus each year. Singapore did not believe in financing development or funding its annual operating expenditure on a deficit. A high savings rate through the compulsory Central Provident Fund, gave the country capital to invest in infrastructure and industries. High savings thus led to a high investment rate. Finally, there must be leaders who had the capacity to implement the above policies. 'Vision alone is not sufficient. Many of us have vision, but it is the will, the ability to implement the vision that is important,' he said.[14]

High-profile government intervention, or official 'paternalism', has been an important contributory factor to Singapore's development, whatever certain Western journalists may say about the lack of press freedom or true democracy. According to one Singaporean study, since 1959, the PAP leaders have appeared to designate themselves as more than being leaders of a political party. 'Given the tasks at hand, they see themselves as architects of a new state and, having wrought an economic miracle from massive unemployment, squalid socio-economic conditions and leftist political adventurism, they next perceive themselves as sole custodians of what they have so ably created.'[15]

Despite the leadership change, there appears to be a perception gap where, on the one hand, the leadership continues to see its paternalistic role as being necessary, and, on the other hand, the new generation of voters is relatively more educated, individualistic, demanding and less tolerant of the style of government where the distinction between state and non-state or private matters becomes blurred under an overly paternalistic approach. The government's approach has transcended all areas directly related to, or peripheral to, economic life, including marriage, procreation, education and others. In the long run, a less paternalistic approach might seem more appropriate, but in some respects – as is discussed elsewhere – the governmental hands-on policy is being extended.

And there is little doubt that a policy of intervention, meritocracy and elitism, and government-knows-best have served the economy very well. The leadership continually justifies this as being necessary because the Singapore economy does operate on a rather thin knife-edge and there are few viable options. Lee Hsien Loong, deputy prime minister, once put it thus: 'Given that the base of Singapore's survival and prosperity is so fine. . .in many circumstances we do need to act rapidly and effectively, precisely because of the knife-edge.'[16] This tends to create a need for government to become more involved to cover all aspects deemed important to development and welfare of the nation. 'For instance, to maintain a conducive environment for investments it has to ensure good industrial relations, orderly wage increases, labour discipline and an efficient infrastructure. Mere economic intervention is often not sufficient as behavioural and attitudinal changes like those pertaining to the labour market, education and other demographics need to be brought about.'[17]As Lee Kuan Yew trenchantly observed on one occasion when he was still prime minister: 'I am accused often enough of interfering in the private lives of citizens. If I did not, had I not done that, we wouldn't be here today.'[18]

PHASED ECONOMIC DEVELOPMENT

Up to the mid-1980s, Singapore's economic development can be divided into three stages:
- Basic industrialization (1966-73)
- Sophistication and broadening of the industrial base (1974-78)
- Restructuring of the economy to higher value-added industries and services (1979-84)

The PAP initially pursued a policy of import-substituting industrialization characterized by low tariffs on a narrow range of industries. As already noted, Singapore's domestic market was too small for this policy to be viable, so the government campaigned to become part of Malaysia. In 1963, after protracted negotiations, Singapore joined the Malaysian Federation, only to leave it less than two years later in a dispute over the insistence of its partners in Kuala Lumpur to create a Malay-dominated society.

With the loss of the anticipated domestic market, the stagnation of entrepot trade and the scheduled British military withdrawal, the PAP turned to labour-intensive manufacturing for export to the world market. Because the local private sector had no industrial experience, multinationals were invited in with generous investment incentives. Political and labour controls were instituted to ensure that multinationals could operate in a stable and hospitable environment.

'This strategy proved to be hugely successful, aided by favourable external and domestic circumstances. Externally, world trade was booming and there was a rush of offshore sourcing by industrial-country multinationals (MNCs). Domestically, Singapore's excellent geographical location and infrastructure, free-trade policies and hardworking, outward-looking immigrant population were great assets. Besides export manufacturing – in which the electronics industry was the most prominent – the city quickly became the regional service and refining centre for the oil exploration and extraction boom beginning in the late 1960s and a regional financial centre with the influx of foreign banks in the early 1970s. The government took over the naval facilities left behind by the departing British forces and transformed them into major shipbuilding and repairing facilities. To quicken the industrialization process, it started new industrial enterprises by itself or with foreign joint-venture partners.[19]

According to one analysis, although as a free port and entrepot trading centre, Singapore was full of merchants, '. . .it had not developed a class of indigenous entrepreneurs who could lead its industrialization efforts, or who would press the government for protection from imports. On the contrary, Singapore's predominantly Chinese merchants favoured continued free trade and most did not object to the large amounts of multinational capital which flowed in to the city-state in the late 1960s and early 1970s.'[20]

Most of the new investment was in 100 per cent foreign-owned enterprises with initially limited local linkages, though there were obvious multiplier effects in the generation of local employment. As industrialization proceeded, more local entrepreneurs were attracted into manufacturing, but mostly as suppliers to multinational subsidiaries, and many local entrepreneurs were eventually to emerge from the ranks of former multinational employees. But through its open-door policy, Singapore by the late 1980s had probably the most heavily foreign-dominated manufacturing sector in the world, with wholly-owned foreign subsidiaries and major foreign-owned joint ventures at that time accounting for over half of employment, two-thirds of output and value-added and over four-fifths of direct exports.[21]

But, as will become clear in subsequent chapters, while still encouraging more MNCs to locate in Singapore – particularly their regional operating headquarters – through various incentive programmes, the government in the 1990s has also begun developing a programme to breed home-grown entrepreneurs capable of operating on a world stage, as well as creating global trading companies along the lines of the Japanese *sogo shosha* (trading companies).

Although the need for increased employment for a growing population would be catered for primarily through greater industrialization, it was also realized quite early on that a financial and banking sector could also make a significant contribution to development strategy. As a regional trading centre already oriented towards serving world markets, Singapore possessed the basic infrastructure on which to build and expand its role in international finance. The policies which were evolved were aimed at giving new dimensions and depth to banking and financial activities to service not only Southeast Asia but beyond, taking advantage of the fact that Singapore's strategic location in a time-zone bridging East and West – a boon to international institutions seeking to provide round-the-clock global financial services.[22]

The government's first move came in 1968 when it abolished the withholding tax on interest payable to non-resident depositors. This saw the beginning of what is now widely known as the Asian Dollar Market. Another significant step was the admission of a foreign bank into Singapore in 1970. The following year, monetary and banking administration was centralized in the establishment of The Monetary Authority of Singapore (MAS), combining regulatory and supervisory with the role of nurturing the growth in the size and depth of the money, capital, gold, securities and foreign exchange markets.

Singapore shared a common capital market with Malaysia until the latter announced in May 1973 its intention to set up a separate stock market. The securities industry was quick to respond to new needs by incorporating a separate and autonomous body, the Stock Exchange of Singapore which began operations in early June the same year. In 1973, the MAS formalized the concept of offshore banking and gave approval for several internationally reputable banks to conduct offshore business from Singapore.[23]

At the same time, its greatest physical asset – the port – was not neglected. The old godowns along the Singapore River were swept aside and the seafront berths and adjacent areas expanded to create the world's busiest container port, now totally computerized to ensure rapid turnaround. The development of the Growth Triangle and the regionalization policy, to be discussed in the following two chapters, have further enhanced the port's importance, coupled with the growth of Singapore as a major shipbuilding, ship repair and oil-rig building centre in Southeast Asia. In 1983, the Singapore Trade Development Board was created with the objective of aiding the country to become a global trading hub and increase international trade.

In 1979, meanwhile, the government launched a 'Second Industrial Revolution' to upgrade the manufacturing sector, in particular moving away from labour-intensive activities and towards higher-technology, higher-skill, higher-productivity and higher-income activities. The new strategy involved (i) a wage correction policy with three years of double digit wage increases aimed at 'restoring wages to market levels' and encouraging capital-labour substitution; (ii) changes in the industrial relations and labour-management system to improve productivity; (iii) increased investments in education and skills training and other productivity-enhancing programmes; and (iv) new and expanded incentives and aggressive investment promotion overseas to attract priority high-tech industries.

The restructuring policy succeeded in achieving some of its goals, including rapid growth between 1980 and 1984 (higher than that in other Asian Newly Industrializing Economies, or NIEs), accelerated technological upgrading and relocation (to neighbouring countries, especially Malaysia) of labour-intensive firms and large increases in the training and supply of skilled manpower. On the other hand, large wage increases sharply raised unit labour costs, which were compounded by high public sector charges and a currency which strengthened against the US dollar. The result was a squeezing of private-sector profitability and a swift erosion in manufacturing competitiveness which – together with a domestic slump in construction and an external market slump in Singapore's major industries (electronics, oil and shipbuilding) and in the commodity-dependent economies of its regional trading partners – triggered a severe recession in 1985-6. After two decades of continual growth, a sudden economic shrinkage of 1.6 per cent was a massive jolt to the country's policy-makers and business leaders.

'The nation went into a state of economic crisis',[24] but responded in a highly pragmatic manner with a heavy emphasis on supply-side solutions to cut business costs. Corporate and property taxes, and statutory charges for government services (rents, utilities, communications, port services etc.) were slashed, along with the employers' compulsory Central Provident Fund (CPF) contributions. A wage restraint policy was instituted and reforms initiated to make wages more flexible and responsive to individual companies' profitability and workers' productivity. This, combined with external factors, created a strong resurgence of growth.

A special high-level economic committee was immediately formed and it eventually charted new directions for the economy. It identified several new growth areas where Singapore could carve a niche in the world market. Two of these – high-tech industry and information technology – have been pursued vigorously and will be discussed in later chapters. A National Technology plan was formulated to provide detailed directives and a new National Science and Technology Board (NSTB) was set up to implement the plan. With a generous budget of S$2 billion, the NSTB's remit is to ensure that R & D expenditure reaches two per cent of the GNP by the year 2000. National research centres have been set up to support selected hi-tech industries. Under a 'Technology Corridor' concept, new hi-tech companies are being established in specially designed science and technology parks in the south-western part of the island where the universities, polytechnics and research institutes are sited.

The government's long-term development strategy is to continue relying on foreign investment and (selectively) on skilled and unskilled foreign labour, while providing more support for local business and adding high-value exportable services to the emphasis on high-tech industry. Some state-owned firms are to be privatized, but the government will continue to promote investments in high-tech and high value-added industry and services, such as electronics, avionics, biotechnology, computer software etc. While it plans to divest its equity shares in government-linked companies and to enlarge the role of the private sector in economic development, the government has said it will invest in new ventures where the private sector will not risk its resources or does not have the capacity to enter. In short, the state will continue to play a major and catalytic role in shaping Singapore's comparative advantage in existing and new activities. The ultimate goal is to turn Singapore into a "centre of excellence" in manufacturing, technology and services'.[25]

BLUEPRINT FOR THE 1990s

The blueprint for the 1990s was created by the Economic Planning Committee and released on 13 October 1991. It was the fourth programme since 1960 designed to guide national development and set a target for Singapore to catch up with the per capita GNP of the Netherlands by 2020 and the United States by 2030.

This new plan was far more complex than the previous ones due to several external and internal factors. The key ones were:

- The economic environment in which Singapore operated had become more complex. In the 1960s and 70s, a simple strategy for export-led growth based on attracting foreign investments into Singapore was adequate to provide a high rate of sustained econ omic growth. But by the early 1990s, there were several low cost competitors rapidly developing their capabilities. Singapore could no longer compete with them purely on a cost basis, but had to evolve a differentiated competitive strategy which was viable and sustainable in the medium to long term.
- In the 1960s and 70s, the world trading system was open and robust. Singapore had little difficulty in selling all that it could produce to the major OECD markets. By 1990, market access had become less certain.
- Domestically, the choices had become more complex. In the past, when a particular activity was promoted – an oil refinery or an electronics factory – Singapore could simply offer tax incentives without worrying about any adverse consequences. With the tight labour market situation, when a company (or industry) was promoted, some other company (or industry) could suffer and have less scope for growth.
- The people of Singapore had become more sophisticated and their value systems more complex. It was no longer certain that a simple salary increase would be capable of fully motivating people. Other issues were becoming important and economic policies had to take these into account.
- Singapore was becoming increasingly interconnected with regional and ASEAN (Association of Southeast Asian Nations) economies, so much so that the role played by the region and Asia needed to be factored into the creation and implementation of economic policies.[26]

The basic strategy as set out in the document was to maintain and extend Singapore's international competitiveness, to be accomplished through eight strategic goals and implemented through 17 programmes.

The eight strategic goals were:

(i)   Enhancing human resources through attracting international talents;

(ii)   Promoting teamwork among government, business and labour through the formation of an Economic Panel to discuss major issues and reconcile differences.

(iii)   Increasing international orientation through the education of the people and alliance with countries in the region;

(iv)   Encouraging an innovative climate by constantly review-
ing government rules which hinder innovations;

(v)   Developing specific clusters or niches within manufacturing
and services where Singapore can match the capabilities of first-
class developed nations.

(vi)   Helping the domestic sector to redevelop economically
and upgrade operations to improve productivity.

(vii)   Improving the ability to maintain competitiveness by
developing better monitoring systems of both short and medium to
long-term competitiveness: and

(viii)   Minimizing economic vulnerabilities through encouragement of MNCs to treat Singapore as a home base and
development of local enterprises.[27]

The committee said that Singapore had reached a developed
country's income level before having become a fully developed
economy. Therefore, it had to quickly catch up in terms of full
development, or the income levels would be hard to maintain. To
be competitive, Singapore had to offer the opportunity of a higher
rate of return than the OECD countries, which meant the entire
economic environment had to be more favourable to business and
enterprise. The island had to become not merely a production base
but an international total business centre for manufacturing and
services.

The main restraining factors towards achieving the high
average growth rates experienced in the 1980s of 7.1 per cent
were full employment and limits set by the government on the
foreign worker population (estimated at more than 400,000).
Singapore has also practically reached the limits of sea-front land
and sea space. In order to continue to grow at relatively high
rates, the committee reported it was necessary to 'reorganize the
way human and physical resources are managed'.

One route was via the Growth Triangle initiative in promoting
the distribution of manufacturing operations between Singapore,
the nearby Riau Islands of Indonesia and Johor, just across the
causeway in Malaysia, in accordance with the comparative
advantages of the three regions in terms of skill levels, land and
labour availability and production costs. The Growth Triangle
initiative would be further expanded by encouraging companies to
undertake distributed processing further afield by establishing
business ventures with indigenous companies in these areas.[28]

Given the severe constraints because of its size, Singapore could only hope to become a developed country if it tapped from the world the best of its talent and technology, besides expanding into its markets and seeking out new business opportunities. In order to do this, Singapore needed to (i) adopt a long-term immigration policy involving an intake, tentatively estimated at around 0.4 per cent per annum of the population, of high quality professional and skilled persons to augment existing low growth rates in the labour force, as well as to refresh and renew the higher echelons of the talent pool in Singapore; (ii) Singapore companies had to be encouraged to set up operations in different parts of the world, where there were business opportunities and substantial benefits for the companies. A globalization plan to be called, 'Singapore Unlimited', was required whereby the various government which operated overseas would provide support for local companies to invest internationally, with the objective of strengthening the companies in Singapore through business synergies.[29]

The city-state faced increased labour constraints in the 1980s, leading in 1989 to a decision to relax the criteria for granting residential status in Singapore. This move was aimed at attracting highly skilled labour particularly from Hong Kong. Further concessions were made in 1990 to ease restrictions on foreign skilled labour, whereas unskilled labour is not looked upon favourably by the government. Other measures included encouraging part-time workers and mothers to join the work force. Education and training programmes were encouraged to adopt a 'life cycle perspective' from cradle to retirement in recognition of the fact that, despite its highly-educated, high-tech profile, around half the work-force never got beyond primary school.

To be competitive, the committee declared, Singapore had to tap global resources, global technology and global talent to overcome the limited local resources. A priority task was to nurture an outward-looking mindset. Singaporeans should go abroad to live and work. There was a need to deepen the country's niche areas such as finance and banking, petrochemicals, health-care, telecommunications and information technology. A globalization plan should be developed to support more local companies to invest internationally. Singapore's infrastructure should be further developed to ensure efficient international communications. The education and training systems should be reviewed to create a climate which supported innovation. Government rules which hindered companies or individuals from adopting innovative ideas to increase business efficiency should also be reviewed. Public commendations should be given for creativity.

The Committee declared that, '. . .developing networks-of-excellence [would help] to enrich Singapore's capabilities in niche areas such as finance and banking, petrochemicals, health care, telecommunications, and information technology. A centre-for-excellence strategy relies on hubbing to assemble resources and expertise in Singapore. [But] developing world-class centres-of-excellence , which are expensive and resource intensive, may not always be feasible. Like Japan, Singapore can overcome its lack of natural resources by harnessing opportunities outside the country, for manufacturing sites and recreational facilities. Singapore has the world as its resource. Be it raw materials, information, labour or tourist resorts, Singapore can create products and services that are not bound by traditional concepts of space and other constraints.

'Globalization can be viewed as a series of concentric circles. The innermost circle which Singaporeans need to work on is their minds. Globalization requires a change in mindset. Then comes the next circle – the institutions which need to acquire a global orientation; then Singapore as a country, the region, the outer world, and finally the global economy in the outer ring. Globalization doesn't merely mean doing things overseas. Singaporeans have to embrace the global socio-economic space and endear themselves to the world. The Japanese gardening approach of *shakkai* or "borrowed scenery" illustrates how a beautiful garden can be made more beautiful by integrating the distant scenery into the landscape of the garden. Using global opportunities in accordance with the principle of mutual benefit is an important new strategy for Singapore's economy in the next lap.'[30]

The committee also placed considerable emphasis on the desirability of creating industrial clusters in the manufacturing and service industries. 'Industries do not operate in isolation. There are vertical and horizontal links to suppliers and customers, which have a major influence on the overall competitiveness of an industry. In several cases, the linkages are so strong that one industry would not be viable or would have its chances of survival drastically reduced, in the absence of others. Such groups of industries, or clusters as they are referred to, must be considered in any development planning, just as much as individual industries.

'Each cluster would have some features common to most industries, representing a common thread which unites [them]. These features or core capabilities could be certain technologies, common customer or supplier bases or some natural advantages. The Government is prepared to invest in these core capabilities or provide special incentives to accelerate their development.'[31]

In December 1993, a $1 billion Cluster Development Fund was set up under the management of the Economic Development Board (EDB) with the objective of enabling customs in the same sector to create a 'critical mass' for expansion. Specifically, it aimed to (i) attract high technology companies to Singapore; (ii) accelerate the development of local enterprises; and (iii) form strategic partnerships with local enterprises and MNCs to expand into the surrounding region.[32]

Turning to economic redevelopment, the Economic Planning Committee said a multi-agency task-force should be set up to upgrade sectors with low productivity, encouraging strategic alliances, disseminating information on market trends and benchmark data, and re-examining public policies. The task-force would also consider retaining retrenched workers in new skills and help introduce more advanced business systems.

International competitiveness has long been a virtual obsession in Singapore. The committee recommended that the indicators used to track the country's competitiveness be improved so that there would be early warning of any uncompetitive situation. A working group, comprising officials from the Ministry of Trade and Industry, Monetary Authority of Singapore and the EDB, was set up to review information on trends in competitiveness.[33] The government quickly accepted virtually all the committee's recommendations and most have already been implemented at the time of writing.

Mention has been made of the high profile role played by the government in not just macro economic management but also in the day-to-day running of businesses. This highly interventionist role is likely to continue, especially in implementing the strategic economic plan. But it is also clear that the government does want private business to play a much bigger role, especially in the internationalization of the local economy. There is a large state-owned business sector which plays a lead role in many of the overseas business thrusts to be described in subsequent chapters. In the late 1980s, the government was involved in some way in over 450 companies, but it has begun a serious effort to privatize some strategic sectors. Singapore Telecoms has been privatized, and feasibility studies have been conducted into the eventual privatization of the airport, ports, gas and electricity utilities, and even the Mass Rapid Transit (MRT) system.[34]

CHAPTER NOTES

1. Fengshui: The Geomancy and Economy of Singapore. Woon, G.K. Shinglee Publishers Pte Ltd, Singapore, 1991, pp24-5.

2. Nation-building in Singapore: An Historical Perspective by Kong, C.S., contained in 'In Search of Singapore's National Values'. Quah, S.T. (ed), The Institute of Policy Studies, Singapore. Times Academic Press 1990, p6.

3. Towards Tomorrow. Essays on Development and Social Transformation in Singapore. Published by the Singapore National Trades Union Congress. Singapore 1973), p8.

4. Nation-building in Singapore: A Historical perspective, as above, p7.

5. 'The New Singaporeans' by Dr Chiang Hai Ding, contained in Towards Tomorrow: Essays on Development and Social Transformation in Singapore, as above, p10.

6. Ibid.

7. Policy options for the Singapore Economy. Lim, C. and others. National University of Singapore. McGraw-Hll Book Co., 1988, pxi

8. The New Singaporeans as above, p12.

9. 'Organised labour in Singapore-past present and future' by C.V.Devan Nair. Towards Tomorrow: Essays on Development and Social Transformation in Singapore, as above, p64.

10. Ibid., p65.

11. Ibid.

12. 'The Port of Singapore' by Howe Yoon Chong. Towards Tomorrow: Essays on Development and Social Transformation in Singapore, p95.

13. Policy options for the Singapore Economy. Lim, C. and others. National University of Singapore. McGraw-Hll Book Co., 1988, ppxi-xii.

14. 'Singapore's success due to 5 factors'. Straits Times 7/1/95.

15. Policy options for the Singapore Economy, as above, p65.

16. Straits Times 8/11/85.

17. Policy Options for the Singapore economy, p66.

18. Straits Times 18/8/86.

19. Foreign Direct Investment and Industrialisation in Malaysia, Singapore, Taiwan and Thailand. Lim, Y.C. and Pang, E.F. Development Centre of the OECD 1991, pp25-6.

20. Strategic Business Opportunities in the Growth Triangle Goh, M et al, Longnams Singapore 1992, p51.

21. Ibid, p52.

22. 'Development of Singapore as a financial centre by Michael Wong Pakshong. Towards Tomorrow: Essays on Development and Social Transformation in Singapore, p86.

23. Ibid., p91.
24.'Strategic Policies & Businesses in Singapore: A Manager's Reference. Huat, T.C. McGraw-Hill Book Co. 1995, p2.
25. Strategic Business Opportunities in the Growth Triangle, p62
26. The Strategic Economic Plan: Towards a Developed Nation, Ministry of Trade and Industry, 1991, pp15-6
27. Strategic Business Opportunities in the Growth Triangle, pp63-4.
28. The Strategic Economic Plan: Towards a Developed Nation, 1991, p5.
29. Ibid., p8.
30. Ibid., pp57-61.
31. Ibid., p66.
32. Strategic Policies & Businesses in Singapore, p28.
33. The Strategic Economic Plan, pp85-6.
34. Strategic Policies & Businesses in Singapore, p63.

3 The Growth Triangle

KEY POINTS

- How the Growth Triangle concept was born
- The economic compulsions
- Industrial promotion of Indonesia's Batam, Bintan and Karimun Islands
- The linkage with Johor in Malaysia
- How the concept works
- Foreign companies' experiences
- Strengths and weaknesses

RATIONALE

THERE IS A UNIVERSAL TREND for economic growth to spread across national frontiers into contiguous areas. In Asia, one can see this phenomenon at work with Hong Kong investments spilling across the border into the Shenzhen Special Economic Zone and from there on into Guangdong province and the rest of China; Taiwanese investments flowing across the Straits of Formosa into Fujien province, and South Korean investments moving across the Yellow Sea to Shandong Province. The spread of economic growth from Singapore into the contiguous territories of Johor in Malaysia and Riau Province in Indonesia, therefore, is far from unique.

What is different is the way governments have become formally involved in setting the framework within which their private business sector can operate. This has involved specific agreements to simplify foreign investment rules so that a company can spread its investments throughout the three legs of the triangle with the minimum of fuss, with the legal and administrative procedures, as much as possible, being handled through the concept of 'one-stop shopping'.

Singapore-Johor-Riau cooperation should also be seen against other regional developments, for a map of Southeast and North Asia increasingly shows the emergence of various overlapping circles of different magnitude. First, there is the long-established Association of Southeast Asian Nations (ASEAN), originally comprising Indonesia, Malaysia, the Philippines, Singapore, Thailand and Brunei, and now in the process of being converted into 'Greater Asean', with the arrival of Vietnam and possibly other Indochina states at a later date. Within that, there is the Northern Growth Triangle comprising southern Thailand, northern Malaysia and northern Indonesia, as well as the economic quadrangle made up of northern Thailand, Laos, Myanmar and the Chinese province of Yunnan. Other economic cooperation circles in the process of discussion or formation include one centred on Southern Indochina as well as the Gulf of Tonkin and the Mekong River, Southern China, the Yellow Sea in north China and Northeast Asia (comprising Northeast China, contiguous areas of Siberian Russia, North and South Korea and possibly, Japan). As the first in the field with the Growth Triangle idea, Singapore is often consulted on how it should be done, prompting Philip Yeo, the visionary head of the Economic Development Board, to suggest half-jokingly that the republic should take out copyright on the idea.

The concept first emerged in the late 1980s when the Singapore government began to look at ways to overcome the constraints imposed on economic growth in terms of available industrial land and potential work-force. Seeking to upgrade its industrial profile , it had already encouraged a number of low-grade, labour-intensive manufacturing operations to move north over the Causeway into neighbouring Johor. But then, the government looked south and saw, literally on the horizon, a necklace of undeveloped small islands belonging to Indonesia. The first idea was that Singapore should simply lease these islands as a new industrial base. But when this did not prove feasible, the idea slowly took shape of building on the shift of industry to Johor to create what is in essence a tri-national industrial park aimed at attracting activities ranging from agribusinesses and fisheries to electronics, petrochemicals, shipping and tourism.

The rationale for this was put forward in a most succinct manner in 1991 by the Institute of Southeast Asian Studies in Singapore:

'The Growth Triangle has taken form as a result of a number of compelling economic reasons, in addition to the facilitating, if not essential, ingredient of political will. The overall cost of doing business in Singapore has risen sharply with two-and-a-half decades of rapid economic growth. The constraints of limited labour and land have resulted in sharp increases in the cost of labour and property, which, together with an appreciating Singapore dollar, have squeezed profit margins. Although the recession of 1985/6 slowed down the rate of cost increases, there has once again been an acceleration in recent years. For example, nominal average earnings in manufacturing increased by an annual average of 12 per cent in 1989-90 when denominated in Singapore dollars, and by an even higher percentage, 15 and 21 per cent respectively, when denominated in US dollars.

'Changes in labour productivity have not kept pace with real wage increases, particularly in 1989 and 1990, implying an increase in real unit labour costs. The increases in property prices are no less steep. Compounding the steep escalation in the cost of doing business is the tightening of an already stretched labour market. Foreign workers are becoming increasingly expensive and hard to come by, because of increases in the foreign worker levy as well as the imposition of a 40 per cent ceiling on the number of foreign workers employed by each company since October 1987. As a result of this, firms have to decide whether to upgrade their activities in Singapore, re-distribute their labour-intensive operations elsewhere, or do both. The Growth Triangle concept facilitates this re-distribution.'

This dilemma was faced in 1992 by a manufacturer of precision engineering components and assemblies for the disk drive industry (which does not want to be named). The result was a decision to open a factory on the Malaysian island of Penang, which although outside the Singapore-centred Growth Triangle still illustrates the point. One reason for the move was that MNC with which it had strategic partnership had already shifted some of its operations to Penang. Other considerations were that for the equivalent of one year's factory rental in Singapore the company could buy a factory in Penang. There was a vast labour pool to draw on and wages were much lower.

The Singaporean managing director of this firm is convinced that if he had not made the decision to shift manufacturing to Penang he would have been out of business within 18 months. Before the shift to Penang, the company had 250 workers in Singapore, but this was reduced to 100 through natural attrition. The Singapore operation carries out headquarters activities such as sourcing and business development; it became the engineering support centre and was used for design, prototyping and production launches.

Company B, meanwhile, is a Singapore-owned industrial electronics manufacturer producing on an OEM as well as full turnkey basis. Although the managing director was approached in 1988 by the Malaysian Trade Ministry about investing, he felt the timing was not right as the company in Singapore was still growing. But eventually, with cost increases in Singapore as well as difficulties in labour recruitment, he anticipated it would be difficult to expand in the republic beyond the present company size of 800. He set up his first factory in Johor employing 400 people in 1992, and opened a second a year later. Main reasons for the move were cost and labour availability. The attraction of Johor, rather than Batam, was that Johor industrial park rentals were cheaper than Batam. But other issue was logistics – transportation was easy via the Causeway. Some companies found it was possible for Singaporeans to commute to Johor to work.[1]

The Institute of Southeast Asian Studies rationale continues:

'The proximity of Singapore, Johor and the Riau islands is a key factor in facilitating such re-distribution, as it implies a minimization of travel and transport costs. For example, professionals from Singapore can transact business in either Johor or the Riau islands, and return within a day. The comparative advantages arising from differences in factor endowments are complementary rather than competitive within the three nodes of the Triangle. Singapore has high-quality human capital and well-developed infrastructure; Johor has land and semi-skilled labour; Riau has land and low-cost labour.

'[. . .]Multinational corporations operating in the region can therefore maintain the capital- and knowledge-intensive operations in Singapore, and the labour-intensive and spatially-driven operations in Johor or in Batam. The proximity of Singapore allows better monitoring and control of operations, and ease of transhipment of intermediate and final goods. Alternatively, to obtain the greatest competitive advantage, firms can locate production facilities according to the production factor intensity in the various locations. For example, the specialized and highly technical operations can be located in Singapore, the less technical processes in Johor and the labour-intensive 'assembly type' operations in Batam.

'The creation of a wider manufacturing base with different factor endowments in each node provides an incentive for MNCs to consider the region as a whole for investment. There is, therefore, a self-augmenting process whereby the initial Growth Triangle becomes an attractive business proposition which then leads to further expansion of the Triangle to other contiguous areas. So the economic imperatives for the development of the Triangle take on a momentum of their own once the initial successes become apparent. Not only is vertical integration possible for manufacturing operations, scale economies in services are also captured within the Growth Triangle.

'Singapore has an efficient financial and business services sector [. . .] linked to global markets, and which is well positioned to provide the ancillary services which are required by industrialization. From the Singapore point of view, having industries in neighbouring areas which are tied to Singapore through managerial, operational and logistics systems allows numerous spillovers to other sectors of the economy. It also allows for yet greater transactional efficiencies because of a larger network. That is not all one-way either. For both Johor and Riau, this is a cheaper development strategy as they can easily tap into Singapore's service network because of proximity.'[2]

'There is mutual benefit for all the participating countries,' argues Mrs Lee Ju Song, Deputy Executive Director of the Singapore International Chamber of Commerce. 'We benefit out of this whole kind of tripartite working arrangement through the provision of our sophisticated international market networking, through our financial infrastructure, through our other business infrastructure and services, while relocating the labour-intensive industries in Batam, Bintan and Johor. [But] most of the marketing aspects and the financial aspects of the businesses are still being conducted through Singapore. Despite the strength of the Singapore dollar, we remain an important financial sector through which our neighbours raise funds for their infrastructural development, because our interest rates are still very modest compared to double-digit interest rates in Malaysia, Thailand and Indonesia.'[3]

The underlying imperative to go regional is nothing new for businesses in Singapore, insists John Chin, Director of the Singapore Manufacturers Association. 'It's being going on for years, but this is the first time it has been focused, framed and hung on the wall. People have been going overseas for a long time, but now it's on the wall for all to see and be encouraged. The government has taken a step towards leading people or pushing them gently.'[4]

The jobs being 'exported' are those generally held by foreign workers, Chin pointed out, adding: 'To put it as coldbloodedly as possible, it suits us' to eliminate such jobs. 'You only have to stand at the Causeway in a morning to see thousands of these guys coming over and earning Singapore dollars quite happily. They go back to Johor Bahru in the evening and immediately one Singapore dollar becomes 1.60 Malaysian dollars, so they're happy with this arrangement. But now, Malaysia wants these people back because it has a severe labour shortage, and already has to cope with one million illegal workers, mainly Indonesians who can't find work at home. So it suits everyone to create a framework that provides an industrial base and jobs that meet all our needs.'

But, did this not create a potential problem for Singapore, the export of manufacturing jobs leading to 'hollowing out' of local industry? It was not a problem *per se*, Chin replied, 'because immediately these guys leave the company here says: "Right, I can concentrate on something that I am better at. With the facilities available in Singapore I'm going to go into higher-tech and higher production facilities, hiring more skilled people and higher value-added products. And I'm not losing the other because I can export it to Johor or to Batam or Bintan." It makes sense to move some things out and replace them with something better. People can see that now.

'Of course, some industries move out and aren't replaced – like textiles. Ten years ago it was in the top 10 industries. Now the manufacture of garments has almost all been exported to neighbouring countries like Thailand and Indonesia. But, usually there is balance. One goes and another comes in – like electronics, where the traditional disk-drive manufacturers are moving out to places such as Batam and replacing this with CD-ROM production which is higher value-added.'

According to Graham Hayward, SICC Executive Director, there was a certain inevitability about the emergence of Growth Triangle given the economic and geographical circumstances. 'Singaporeans were already moving offshore to Johor in the early 1980s because of labour costs, so that leg of the triangle developed naturally. What was politically created was the Batam island concept and that was very much the result of Lee Kuan Yew's vision and a meeting with President Suharto of Indonesia, where the latter made several concessions such as allowing Batam to become a duty free zone and permitting foreign investors to hold 100 per cent equity with little requirement for later divestment – completely different from the ownership rules in Indonesia proper. But although it was a forced situation, I think it would have come anyway because Johor was running out of space for more factories, requiring manufacturers to look for something else nearby.'[5]

Initial doubts about the Growth Triangle tended to evaporate after MNCs realized that the Singapore Economic Development Board and government-linked companies (GLCs) were actively involved in developing and managing many of the industrial parks and resorts on Batam and Bintan. This important signalling element gave a sense of confidence to investors who had become accustomed to the rapid-fire success of Jurong and other industrial estates in Singapore. GLCs gave security through their dealings with higher authorities in Indonesia and provided the key interface between the Indonesian bureaucracy and investors. This was important since the red tape and bottlenecks of dealing with Indonesian bureaucrats were now transferred to a third party which had a reputable track record. In this way, investors felt they were insulated from the maze of regulations and procedures in the Indonesian adminstrative system.

BATAM LEADS THE WAY

Indonesia's Riau Province mainly consists of the Riau Archipelago in the South China Sea and Riau hinterland located on the central eastern part of Sumatra. The economy of Riau is largely dependent on the oil industry. Plans are now being made to diversify and broaden its 'economic rice bowl' to include industries like tourism, agribusiness, aquaculture and manufacturing. Riau's development is to be mainly driven by the private sector, in line with the Indonesian government's strategy to encourage private sector participation in nation building and to create a more open market economy.

Riau archipelago stretches from the Straits of Malacca in the West to the South China Sea in the East. Only about 740 islands have officially recognized names. Apart from oil and gas, the archipelago is also rich in other natural resources like tin, quartz, bauxite, granite, gold, kaolin and timber. The bigger islands are also suitable for agribusiness. There is also good investment potential in the tourism sector, particularly for marine and resort tourism developments. Basic infrastructure like utilities, telecommunications and transport must be laid before any major projects can commence. In this respect, Batam leads the way.

Despite Batam's strategic location in the busy Malacca Straits – only 20 kms south of Singapore, and only 20 minutes away by ferry from Finger Pier – industrial development of the relatively barren and under-populated island did not begin until the mid-1970s. Based on the recommendations of a study carried out in 1971 by the government and some Japanese and American engineering firms, Batam was initially designated for development as a logistic centre for oil and gas industries with related processing of energy products. But a subsequent downturn in the oil industry resulted in further studies being made in the late 1970s for a broader based development masterplan which led to the island being turned into a bonded zone to encourage the development of export-oriented industries. A comprehensive blueprint was drawn up to establish a framework for Batam's development to the year 2006.

Some Singapore-based manufacturers had already begun setting up factories in the 1970s. Property developers also began promoting the island as a weekend getaway for Singaporeans and expatriates. Holiday homes and hotels were built to cater to the demand for resort-styled vacations. But it was not until 1989 that plans to develop Batam on a large scale began to take off. Investment guarantee and joint economic cooperation agreements were signed between Indonesia and Singapore to create a conducive environment for foreign investors in Batam and other parts of Riau.[6]

The whole of Batam plus the small surrounding islets, collectively known as the Batam Economic Zone, enjoy duty-free status and some investment incentives which are not yet available in other parts of the Riaus. Used as a launch pad for the Indonesian arm of the Growth Triangle, Batam's ability to meet the expectations of foreign investors will largely determine the success of Riau's development as a whole.

With Batam's industrial development now under way, attention is moving on to the Bintan as the next commercially viable island in the Archipelago. Other islands being primed for future development include Karimun and the Natunas. Karimun, near Singapore's Pulau Brani and other oil-refining locations is earmarked for heavy industries like shipping and oil related operations. In the South China sea, the Natunas belt is rich in natural resources, and with its deep waters it is potentially suitable for marine tourism developments. Three ports are to be built there as part of a US$42 billion gas project.

But, for the moment, let us concentrate on Batam. By the turn of the century, the island's population is expected to reach 700,000, compared to the 105,000 recorded in 1991. Some of this population, as will be discussed later, is transient – workers who come from other, generally impoverished parts of Indonesia for a couple of years to earn money before returning in relative prosperity to their village.

At present, there are eight industrial estates officially approved and being developed by private investors. Due to the relatively undeveloped state of the infrastructure to cater to the more sophisticated needs of large-scale production, each estate is expected to provide its own supporting facilities and independent management and provision of secondary roads, water, electricity and telecommunications. They are also expected to set up in-house medical clinics, housing and recreation facilities for live-in workers; as well as provide tenants with administration, transport and warehousing services. Some industrial parks also provide other package services including the handling of labour recruitment, investment applications, immigration and work permits for expatriate staff.

Examining some of the areas in more detail, the Batu Ampar region is being rapidly developed into a region for light and medium-scale industries. Some thirty to forty industries, mostly of medium size, will be accommodated in the planned industrial zone. Some existing heavy industries, situated for the most part close to the present harbour facilities, are also located in the area. This zone is serviced with connected roads and supported by harbour facilities that include open and covered warehousing. This development region will eventually have harbour and port facilities that can handle ships up to 350,000 dwt. Commercial organizations will generally be located close to the harbour, while government departments will be more centrally located. Mukakuning, a landlocked area adjacent to Batu Ampar, will also be used for light and medium industries, government and commercial offices and housing.

A large-scale industrial project taking place in the Mukakuning sub-region is the 500-hectare Batam Industrial Park (BIP). This is the centre-piece of the Singapore Government's effort to encourage Singapore manufacturers to relocate their labour-intensive operations to Batam.

The Sepupang region, comprising Sepupang, Tanjung, Uncang and Sagulung, has already undergone significant development. Office buildings have been constructed, water supply lines have been installed, and electricity generation and transmission systems have been laid down. This zone will be the focal point for a core of light-to-medium-sized industries. The development plan for Sekupang includes provisions for small-scale shipyard and ship repair industries at Telok Senimba; primary agricultural activities (cattle fattening, meat processing, canning etc). and, fisheries in mangrove and catchment areas. Special attention will also be given to timber processing, a target growth sector in the development plan. The Sekupang harbour will be expanded to accommodate vessels of up to 15,000 dwt and will be serviced by a complex of warehouse facilities. The harbour and port facilities will service the island's export-based industries as well as inter-island trading, cattle exporting, transhipment and other shipping activities.

The Pantai Timur (East Coast) region, which comprises the sub-regions of Kabil-Batu Besar, Duriangkang-Tanjung Piayu and Nongsa, is slated to be the 'heart and core' of the island. The development plan has allocated some 4,000 hectares in the Kabil-Batu Besar vicinity for medium-scale and heavy industries, with a smaller area aside for integrated wood industries. Several industrial parks are under construction here. The sub-region of Nongsa, with its beaches and clear waters, is set to be the island's tourist centre. Nongsa already boasts a number of hotels and recreational facilities while several more hotels and motels, golf courses and marinas are under construction. A road network connects these tourist facilities to airport, harbour and ferry terminals, and other centres on the island.

Batam Centre, looking out across Tering Bay, is being developed into the administrative and commercial core of the island, with government offices, educational facilities, shopping centres, commercial complexes, hotels, leisure and recreation facilities. An industrial estate for light manufacturing industries is also under construction here as well. Residential districts will be arranged around this urban core will accommodate eventually an estimated 147,000 of the island's entire population.[7]

Batam today supports a workforce of 68,000 employed primarily in industrial parks, hotels, golf clubs, and an assortment of small businesses. Exports totalled US$1 billion for 1994, nearly seven times the value in 1990. Investment commitments were estimated to total US$4.8 billion as of June 1994, of which a quarter came from Singapore investors. Most of the money has gone into industry, tourism and real estate, with the industrial sector getting half the promised investments.[8]

According to Indonesia's Minister for Industry, Mr Tungky Ariwibobo, total private investment in Batam by the end of 1994 had already passed the US$14 billion mark. 'At last count, over 100 companies are operating on the island, with another 70 or more companies at various stages of application and construction.'[9]

FOREIGN INVESTMENT

Nestled in the Mukakuning hinterland, Batam Industrial Park (BIP) became operational in early 1991, and its tenants now include multinational household names such as Sumitomo Electric Industries Group, Smith Corona, Philips, Seagate and Sanyo. To get a better picture of its operation, a few foreign investment case studies can be presented to illustrate why companies have moved to Batam and how successful the move has been. Later in this chapter, we will return to this point when considering the strengths and weaknesses of the Growth Triangle concept from an investor's viewpoint.

American disk-drive maker Quantum Corp. announced plans to build a second plant in Batam even before its existing plant there had gone into full production. At the opening of the first high-end recording heads assembly plant on the island in January 1995, Chief Executive Officer Bill Miller said it was taking steps to ensure efficient production capability in Batam to meet future increases in demand for its drives. According to the plant's resident director, Mr George Ranjuk, another 100,000 sq.ft. facility would be built beside the existing one to be ready in early 1998. The group's Singapore operation produces mainly three-and-a-half inch disk drives, while the Batam plant assembles the heads, a component of the drive. Marketing Director David Rawcliffe cited high labour and business costs as among the reasons for shifting some of the operations to the much cheaper environment of Batam.[10]

American industrial giant McDermott was among the first to start tapping the synergies of operating in Batam almost 20 years ago with the formation of PT McDermott Indonesia. Its multi-million dollar fabrication yard at Batu Ampar is reputed to be the largest in the region and ranks as the world's top five in the industry. The company is also a major supplier to Indonesia's offshore oil exploration and drilling operators. Its workforce of 3,700 employees at the 88-hectare yard are mainly involved in the fabrication of offshore drilling and production platforms for oil companies in the region.

Batam not only lies in the midst of the region's shipping routes, but is also the nearest link to Singapore's well-developed oil storage and refining facilities. Much of Riau's crude oil is also shipped via Singapore. The US accounts for 70 per cent of Riau's trade, most of which takes the form of oil exports. Pertamina, Indonesia's state-owned oil and gas company, has teamed up with oil multinationals like Caltex, Stanvac, Conoco and Hudbay Oil to produce oil off Riau. About half the country's daily oil output is pumped from Riau's Duri and Minas oil fields. Incentives are being offered to promote the use of more efficient and sophisticated drilling and pumping technology to prolong the life of the country's oil industry. Duri is expected to overtake Minas in oil production in 1995 when a US$1.8 billion installation is completed using steam to force the heavy crude oil out of the ground. With more oil and gas projects in the pipeline on Riau hinterland and the archipelagan islands of Natuna, the province is likely to see an influx of oil multinationals and support service companies in the 1990s to meet market demand. From this viewpoint, McDermott, at least, has no regrets about its move to Batam.

The first tenant to begin manufacturing in BIP was Bowaters Bulk Packaging, which produces large bags for fertilizer. The British-based company decided it had to reduce its cost base for what is a labour-intensive operation as well as move closer to one of its biggest markets, Asia. It looked first at Thailand, but failed to obtain a manufacturing permit because the Thai Government thought it would create too much of a challenge to domestic firms.

It was then that the company began to look at Batam, attracted primarily by the fact of heavy Singapore Government involvement which it was considered would smooth over any potential difficulties. Production began there in 1991 in tandem with a similar operation in Britain. But, with fertilizer demand falling in Britain, it was eventually decided that the company could not afford the luxury of two factories, and the decision was taken to stick with the lower cost one on Batam. From there, with the operation overseen from the regional office in Singapore, Bowaters has built up annual sales now in the region of US$7 million covering 26 countries. Raw materials primarily are imported from Europe due to difficulty in finding the right grades closer to home – even though this inevitably pushes up costs.

UIC Electronics, part of the publicly-listed United Industrial Corp group, now has a glittering multi-million dollar factory in BIP to complement its Singapore operations. The expansion into Batam was considered crucial for UIC's growth in world electronics, helping the company to remain competitive and secure a larger market share. Labour shortage and the lack of suitable premises in Singapore spurred the company to look for nearby production sites overseas to support its Kallang Bahru factory.

Electronic components are shipped to the Batam factory to be made into printed circuit-boards, then shuttled back to Singapore for final assembly, packaging and export. UIC mainly produces printed circuit board assemblies and sub-assemblies of computer and telecommunications peripherals for multinational corporations. Eventually most of UIC's high volume items will be made in Batam, with Singapore to be mainly used as a marketing, procurement and engineering support service centre. The Singapore factory will be used to produce more sophisticated products, such as prototypes and higher value-added printed circuit-board assemblies. A total of 500 Indonesian workers will be needed when the Batam factory operates at full capacity, with more space already booked at BIP for future expansion.

Japan's Sumitomo Electric Industries Ltd and its subsidiary Sumitomo Wiring Systems Ltd, for instance, were among the first tenants in BIP. The Batam operations were established for the production and assembly of wiring harnesses. A regional company has also been set up in Singapore to support the Batam operations as well as Sumitomo's existing automotive wiring operations in Johor. These investments, according to Sumitomo officials, are in line with the group's strategic plans to capitalize on the complementary strengths of the different locations in the Growth Triangle.

PT Thomson Television Industrial (TTI) is another classic example of an MNC that has capitalized on the different factor endowments and cost structures within the Growth Triangle. TTI has its regional headquarters in Singapore; it operates three plants in Singapore, two plants in Johor and employs more than 700 workers in its Batam plant for the production of television components.[11]

American telecommunications multinational AT&T established a consumer products plant in the BIP in 1991, where 500 workers produce one of its top selling cordless phone models, while the company's Singapore plant concentrates on high-end telecommunications products. The German-based Varta Batteries, meanwhile, has given its Batam factory responsibility for assembling and packaging rechargeable batteries designed in its Singapore plant.

BINTAN NEXT IN LINE

Bintan, the largest of the Riau Islands and about twice the size of Singapore, is located some 45 km away – a distance covered by a direct ferry service taking one hour. Some 43,000 hectares of land are earmarked as water catchment and forestry areas. The water project, costing an estimated $1.4 billion, will provide not only for the island's own needs but also a good deal for export to Singapore by undersea pipeline.

The Bintan master plan has carved out the island for tourism, industrial projects and agribusiness. The development of this island is expected to be led by the private sector. Tourism has been given top priority at the moment. Some 19,000 hectares of land on the northern coast have been earmarked for tourism projects. The Singapore Technologies Industrial Corporation, resort-development specialist Wah Chang International, the Keppel Group and local banks, have reportedly formed a consortium with Indonesian partners to develop Pasir Panjang beach into a top-class resort destination with hotels, holiday resorts and golf courses. The biggest of these is Bintan Beach International Resort, a project funded by Singapore and Indonesian companies, is to be developed over a 15-year period at a cost of $3.5 to S$5 billion with about 20 hotels, 10 condominium projects and 30 clusters of bungalows, located along the Pasir Panjang stretch of beaches. To support these developments, construction of roads, jetties and other infrastructure is underway.

Industrial development plans include a 4,000-hectare estate near Tanjung Uban on the western part of the island, described as a 'modern mega-industrial complex'. It will start with an initial first phase of 100 hectares, due to be completed within 1995. Bintan officials have also singled out agribusiness for development. Rearing of pigs for export to Singapore and the processing of seafood, have been identified as industries with good potential. Bauxite, kaolin and tin are also mined on Bintan and nearby islands. The Indonesian government plans to develop the petroleum industry and related downstream activities such as the production of plastics.[12]

BIE is being developed by a joint Indonesia-Singapore consortium comprising the Salim Group from the host country, Singapore Technologies Industrial Corporation and Jurong

Environmental Engineering, also from Singapore. They in turn formed four companies to undertake the venture. The developer of the factories, workers' dormitories and town centre is PT Bintan Indi Industrial Estate (PT BIIE). It is also the operator of the utilities and supporting facilities. PT Bintan Industrial Estate Servicatama (PT BIES) is the developer of all the estate utilities. The project management is undertaken by Bintan Industrial Management Pte Ltd (BIEM), while Interisland Marketing Services Pte Ltd (IMS) is an offshore company formed to undertake the marketing and treasury functions of the other three.

The first phase of industrial development, costing $60 million, covered 55 hectares of land, comprising 18 semi-detached factories, two detached factories and 10 fully prepared land lots. Indonesian and Singaporean companies were the main early takers. The first MNC was the Japanese sports shoe manufacturer Mizuno. To date, virtually all the semi-detached and one of the detached factories have been taken up. The target industries are: textile and garment, furniture and woodcraft, toys, plastics, packaging, food processing, shoe and footwear and 'other related industrial and supporting facilities'.

For the foreign investor, the promoters are stressing the attractiveness of a 'one-stop agency' service. Thus, a businessman only has to visit the BIE management office near the Singapore port to negotiate all the details of his project. The BIE provides not only the land and factories, but labour recruitment, work-force training locally or in Singapore, a daily ferry service from Singapore, a thrice-weekly barge service to and from Singapore – both to the consortium's own ferry terminal and cargo wharf on Bintan. A deep water port up to 40 metres is being constructed to accommodate all shipping requirements, with shipping and warehousing requirements operated by a subsidiary company, Batamindo Shipping & Warehousing Pte Ltd. Dormitories to house 6,000 workers have also been built to cater for phase one requirements.[13]

But the emphasis on Bintan is definitely on tourism, as this text from a Singapore magazine suggests: 'Picture this. Balinese-style villas wrapped around serene pools, nestled on a hill overlooking secluded beaches, clear waters and the expanse of the South China Sea. That's what visitors will get when they check into Banyan Tree Bintan which opens in April [1995].The $50 million resort [. . .] hopes to set the tone for a $3.5 billion plan to develop 23,000 hectares of Bintan's best beaches into a mega resort.'[14]

Overall responsibility for development is the responsibility of Bintan Resort Corporation, a blue-chip consortium which includes, as with Batam, the Salim Group from Indonesia, and well-known Singaporean names such as Straits Steamship Land, Singapore Technologies Industries Corp, and the republic's Big Four banks. They, in turn, have attracted other consortiums to specific projects, including Sembawang Industrial of Singapore, Club Med and Shangri-La International.

Under a 20-year master plan, the strip of land is supposed to house 10 golf resorts, 20 hotels, 10 condominiums, three village clusters, a township, several marines and 'eco-tourism attractions'. According to Yeo Nai Meng, general manager of Bintan Resort Management, which is overseeing the development, the aim was to attract 300,000 visitors in 1996, its first year of operation, making Bintan a second destination for Singapore-bound tourists.

BRC reportedly had some initial difficulties in attracting more investors because of negative publicity generated by problems on Batam, such as shoddy buildings, the product of poor workmanship, gaps in the infrastructure, and failure to meet time-frame commitments in getting projects off the ground, which will be discussed in detail later in this chapter. But Bintan's developers feel that in the long-term they have a good chance of succeeding. According to one Singapore-based analyst of the leisure industry: 'Bintan has better prospects because of the people behind its development. They are big names who will have to maintain their reputation.'[15]

KARIMUN IN THE PIPELINE

The development of the Karimun islands, located just 40 km southwest of Singapore, is a natural extension of the Riau development concept. Their strategic location along tanker routes, a deep draft to accommodate ships as large as VLCCs, and the availability of low-cost labour and large tracts of land are key attractions. A consortium of companies led by Singapore's Sembawang Group and an Indonesian construction/property development conglomerate, the Bangun Cipta Group, has taken on the development challenge.

The initial focus will be on shipyard and oil-related industries. In subsequent phases, other industries such as industrial plants and marine-related activities will be developed for use by third-party companies and joint-ventures. The heavy industries in Karimum are poised to complement the already buoyant marine and petroleum-related industries in Singapore and Indonesia.

The development of the Karimum islands has proceeded at full steam since the signing of the memorandum of understanding in August 1991. The Master Plan for the 3,000-hectare industrial development has been completed. Phase 1 of the ship-repairing activities includes a 30,000-dwt floating dock as well as basic shipyard supporting facilities. Plans are also in the pipeline for the development of oil terminalling activities in a consortium with international petroleum trading companies. Negotiations are also underway for the development of an industrial estate to accommodate petroleum-related heavy industries. On a broader front, there should be sample opportunities for the growth of peripheral supporting activities.

A first-tier Indonesian company PT Karimun Investama has been incorporated to act as the land owner and developer; this company, majority-owned by a consortium led by the Bangun Cipta Group, will laise with various Indonesian authorities and provide the basic requisites for the Karimum project. Karimum Industrial Management Pte Ltd will provide management, marketing and design expertise. This Singapore-based company, which is majority-controlled by the Sembawang Group, will manage the infrastructural developments on the islands.

JOHOR

Johor, the second largest state on the Malaysian peninsular, has always had close links with Singapore given their close proximity. The physical links spanning the Johor Straits, are a road and rail causeway built before the Second World War and a second causeway, work on which began in 1995 to link Tuas on the western side of Singapore – where a new high-tech science and industrial park is being developed – and Tanjung Kapang in Johor. This links up with the Malaysian North-South Expressway near

Senai, site of the local airport, and on the Singapore side joins the Pan Island Expressway, which carries traffic as far as Changi Airport on the east coast. Singapore is proposing to extend its Mass Rapid Transit (MRT) rail system to Johor, and Malaysia has accepted in principle.

Senai airport can handle short and medium-range jets, but it is undergoing a long-term development into an international airport. Johor's port facilities are well located and navigable all year round. The port at Pasir Gudang has general cargo wharves and an oil jetty, capable of handling tankers up to 25,000 dwt. The third and fourth phases of a development programme are underway to cope with user demands up to the year 2000. An upgrading completed in 1991, enabled the port to handle container capacity up to 100,000 twenty-foot equivalent (TEU), and capacity was scheduled to double again with the completion of phase three in 1995.

Johor's gross domestic product is projected to reach M$15.86 billion in the year 2000. double the 1990 figure. The state traditionally has been largely dependent on agriculture with the primary sector employing over half its work-force and contributing a third of GDP. But it has been undergoing a restructuring involving a move to the secondary sector. It has been one of the most aggressive states in Malaysia in seeking industrial-related investment, and the gap between manufacturing's contribution to the GDP and the share of agriculture is shrinking each year, and the former is expected to move in front by the year 2005. Further support for manufacturing is provided by the number of plant relocations undertaken by companies from several countries such as Japan, Korea, Taiwan and the United States.

Initial migration of industries to Johor took place because of the availability of labour rather than its cost. As the labour market tightened in Singapore, many investors chose to relocate or expand operations across the Causeway rather than restructure and become more capital-intensive in manufacturing in Singapore. There were good reasons for this. Almost inevitably low-skilled labour acts as a variable element which can be increased when the need arises, and shed during times of low demand. Capital-intensive manufacturing requires large and assured production volumes in order to be cost-effective and the demand for these has to be fairly stable over long periods. Many of the industries that migrated north were those producing low value-added textiles, leather and electronics assembly products. These are products with a low shelf life. If these industries had continued to stay in Singapore, using labour-intensive techniques, they would have had to develop better product quality and variety in order to stay competitive. In effect, they chose to continue to use pricing as their main strategic weapon for maintaining market share and to remain labour-intensive, and hence decided to move to an area where there was an ample supply of labour. Another factor behind the decision to move for some intermediate producers was that their main customers shifted to Johor, so it made sense for them to follow suit in order to maintain the close geographical relationship.[16]

Although the infrastructure in Johor is not as well developed as that of Singapore, it has a reasonable road network linking most of the major towns and a number of industrial townships along the major routes. Electricity, water, transportation and communications links have been catered for under the various Malaysian Plans. These factors and the road-and-rail link to Singapore were important parameters in the investment decisions of many investors. The fact that Johor could plug into Singapore's extensive world-wide shipping and air networks meant that manufacturers could ship their products to any market with the shortest possible transit times.

'Having operated in Singapore for many years, many companies looked towards other close locations in the region which could approximate Singapore's business environment and characteristics. This happened when Malaysia unveiled its new investment policies and its transparent ''property rights'' framework. These were important determinants for many companies moving to Johor. Clear confidence signals were apparent when many investors were assured of a legal system similar to that operating in Singapore and one which the government would uphold. Once the decision to move to Johor had been made, there were other benefits that these industries obtained. Malaysia's new investment policies provided for pioneer status, lower import tariffs for export production, and privileges of the Generalized System of Preferences [no longer available in Singapore, which enabled Malaysian-made products to be exported to the US and Europe duty-free]. Pioneer status gave companies tax exemption for five to seven years and in some cases these were renewable. All these factors were then augmented by a depreciating Malaysian ringgit.[17]

JOHORE CASE STUDIES

A fairly typical industrial operation is that operated by two Japanese companies, Onishi Sangyo Co Ltd. and C. Itoh, which joined forces to set up Corepax (M) Sdn Bhd to manufacture 'hotmelt sealed' kraft-paper bags for the petrochemical industry. Based in Pasir Gudang. the company uses materials which are imported from the United States and Japan to produce about 800,000 to 900,000 bags per month. The company has an output capacity of two million bags since it became fully operational in August 1991.

Smaller companies are also find Johor a good place to be. GOKO Kamera Sdn Bhd, a Japanese-owned company, started with a rented space in a shopping complex in Johor to manufacture cameras. It has since multiplied by leaps and bounds and now has a factory in Pasir Gudang employing 600 people. Its 35mm cameras are exported to Europe, United States, West Asia, Australia and Japan.

A few companies now operate in both Batam and Johor, such as Giken Sakata (GS) a Japanese precision component manufacturer. The Batam subsidiary began operation in BIP in March 1991 with a work-force of 450. The Johor subsidiary assembles tape recorders, video tape recorders and compact discs while the three factories in Singapore produce high-precision machine parts like microshafts and assemble cassette recorders, compact discs and floppy disc drives.

Since 1968, Singapore Marine (S) Pte Ltd has been building powered and sailing boats at its Jurong yard. It has a work-force of 500, including 90 highly skilled carpenters. Robert Livingston, now Chairman and CEO of this operation and its parent GB Holdings Ltd, recalls that when he arrived in Singapore in the mid-1970s it was possible to smile at talk then that the republic would achieve a living standard comparable to Switzerland by the year 2000. The target was actually reached in 1994, so that 'when they now talk about reaching an American standard of living in the next century nobody laughs anymore'. For expatriates, he says,

Singapore is as close as many of them can get in the developing world to a lifestyle similar to what they are used to be back home in, say, America or Australia. The fact, notwithstanding, Singapore Marine made a decision in the early 1990s to eventually move its manufacturing activities to Johor.

Livingston explains: 'The exchange rate has slipped from three to one to 1.45 dollars in my time here, and for an operation that depends on exports for 99.9 per cent of its business, it's obvious that we are a "sunset industy". We looked at Batam but decided it wasn't for us. The Batam people were keen to have us, so we said we needed 300 workers and they promised to have them for us the next day. But then we said, "wait a minute; we need skilled carpenters, specialists in this and that", and that wasn't available.

'So we decided to build a plant in Johor which opened in April 1994, just opposite Ponggol [on Singapore's northern coast]. It takes about an hour to drive from Jurong to the Johor plant, but we can bring our finished boats across the Johor Strait for eventual shipping out in 10 minutes. In addition, for the past three years, it's been very hard to get workers in Singapore. We have had to bring in people from Burma, Thailand and Malaysia. The other problem is land costs. We pay $360,000 a year now, but it's going to keep going up and will be a $1 million before too long. We can get a site in Johor on a fixed rent for 30 years at a fraction of the cost. In a couple of years we'll be down to 200 people in the Singapore operation, although we have to be careful because of retrenchment costs. I have to pay one month's wage for each year of work. If I let everyone go it would cost me $12 million, so we'll do it very gradually.

'I see Johor becoming a satellite of Singapore in 10 years time. Everything is moving that way. There is a lot of development going on in the northern part of Singapore around Woodlands, at this end of the Causeway. The new American companies moving into Singapore are gravitating there or are basing on the Johor side.'[18]

This is one reason why the Singapore American School will be closing its two campuses in the heart of the traditional expatriate belt – postal districts 9-10 – in 1996 and moving to a new integrated campus in the Woodlands area. For Americans, the hub of their social life is the American Club just off Orchard Road, Singapore's premier shopping street. There is now talk of establishing a new American Club in the Woodlands area.

POLITICAL ISSUES

So far in this chapter, the emphasis has been on the positive elements of the Growth Triangle. But, inevitably, everything has not gone smoothly. There are a number of operational and social issues which will be discussed shortly. But first, we will examine those problems which are more political in nature.

Where Johor is concerned, these may be categorized into inter-country, intra-state and inter-state. 'Relations with Singapore can at times be a thorny issue for Malaysians. Johor is no exception to this. In order to continue to push for greater economic coordination, joint-venture development and large-scale investments from Singapore, the state government has had to manage this marketing process very gingerly. There has been outright indignation in some quarters in Malaysia about the close links and cooperation in matters relating to water agreements and the transportation of gas between Singapore and Johor. At another level, the increasing influx of Singaporeans to Johor and the large-scale investments in the retail and property markets by them are matters of concern for Johoreans. The advantageous purchasing power of the Singapore dollar is one factor which has driven up costs of housing, food and other necessities in Johor, this being yet another major source of complaint.

'Intra-state issues centre on the problems of income distribution. With Johor Bahru and other urban areas acting as growth points, rural-urban disparities could sharpen. More difficult to stomach would be the possible divergence in incomes between ethnic groups, particularly since the Malays dominate the rural sector. Federal-state and inter-state relations are yet a third difficulty. Not all Malaysians (particularly non-Johoreans) are enthusiastic about the Growth Triangle concept. While these are often fuelled by wrong perceptions, there could once again be an element of the issue of who gains from this whole exercise.[19]

'One common element in the political problems associated with the Growth Triangle is a resentment of the marketing of the concept – with Johor and Riau being providers of cheap labour and land, as if they are bereft of technical and managerial expertise.'[20] A question to be asked here, therefore, is whether Singapore is trading on the economic weakness of its neighbours in this way.

Mrs Lee Ju Song of the Singapore International Chamber of Commerce, does not agree. 'We are all at different levels of industrial development. So, to classify us as exploiting our neighbours weakness is not correct interpretation of Singapore's activities. In the 1980s we realised that it is best to help our neighbours to grow. This is because the success of our economic performance is going to be highly dependent on how successful they are,

'Actually, many companies first come to us to ask if the investment elsewhere is going to be viable. Based on what they have in mind, we offer to fix an appointment with our counterparts in Johor, Penang or Kuala Lumpur, and because of the sincerity which we have demonstrated we are able to enjoy such a good working relationship with out neighbours. We are surrounded by a huge Muslim community [Malaysia and Indonesia] and we have to work very hard to convince them that we belong here, we belong to the region. We may be ethnically Chinese, but we are definitely Singaporean, we are definitely ASEAN and we are definitely Southeast Asia. We are not shortsighted. We cannot afford to offend and let our neighbours to be suspicious of our intention.'[21]

Tackling this issue, the Institute of Southeast Asian Studies has commented: '[T]here is a need to be more sensitive to the fears of our neighbours, even if they are not well founded, and to be more sympathetic towards their ambitions. There is a need here to emphasize the mutuality of benefit which flows from such cooperation, the need to emphasize the concept of partnership rather than the division of labour. Singapore should respond positively to requests from its neighbours to help them upgrade their human skills. Singapore should respond favourably if Johor were to ask it for help to build its science park. It is in Singapore's interest to help its neighbours "scramble up the technology ladder" as quickly as they can.'[22]

In December 1994, an internal agreement was signed between the federal government in Kuala Lumpur and state government of Johor to mark a significant step forward in the administration of the Growth Triangle. Previously, the central government had control of all the federal activities in Johor, including customs and other activities. Under the new agreement, the Johor Menteri Besar (Chief Minister) was given the right to do a lot more and take decisions in a lot more areas, including immigration and customs regulations. To many this was highly symbolic in that the Growth Triangle concept finally seemed to have been given the official seal of approval from Kuala Lumpur, raising hopes for many in Singapore that they would no longer have, in the words of one source, 'to play politics' at a federal level.

Relations between the two countries seem to be better at the time of writing than they have been since they parted company in the mid-1960s, but it requires constant efforts on both sides to maintain harmony and it does not appear to take much to upset the delicate balance.

'On Batam, political problems take on a slightly different slant. Because Indonesia is a large country and the population bases are in Java and Sumatra, the population at large is not relatively well-informed about developments in the Riau Islands. For those who are in the know, one of the main issues again centres on the question of sharing the benefits. The development of the Riau Islands, in general, has been spearheaded by the political elite and a group of leading Indonesian business conglomerates. It would be good if this base were widened so that spillovers could occur to a larger populace. Some also comment on the absence of the 'third leg' of the Triangle and that it is more a case of Singapore-Johor and Singapore-Riau rather than a genuine 'Triangle'. Steps have been taken to strengthen the Johor-Riau link, although this is relatively weak compared with the other two.'[23]

While Johor and Singapore generally have clear 'property rights' within the legal system, Batam suffers from the vagueness of Dutch law. Promulgation of clear 'property rights' laws and its interpretation would help reduce the uncertainties of investing in the Riaus. 'Thus far, the joint-venture companies such as BatamIndo Management, which manages the Batam Industrial Park, have insulated investors by taking on the 'property rights' risk. However, as supporting industries follow suit there will be a need for clear land laws and a more transparent legal framework. Supporting industries are often spearheaded by small and medium-sized enterprises which have less financial and political muscle and for them such laws provide for a sense of security and business confidence.'[24]

SICC's Graham Haywood agrees with this assessment: 'Things like leases in Indonesia are very difficult. You do not own the land in Indonesia, nobody does. All the land belongs to the people via the government. What you get is an assortment of rights to use the land for 30 years. They are prepared to roll it over sometimes 20 or 30. But the problem is that in 30 years' time, what is their reaction going to be? To extend the lease it also costs money. So the land is always a problem for investors. If you are getting your land from a local developer, which is in many case is what you have to, frankly your legal right to use that land depends on the financial integrity, strength and longevity of the developer. And this worried a lot of people who initially rushed over from Singapore to Batam to buy houses. Then people began explaining to them the legal position and they rushed back again. So, you will see a lot of developments sitting around. They had cleared roads, or bits of jungle and started building infrastructure or the skeleton of buildings and then they stopped because the demand ran out when people discovered the fragility of the legal hold they had on their so-called investment.'[25]

At the time of writing, the Indonesian Government has begun a review of the land laws which may eventually lead to a lifting of the ban on foreign ownership.

PROBLEMS ON BATAM

The going has been far from smooth on Batam, where several projects have been scaled back, delayed or dropped, and many investors have had their fingers burnt. Batam, seen as a test case in the Growth Triangle, has suffered a bad press over golf club developers who did not deliver, inadequate infrastructure, and a glut of housing. Investors, naturally, became wary.

A Singaporean asessment[26] of the development provided a picture of 'defaulting golf club developers, poorly built houses with brand-new windows falling out, inadequate power and water supply. That is the side of Batam that has been in the news in recent years. It seems a long way off from the Indonesian government's vision of transforming Batam into an industrial, commercial and tourism hub by the year 2005.

'While major projects such as BIP [Batam Industrial Park] are joint-ventures between big Singapore and Indonesian groups, the bulk of the developments are undertaken by small companies. This is where the cracks are showing. Developers grouse that there is not enough direction and coordination in the overall development plan. They also say that there are too many entrepreneurs doing the same thing. And as the response to Batam cooled over the years, the number of projects has slowed. "Batam suffered from a case of too much, too early, after which nobody believes you," says Geoffrey Blake, project manager of the Tering Bay golf resort, which is owned by heavyweight Indonesian investors. "Too many rushed their projects and delivered bad quality or failed to live up to their promises."

'With the exception of some developed industrial areas like Batu Ampar, much of the island is pockmarked by abandoned construction projects and ghost town housing estates. It's a "Catch 22" bind. While the authorities are pushing developers to get projects going, many are reluctant to commit further until demand picks up. [. . .] Many developers say slow infrastructure development is partly to blame for their woes. "You cannot blame developers who were pushed to build as fast as possible," says Bernard Syauta, executive director of Indonesia's Srimas Group which owns the Palm Springs housing estate and First Triangle Industrial park. "When they did, they found the supporting infrastructure lagging behind."

'In Batam, the government provides the basic infrastructure from roads to telecommunications. But there have been complaints of inadequate water and electricity supplies. Several developers provide their own power and water for tenants. "The government cannot rely on private developers to provide the infrastructure as it's a huge investment," says Chan Chan Kung, general manager of PT Suar International Development. PT Suar, a Taiwanese-Indonesian venture, operates Kuang Hwa Industrial Park, which has four tenants.'

'Of the eight industrial parks registered, only four are up and running. Of the four only BIP is considered a success. Unlike BIP, most other parks function more as landlords, leasing out plots of land to companies which in turn have to build their own factory and invest in infrastructure. This makes it harder to lure investors.'

In answer to these complaints, the Batam Industrial Development-ment Authority (Bida) head Soeryohadi Djatmiko insists it is working on improvements, citing the following:

- Bida privatized water management in January 1995 to boost efficiency and promised the whole island would have water by early 1996.
- In 1993, the electricity unit was handed over to a state electricity company which has budgeted US$600 million for power investments up to the year 2003. Twelve more power plants will be built over the next 10 years and existing ones upgraded.
- Batam's road network has reached 576 km, linking all major centres.
- Batam's Hang Nadim airport, being upgraded into an international airport, was due for completion by the end of 1995. The airport's upgrading is viewed as a much-needed catalyst for Batam's growth, serving as a hub for tourist charters as well as cargo flights. The new passenger terminal will be able to handle three million passengers a year. Aside from these projects, there is also an ambitious plan for a US$1 billion container cum transhipment port in Kabil. The first phase, ready in 1997, will be able to handle 550,000 TEUs (20-foot equivalent units).

BATAM: INDUSTRIAL CASE STUDY

Turning to the industrial side once again, the following is a description of one manufacturing operation on Batam which will illustrate some of the continuing problems investors face there. The executive who provided the information did so, however, only on the understanding that the company would not be identified.

The factory employs 400 people and is run by Indonesians. The executive explained that '. . .when we came out here we decided to have an expatriate at the top in Singapore, but then to delegate to senior people of the culture who are doing the work the responsibility for actually running the manufacturing side of the business. I think we are the only ones on the industrial park who are doing this at present.

'You don't have quite the same close control as you would with an expatriate in charge, but we haven't had the industrial relations problems that many people have had on the industrial park. Singaporeans have a somewhat downbeat view of the Indonesians and many of the companies are run by Singaporeans

– mainly because BIP is a manufacturing overspill from Singapore.'

What did he mean by 'labour problems'? 'I think that other people who weren't knowledgeable of Indonesian culture did have some difficulties. There's been the odd strike and dispute. In four years we've never had a problem. You have to look at it from a workers' viewpoint, however. Batam was an island with about 10,000 people six years ago. Now it is 170,000 to 180,000. And all the people who come to work on industrial park are people on a two-year contract basis. They are 17-19 years of age – people away from home for the first time, in a new environment and working hard to remit money back to their families in other parts of Indonesia. As a result, one of the main problems is homesickness and stress. And if you get a strong management push, with a lot of people already lonely and away from home, then it tends to escalate very fast.

'Worker turnover is very high. A large proportion of the people at the end of their two years go back to their home village. We have 25 per cent annual turnover because people don't want to stay. They can extend after the two-year contract, and we do our best to persuade them to do so because otherwise, from company point of view, you are never building up the real depth of skill and experience that you would in a more stable community. And generally in manufacturing it's that depth of knowledge from people having been there eight to 10 years which actually gives you progress in optimising your manufacturing process or improving your products. It comes from the shopfloor to a large extent. Because people aren't staying and you don't get this build-up of deep experience, I think there is a problem you will always have to put more imput in formally either from technical department or from your industrial engineering department back home than you would in a Western-based company.

'Our process is one where people can make a contribution due to variety in what we make. If you are assembling disk drives, until model changes, it's the same thing. So many others don't have problem. But if you get into real high-tech areas like aircraft manufacture which Indonesians really want to do, then I think they will come across the same problem. An aircraft mechanic with two years experience is not as good as one with eight years experience.'

Recruitment is also a problem for Batam-based manuafcturers. The BatamIndo Authority has a subsidiary called TunasCarrier that recruits on behalf of companies on the site. They go out to all the high schools all over Indonesia, screen the best people, and then bring them to Batam for further screening and training by the employers. For the initial two years, the employment contract is with TunasCarrier not with individual company.

'Again, we have done it differently,' says the executive. 'We decided we wanted to recruit our own people. Because we have Indonesian management and hierarchy we have not used that service. One of the complaints of our sister companies is that they cannot get quantity and quality that they want. First, they can never get quantity. Some of the companies want to recruit 500 workers at a time, but what they find is that they only get 380 or something like that. So there's a quantity *per se*. Obviously, TunasCarrier have a problem finding enough people of the requisite quality. When they presented to the employer on Batam, they do their own screening and perhaps reject some more. So companies who want to grow quickly have a permanent problem of finding enough good people.

'TunasCarrier recruit the better people from the high schools. Initially, we used the same channels and it wasn't until a few months into the process that we decided to go our own way. One reason is that the culture I am trying to engender in my people is that you should use less people. The Indonesian culture is that if you control 1000 people you have a higher status than if you control 200. So the culture is to build people, push them in. I've managed to convince our managers that that is not the way we must go. We must go down in numbers. It must be like the West and Japan: the better manager is the one who can do the job, promote output with fewer people. My managers now have stopped trying to always solve the problem by recruiting more people. I've said we must produce in next three or four years perhaps 40 per cent more output with no increase in numbers But that's a break in Indonesian cultural thinking. I don't think government realizes there is a problem.'

Another difficulty the company is now facing is that Batam is no longer the low-cost site that it once was. Minimum labour rates have increased drastically. In 1991, the company being studied was p[aying 2,400 Rupiahs a month, which was the minimum wage, and by early 1995 it was paying 6,750 Rupiahs. The rising cost of labour, therefore, is a matter of concern, even though the Rupiah has been devaluing at around seven per cent per annum against the US dollar.

And costs are high in other areas due to Batam's geographical position as a small island with no agricultural base to support its growing migrant population. According to the executive: 'Everything is more expensive, even for local people. Food has to be imported. So it's not as low cost as other places and it is rising fast and that is a concern. We no longer see it as a low-cost plant. With our products we are having to move up the technology, the quality and the added-value ladder far more quickly than we anticipated. Increasingly, Batam would be one of the less competitive new sites that is vying for inward investment in the region. I think that Vietnam would be much less costly, but you don't have the close proximity to Singapore, so you could argue that Batam should command a premium. And it does. You then get into the debate as to how much is the premium worth? How much is it worth to be close to Singapore? If the Singaporean authorities don't shelter you from some of the worst aspects of doing business in Indonesia, then again there becomes a problem.

'These are valid questions. A lot are subjective. We can all point to our increasing costs and that's definitive. But I think that most companies on Batam are just beginning to get to grips with the tax authorities etc., because during first couple of years they have losses in start-up operations, but the tax authorities are becoming far more interested in what people are doing. The next couple of years will be very interesting, especially if the Indonesian Government and officials are too aggressive in pursuing companies. It's not just the issue of what you pay it's also management time to try and make counterpoints to the authorities. For instance, if you are asked for tax, the assessment is always higher in Indonesia because the rules are not so firm; it always becomes a matter of debate and negotiation. So there is a question of management time that you are putting into dealing with the array of import duties, customers people, tax people, labour department. You tend to need a whole battery of people just to contend with the government machine in Batam. That in itself is an issue apart from level of taxation.'

The executive also complained about the high freight costs of shipping his products from Batam to Europe via Singapore, with between a quarter and a third of the cost coming in the very short inter-island journey – US$700 to go 12 miles, out of a total cost to Europe of US$2,500. Ideally, Batam needs a roll on-roll off operation enabling cargo to be shipped direct to its final destination, which would make the Port of Singapore unhappy due to the loss of business. As a result, at present, a container is loaded onto a truck at the Batam factory, unloaded and placed on a barge for the short journey to Singapore, where it is offloaded onto a lorry to be carried a short distance to a storage area in the port to await reloading on a lorry for movement onto the ship bound for Europe or elsewhere.

Added to this, the exective complains, is the fact that the Batam electricity rate is four times higher than average elsewhere; and the water rate is 10 times higher; at the same time, in early 1995 Batam Indo approached firms on the BIP and asked them to pay a 'management levy' of $6 per worker per month, which provoked strong resistance.

Batam might be more attractive for some foreign investors if it was the gateway to the rest of Indonesia. But, given its duty-free status, that would be difficult while the government in Jakarta remains concerned to protect some of its fledgling local industries from the competition of foreign products. For the company being studied, the domestic route would involve the immediate imposition of a 40 per cent duty. Its business in Indonesia primarily is with one company which then uses the products for re-export, enabling it to claim back its outlay under a duty drawback system. The same applies to payments of VAT. The executive says: 'We don't have any domestic market share because it's not worth developing from Batam. If you're interested in the domestic market, then it's better to go into Indonesia proper.'

BATAM: SUMMING UP

It would seem, therefore, that although Batam started out promisingly as a low-cost alternative for manufacturers in the region, the reality may prove to be somewhat less enticing. According to Marcus Chan, managing director of Varta Batteries, which relocated its battery-assembly unit from Singapore in 1991, 'savings have not been what we projected'. Items cited as costly in comparison to other low-cost production centres like China were freight, utilities, medical care and rents. The extra costs of recruitment and taking care of Indonesian workers and expatriate staff added to Varta's burden. This is higher than some low-cost countries like China, says Mr Chan, adding: 'We would have moved to China originally if it were not for Batam's proximity to Singapore. But if costs continue to escalate, we will have to consider other options.'[28]

So how competitive is Batam, compared to other low-cost areas in Asia fighting to attract investment? According to one businessman: 'If you already have an operation in Singapore and are struggling for labour and facing high costs, then I think Batam is still probably an attractive proposition to download your operations or increase capacity. But I think if you were looking from a Japanese or a Western perspective as to where to locate in Asia, I think Batam would struggle to be competitive.'

The manufacturing operation described in detail at the beginning of this section was actually set out by someone else who has since moved on to another company. And this particular executive has a more positive approach to Batam, although he ackowledged some initial teething problems. 'Effectively Batam-Indo is a Singaporean company, but it was was under great pressure to use Indonesian contractors for the early construction. Unfortunately, the one who did our factory wasn't up to standard.

'There are frustrations, certainly. The Indonesian Government is following a few populist measures like increasing the minimum wage every year. The minimum wage on Batam is higher than anywhere else in Indonesia, and every year it keeps going up, failing to take into account that a lot of MNCs supply other things like accommodation, meal allowance, medical care and a whole range of things which you wouldn't get in Java and Sumatra.

'In 1990 when we began, there wasn't really anywhere else to go, but it was the correct move because we were producing very labour-intensive, low-skill stuff. But now, with the range of China, Vietnam, Cambodia, it is getting less and less competitive and very quickly uncompetitive. It may still have a niche, because the higher-tech businesses in Singapore are going over there. So in comparison with Singapore, although it is getting uncompetitive on the very labour-intensive stuff which is easy to move to Vietnam (making components for televisions etc.) for a higher-tech firm it might be the thing to do, using a slightly more skilled Indonesian work-force, but which is still a tenth of the cost of a Singaporean work-force. And you have the added advantage of Singapore's infrastructure, finance, shipping etc. on the doorstep.

'So, for Singapore the Growth Triangle still makes sense, and for Indonesia it makes sense, because, with a population of 190 million, it's got to create two million jobs a year to stand still. But for Malaysia, it doesn't make sense really. I know this well because I have a factory in Johor now, and because I can't get labour for love nor money. I'm having to bring in Bangladeshis.

'Johor is worse than Batam, bureaucratically, racially, administratively. Batam is designated as a free-trade zone and things can go in and out; it's isolated in a sense from the rest of Indonesia so it's a dedicated business island and you can overcome all the nonsense that you might have to go through if you are anywhere in Indonesia. In essence, it is becoming an Indonesian microcosm of Singapore, which is fine. But Johor is still part of mainland Malaysia. It has all the rules and regulations – racial quotas on the work-force and equity holdings (to safeguard the interests of the Malay population *vis-a-vis* the Chinese minority); duties to take stuff in, duties to take stuff out; various other payments to take stuff in and out, and so forth.

'Batam is isolated and this is the essential problem they having with the Growth Triangle and why Malaysia isn't really playing along with it – because there are a group of bureaucrats in Kuala Lumpur who, it seems to me, don't want to play along with it. Their power base rests on maintaining the old ways. The administrative sclerosis that goes in isn't there in Batam. You can get things moving. Therefore, I'd say to any potential investor: take a look at Batam, but I don't think Johor is the answer.'

One of the chief selling points put forward in favour of Batam is that the management company, as this executive mentioned, is mostly staffed by Singaporeans, and their marketing pitch stresses the combination of the 'best of both worlds' – Indonesian cheap labour and Singaporean efficiency. BatamIndo promises to look after everything, and, in effect, says: 'Don't worry. . .if anything goes wrong we'll look after you.' Increasingly, however, foreign executives say this can no longer be taken for granted. As one commented: 'Once you get [to Batam], you find the Indonesians saying, "well it's not quite like what they told you in Singapore. This is Indonesian territory and we want a bit of a say in this as well, so don't put us down". So the Singapore sales pitch that, effectively, you are operating on Singaporean company is not quite right now – if it ever was – and that is where I think some of the problems are arising or will arise. It's vital, therefore, that you go out of your way to get to know the local Indonesian authorities as well as those in Singapore.'

But even while Singapore continues to promote the Growth Triangle concept – or at least that part of it centred on Batam, Bintan and surrounding islets – it is looking much further afield in the growing outward reach of its economic strategy. And is this broader area that we need to look at next.

CHAPTER NOTES

1. Cited in 'Overseas Investment: Experience of Singapore Manufacturing Companies'. Lee, T.S. Singapore, Institute of Policy Studies/McGraw-Hill Book Co., 1993.
2. *Growth Triangle: the Johor-Singapore-Riau Experience*. The Institute of Southeast Asian Studies, Singapore, 1991, pp4-9.
3. Interview in Singapore 7/1/95.
4. Interview in Singapore 24/1/95.
5. Interview in Singapore 16/1/95.
6. Doing Business In Riau. Ernst & Young, 1992.
7. *Strategic Business Opportunities in the Growth Triangle*. Goh. M et al, Longman Singapore 1992 pp17-18.
8. 'Can the Triangle grow?' *Singapore Business*. February 1995.
9. *Straits Times* 19/1/95.
10. 'Disk drive maker Quantum plans second Batam factory' *Straits Times* 19/1/95.
11. *Strategic Business Opportunities in the Growth Triangle*, pp88-9.
12. Ibid., pp30-31.
13. Briefing by BIE executives in Singapore, 16/1/95.
14. 'Bintan: Mega-resort in the making.' *Singapore Business*, February 1995.
15. Chris Wong, leisure consultant of Horwath Asia-Pacific, quoted in *Singapore Business*, as above.
16. *Growth Triangle: the Johor-Singapore-Riau Experience*, pp11-12.
17. Strategic Business Opportunities in the Growth Triangle, p12.
18. Interview in Singapore 20/1/95.
19. *Growth Triangle: the Johor-Singapore-Riau Experience*, p16.
20. Ibid.
21. See note 3.
22. *Growth Triangle: the Johor-Singapore-Riau Experience*, px.
23. *Growth Triangle: the Johor-Singapore-Riau Experience*, p16.
24. Ibid., p21.

25. See note 5.
26. 'Can the Triangle grow?' *Singapore Business*, February 1995.
27. Ibid.
28. Ibid.

4 Regional partnerships

KEY POINTS

- Role as regional hub
- Importance of regionalization
- What Singapore has to offer
- Government incentives for firms to move overseas
- Partnership concept
- Case history: Keppel Shipyard
- Developments in China
- Singapore's drive into India

SPRINGBOARD FOR ASIA-PACIFIC

GLANCE AT A MAP of Southeast Asia and it is possible to miss Singapore. This is a nation of only about three million people living on a land mass little larger than central Tokyo. Yet, astonishingly, it is the fifteenth largest importer in the world – more than 70 per cent of the goods being re-exported to neighbouring countries, either directly or after some processing.

Thousands of companies, from multinationals to small local dealers, are involved in links with ASEAN, Indochina and as far afield as China, Taiwan, Japan, Korea and India. Some of the reasons are obvious: an excellent location on strategic shipping lanes and a natural deep water port, and an infrastructure which manages to keep pace with economic growth. Singapore has led the way in the region in developing highly efficient port facilities, a superb airport, extensive road networks and world class telecommunications.

It has always encouraged foreign investment and has one of the most transparent and straightforward investment regimes in the region. An estimated 3,000 foreign companies have bases on the island, including 200 manufacturing operations. Ever since Raffles, Singapore has been outward-looking, relying for survival on business and trade with the surrounding region. Regionalization of the economy, therefore, is not new. What is new is that it is now a key plank of government policy, having been put at the top of the agenda following the 1992 visit to China by Senior Minister (former prime minister) Lee Kuan Yew which opened up a wide range of cooperative projects between the two countries.

Striving to stay ahead in a fast-developing region, Singaporean companies are now strongly urged by the government to invest in regional ventures, especially where the government provides the political framework. The first major project to emerge from this policy was the 'Growth Triangle', which continues to grow, radiating out from the original base of Batam to encompass other islands in the Riau Archipelago, as well as expanding the environs of Johor.

The second phase was the move into China, beginning in 1993, when Singapore negotiated with the Chinese government an ambitious plan to develop an industrial township, run on Singaporean lines in Suzhou, near Shanghai. The Singapore Government undertook to train officials from Suzhou in infrastructure planning and public administration, while a consortium of Singaporean firms produced a blue-print for the physical development. Since then, Singaporean firms have become involved in numerous other infrastructure projects in China, including power stations, ports and airports, hotels and leisure developments and a high-tech industrial park at Wuxi. Another consortium is developing an industrial park at Bangalore in India, and investments are beginning in Vietnam and Myanmar.

According to Graham Hayward,[1] Executive Director of the Singapore International Chamber of Commerce, the government-led regionalization programme has gone through three phases in the 1990s: 'The first phase was to go out to the world and invest. And that didn't go too well because some people made some unhappy investments, including the government. There was one in New Zealand, which got off to a bad start and was further undermined by the declining value of the New Zealand dollar. Then [drinks producer] Yeo Hiap Seng bought into a US company called Chungking which did not go at all well. So it became quite clear very quickly that Singapore did not have the resources or cultural understanding to go too far offshore. The next phase was: "OK, let's go regional as opposed to international. Let's invest offshore but let's keep it within Southeast Asia because, logistically, we can control it, and, culturally, we are in harmony with them." That worked well, especially in China with the added dimension for the bulk of the Singaporean business population of a shared language and ethnic roots.

'But then, some people quite quickly realized that, maybe, they were putting too many eggs into the China basket. This is why, since early 1994, there has been an increasing emphasis on India to balance China, which makes a lot of sense, considering the hard core of educated Indians in Singapore and a potential middle-class market of 200 million quite affluent people in India.'

At the time of writing, Singapore was the fifth largest investor in China (US$8.5 billion), eighth in India (US$117 million), third in Vietnam (US$1.3 billion) and the largest in Myanmar (Burma) with US$272 million, according to the EDB.

PROMOTING PARTNERSHIPS

The third focus is the notion of 'partnership', the idea that companies from countries such as America, Britain, France, Germany and Japan should team up with Singaporean counterparts, whether government-led or from the private sector, to invest and carry out business in areas like China, India and Vietnam. Hayward believes this makes a lot of sense, because '. . . there are many foreign companies who are happy with Singapore. They are at ease here. The people speak English; the Chinese are westernized; it's a user-friendly country; the legal system is good and there is a transparent economy.

'Added to this, the local entrepreneurs have a good rapport with the surrounding market and some specific advantages in areas like China and India. There is also a very considerable reservoir of goodwill towards Singapore because it is not a threat to anyone politically, it is seen as a reliable and trustworthy partner in the region, and Lee Kuan Yew has earned incredible respect world-wide, especially among Chinese, as an elder statesman and father figure. That is why I think Singapore will be a very good partner for a lot of Western companies who are hesitating to go it alone in this part of the world for a variety of reasons – like lack of trust, lack of contacts and lack of knowledge of local operating conditions.'

Ideally, the creation of such partnerships should come from a Singapore base – namely through Western companies that have already established a significant presence in the republic, or are willing to do so, given the right incentives. This can be done in stages. For a start, Singapore can become an ideal product distribution base for the surrounding region – essential given the small domestic market – either by providing a simple warehouse operation or a manufacturing facility.

Atlas Converting Equipment, a medium-sized British manufacturer, set up regional sales and technical service office in Singapore in the early 1980s, and sells direct from Singapore to China, Korea, Indonesia, Thailand and Malaysia. General Manager Keith Sutton explained some of the benefits: 'Asian customers have high expectations of after-sales service. they expect to be able to pick up a telephone, discuss the problem and expect a prompt follow-up visit from your technical representative. A customer in northern China or Korea will be extremely reluctant to buy from the UK because of its distance, but he will have no psychological barrier to buying from Singapore.'

F.G.Wilson is another British manufacturer which has had enormous regional success after setting up an operation in Singapore in 1992. From Singapore the company's generating sets are sold to 18 countries from Sri Lanka in the west to Fiji in the east, and from Taiwan down to New Zealand. Sales Manager Clive McKeown explained that one of the advantages for him of using Singapore as a stocking centre is the absence of high tariffs: 'With tariffs as high as 20 per cent in Indonesia and 40 per cent in Malaysia you simply cannot afford to hold stock there. And once you have imported the goods tariff-paid you are left in a very weak position to negotiate with your customer.' Singapore is virtually tariff free and the processing of documentation and turn-around times for cargo are still far faster than elsewhere in the region.

The above points to another benefit of using Singapore as a stocking and distribution centre: speed of response. The manager of one British company which uses Singapore as the supply base for its operation in Vietnam said: 'When you receive an enquiry from Vietnam you have to move really fast. Your customers have very little foreign exchange; they need to move deals extremely fast and will give you two or three days to supply. From Singapore we can meet that kind of deadline.'[2]

Through such distribution operations, companies gain confidence from the comfort of a secure base, adding more functions in the marketing, administration, servicing and research areas. Contacts are developed with various Singaporean business and finance sectors counterparts. The foreign companies are encouraged to take advantage of every incentive the government has developed to upgrade their operation and for the benefit of their export business. From there, they may be ready to listen to proposals for a synergistic alliance with a Singaporean partner or partners to take a higher-profile role (e.g. project management or local manufacturing) in one of the countries on the established customer list.

Of course, Singapore is not acting out of purely altruistic motives. The government, for a start, wants to see more of its home-grown companies venturing out into world markets. In part, they can be nurtured through financial and other incentives to make the big step. But in some cases, it will be wiser if they can have a Western or Japanese partner to provide added strength, perhaps shared special knowledge, and to spread the risk. Equally, for those Singapore consortia involved in building industrial and scientific parks in China and India, the partnership concept creates potential instant tenants for the factories and office buildings being put up.

John Wilson,[3] President of Singapore-based John Crane Asia Pacific, as well as President of the British Business Association in Singapore is one who sees the regional strategy as a very positive move, and is convinced that no bureaucratic hurdles will be allowed to stand in its way. 'Given the fact that an oriental face is often more acceptable in many places, Singaporeans can act as a very important bridge between East and West.

'It's not impossible to go it alone. There are British companies who have gone alone into Vietnam, for example, and done very well. But for others to go in as partners with a Singapore company will strengthen the business because there are definite synergies. In terms of China, there is an even stronger advantage because of their ability to speak the language and therefore communicate easily. Having worked in China for many years, one of my biggest difficulties was translation, which added to the difficulties of both negotiating and also operating. Singapore is particularly strong in certain areas like the north and the central coast, while Hong Kong is very strong in the south. As far as India is concerned, there are advantages probably for foreign companies in certain sectors like building, industrial parts, hotels and leisure where Singapore has a lot of experience.'

Singapore's ambitions were clearly spelt out by Prime Minister Goh Chok Tong, when opening a German trade centre in Singapore in mid-June 1995, he warned that European companies in particular risked being left behind in the investment rush into Asia and made a strong pitch for his government as the essential middleman to overcome any deficiency. 'We are strategically located at the heart of the Asia-Pacific. Our cosmopolitan society, our multi cultural make-up, our Confucian upbringing and Western education enable us to serve as a bridge.' To further this concept, Singapore took the initiative in proposing an 'Asia-Europe' summit to deal with trade and investment issues, which was due to be held in Bangkok in mid-1996. The choice was significant because Thailand has already recognized Singapore's hub role, declaring the republic will in future be its '. . . gateway to sell its goods to the rest of Asia and the world', taking advantage of Singaporean skills in finding new markets for the products passing through.

At the time of writing, the partnership concept was still in its early stages of development. But some projects have already emerged. For example, two Singapore-listed companies teamed up with a major New Zealand group to invest in one of the largest cement plants in China. The local companies – a steel maker and investment management firm – took a 49 per cent stake in Yangtze Cement Holdings Pte Ltd, a joint-venture formed to invest in one of the major cement works in Suzhou. The other shareholder is Milburn New Zealand Ltd., the largest cement producer in New Zealand, which, in turn is a subsidiary of a large Swiss cement group. Yangtze Cement had an initial paid-up capital of $58 million and owned 50 per cent of the Suzhou cement plant, which serves the greater Shanghai area.[4]

Britain's TI Group, with sales of £100 million and 2,000 employees in its own or associated companies across the Asia-Pacific, is no stranger to the region. But it still recognizes the advantages of a helping hand to develop further. In February

1993, it found one in the shape of Sembawang Group, a big Singapore-based industrial conglomerate located on the island's largest shipyard in which the Singapore government indirectly holds a majority stake. The two companies signed a memorandum of understanding to develop business opportunities together in the region, focusing initially on Singapore and China.

TI's businesses have long been active in the region. The John Crane seals business established its first operations there 27 years ago, and its seven-year-old joint-venture in Tianjin is China's largest seals manufacturer. Bundy, which makes automotive tubing and systems, has a number of ventures in the region and both the TI companies are well-known names. Dowty, with the region's only independent service and repair facility capable of handling landing gear from wide-bodied jets, has expanded its operation close to Changi Airport. TI believes the region offers strong growth opportunities for all three of these core businesses.

'John Wilson says: "We have knowledgeable people here and all three divisions have exposure in China. But the link-up with Sembawang gives us extra knowledge and a different approach to the market. We are able to draw on a pool of Chinese speakers. And Sembawang are able to take an objective view of our businesses, because they are not experts in them. We bring that expertise." The Chinese business culture of *guanxi* – relationships, contacts, networking – is a most important aspect of doing business in China and establishing such relations are easier between Chinese. Lai Chun Loong, president of Sembawang Industrial, agrees that knowing the culture and language helps bridge the gap between West and East. "We have proven that we can convert Western technology and management systems into the regional environment, and are able to guide the Western company and the receiving party for the technology in the region".[5]

In late 1994, the Economic Development Board, and the Sembawang Group and Germany's Daimler Benz took a stake in a joint-venture company, Daimler-Benz Vietnam Investments, which plans to assemble Mercedes Benz vehicles in the Indochina state. Saigon Motor Co., Vietnam's Ministry of Transport, Indonesia's Salim Group (heavily involved with Singapore interests in the Riau island projects referred to in the last chapter), and Autostar, a subsidiary of Hong Kong's Peregrine Group, were the other partners.

Commenting on this development, a local commentator wrote: 'In my view, the Republic's vast financial resources and strong political connections can be used as a magnet to draw quality European MNCs for ventures in and around the region with top-end manufacturing to be located here. This is entirely plausible if one considers the views of some of Singapore's friends. Daimler Benz Chairman Edzard Reuter told me in an interview that India's top leaders would like the company to come to their country in partnership with Singapore.'[6]

In early 1995, meanwhile, property tycoon Ong Beng Seng's private investment arm, Kuo International Pte Ltd., won approval to set up a car plant in North Vietnam with Japan's Toyota Motor Company along with a yet-to-be designated Vietnamese state firm under the Ministry of Heavy Industry. Vietnamese officials said the firm might later be privatized. The approval marks a change in Vietnamese government policy, which was previously aimed at persuading multinationals to buy into two existing car assembly operations.

According to Toyota, the proposed $252 million project would eventually produce 20,000 cars a year. Toyota models are highly popular in Vietnam, where demand for cars and commercial vehicles is expected to increase sixfold to 60,000 a year by the turn of the century.[7]

PROMOTING ENTERPRISE OVERSEAS

To develop the regionalization drive, the government set up a Committee to Promote Enterprise Overseas, which produced an interim report in May 1993, with recommendations on tax incentives, government support through financing, partnering and facilitating overseas ventures, and measures to improve the regulatory environment for private enterprise. This was discussed by more than 500 top public and private sector executives at a forum organized by the EDB in the same month.

In a keynote address, Prime Minister Goh Chok Tong emphasized that the drive to go regional must bring benefits to the domestic economy, make it more resilient and raise the standard of living for Singaporeans. This was also stressed by the then Minister for Trade and Industry, S. Dhanabalan, in his closing speech, when he explained that the aim of regionalization was not just to have more Singapore investment overseas and more Singaporeans working abroad. If companies shut down their operations in Singapore and relocated to another country, the owners presumably would be better off, but there would be no spin-off for the Singapore economy. On the other hand, if a company relocated its existing activity to another country but upgraded its Singapore activity to one which was more technology, knowledge and skill intensive, there would be clear benefits.[8] Goh stressed that projects should make use of the expertise available in Singapore according to an organized 'Singapore Inc.' public-private sector cooperative basis. They should have economic linkages and spin-offs to a wide range of Singapore business entities, typified by the Batam/Bintan project with Indonesia.[9]

In its final report, the committee declared: 'We must invest abroad to develop an external dimension to our economy to give our GNP an added boost; create opportunities for smaller businesses and good jobs for Singaporeans (by venturing overseas, we are creating new opportunities for Singaporeans both overseas and also in Singapore). When our companies venture overseas, like the Japanese, they can bring in their suppliers, In this way, the small and medium enterprises also expand overseas. The Japanese do this when they go overseas. They bring along their suppliers, and their supermarkets. In this way, even their sushi and sashimi chefs, their newspapers (like *Asahi* and *Nihon Keizai Shimbun* in Singapore), and their television stations, and many ancillaries follow their major players overseas.'[10]

From the Regionalization Forum, the committee took up several suggestions:

- The Civil Service College to hold a seminar every two or three years on major economic issues which would enable senior civil servants from various ministries and statutory boards to map out a common national strategic response and set directions.
- Mechanisms to be developed for public sector personnel to be seconded to the private sector. Much expertise in infrastructural development like airport and seaport management, town planning, and industrial estate development resides in the public sector, and this can be shared with the private sector, it was argued.
- An International Business Institute should be set up to train local

managers and entrepreneurs venturing overseas to prepare them and their families for the different business and living environment abroad. It should have a strong practical orienta tion and be driven by the business community.

- The Local Industry Upgrading Programme,[11] developed by the EDB, to be extended so that various statutory boards are encouraged to identify and help a core of their high potential suppliers and contractors to upgrade their capabilities.[12]

The government, it was suggested, should be an active partner in overseas ventures along with the private sector because of the 'technical expertise, depth of experience and proven track record in public sector operations and infrastructural development' of its various agencies and that of government-led companies (GLCs). 'Government's participation should not be such that it ends up bearing the majority of the risk while the private sector assumes only a small part of it. Government ministries and departments are not geared for undertaking overseas ventures themselves and should confine their role largely to that of being a facilitator.'[13] The key recommendations, therefore, were that:

- GLCs and statutory boards to partner private sector companies in overseas ventures by selling their expertise to the private sector, forming joint-ventures or consortia, leading in large infrastructure projects.
- Statutory boards to identify and help a core of their high potential suppliers and contractors to upgrade their capabilities. Government working out a mechanism to allow public sector officers to be seconded to work in public-private sector joint-ventures.

The committee also urged the creation of a 'country investors' club' for each major country, comprising private sector investors and public sector representatives in the country concerned to help track investment trends. Thus, Investment Guarantee Agreements have been negotiated with India and Pakistan. A Vietnam-Singapore Commission for Cooperation was established in May 1993, and in the following year, a Singapore-Shandong Business Council was formed to promote and facilitate trade and investments between Singapore and the North China province.[14]

The Committee acknowledged that although the whole regionalization concept was built around home-grown enterprises and home-grown entrepreneurs hopefully leading the way, there were many who believed the average Singapore company was not sufficiently well-developed to compete abroad as compared to those from the developed countries, or Hong Kong and Taiwan, and, in addition, Singaporeans are generally risk averse – preferring to take safe professional and managerial jobs rather than strike out on their own.[15]

'The largest local companies tend to be concentrated in traditional sectors such as banking, property development and food and beverages. There are also a number of GLCs, for example, in ship-repair, transportation, and communications and certain high tech nology areas. Most local companies remain small and have concentrated on serving the local market – this is to be expected. In 1990, of the 80,066 local enterprises in manufacturing, commerce and services, less than one per cent were major companies; essentially, they were all small and medium-sized enterprises with less than $12 million in fixed asset investment. However, an increasing number of them are making the breakthrough into the major leagues, and these include companies engaged in fashionwear, retailing, manufacturing, engineering, computers and software. There are also companies providing consultancy and professional services overseas. Most of these companies are seeking listings on the stock exchange and some such as Creative Technology and IPC Corporation have developed multi-national operations of their own.'

To nurture more such success stories, there are, at the time of writing, more than 60 programmes introduced over the past two decades to promote the growth of local enterprises at each stage of their development, covering technology acquisition, business development, human resource management, marketing, design, research and development. They are centrally coordinated by the EDB, and administered by agencies like the Singapore Institute of Standards and Industrial Research, Skills Development Fund and the National Productivity Board.[16] Typical examples are the Local Enterprise Finance Scheme ((LEFS) Overseas) and the Regionalization Training Scheme (RTS). LEFS (Overseas) provides low-cost loans for the purchase of equipment and industrial facilities needed for the overseas operations, while RTS provides a grant to help local companies to defray the cost of training overseas personnel in Singapore. In its first full year of operation (1993), 28 projects were approved for the former scheme, and 37 for the latter.

In 1993, the EDB helped local companies in more than 150 investment projects. Its involvement included identifying investment opportunities, supporting feasibility studies, arranging business consortia and implementing overseas projects. Of these, 33 per cent concerned infrastructure, 34 per cent were manufacture-related and 31 per cent service-related. The breakdown of location was: China 25 per cent, Southeast Asia 27 per cent, South Asia 45 per cent and other countries three per cent. In the same year, the EDB also organized 10 country roundtables for Singapore executives to explore collaboration opportunities in the immediate Asian region with businessmen from Australia, Britain, France, Germany, Hong, Kong, India, the Philippines, South Korea, Sweden and Thailand.[17]

And, as a further move to develop the foreign segment of its partnership plan, the EDB then introduced the Business Head-quarters (BHQ) programme to attract companies to use Singapore as a base to expand their services to the region, including product development, logistics, merchandising, customer support, financial management and procurement. BHQ is an extension of the Operational Headquarters (OHQ) programme which the EDB introduced in 1986 to encourage companies to use the island as their headquarters to manage the activities of their subsidiaries in the region. The BHQ programme incorporates a wider range of incentives to cater to the needs of different types of services, which include: product creation: market research, competitive analysis, concept formation, product and process development; customer service: marketing, after-sales service, information management and customer account management; financial management: budgeting and treasury management; regional management: strategic planning, business development, legal advice, financial and administrative support, and human resource management.

The incentives included:

- Pioneer service status: up to 10 years tax exemption for activities where the technology is new to Singapore, and where substantial technology transfer and expertise is evident.
- Export of service: tax exemption on 90 per cent of the chargeable income for the qualifying portion of export services, for up to 10 years.
- Warehousing and servicing: tax exemption on 50 per cent of chargeable income for the qualifying portion of export sales or services, for up to 10 years.

Companies awarded BHQ status can also apply for an

Investment Allowance, Initiatives for New technologies (INTECH) grants, approved royalties, fees and development contributions, tax exemption on offshore dividend income and double deduction for R & D expenses.

CASE HISTORY: KEPPEL SHIPYARD

Singapore's ship and oil rig-building/ship-repair sector has been among the most enthusiastic supporters of the overseas investment drive. And within the sector, the government-owned Keppel Shipyard has been the most aggressive, driven by the imperative of growing competition from neighbouring Indonesia and Malaysia who have both stepped up their efforts to develop a marine industry. It has invested heavily in repair yards in the Philippines and Vietnam, and has entered an Australian joint-venture, Keppel Caincross Shipyard in Brisbane, which offers 24-hour integrated repair and refurbishment services and dry docking facilities. There is also a growing competitive threat from the Middle East, which Keppel has sought to meet by setting up two yards in the United Arab Emirates, Arab Heavy Industries and Al Majid Engineering, which carry out repairs and conversions. Both yards are managed by Singmarine Industries, which is part of the Keppel group.

Meanwhile, Sembawang, a diversified marine industry group also partly government owned (an inheritor of Britain's largest naval dockyard beyond Suez), is establishing a repair yard on the Indonesian island of Karimun (see previous chapter).

This sector illustrates clearly the imperatives that have pushed the regionalization programme forward. The emergence of shipbuilding mirrored the development of Singapore from its earliest days, but there was a time in the mid-1980s, amid recession, when it was designated by the government as a 'sunset industry' that no longer fitted into the island's future image. It was kept afloat largely by the fact that many of the large tankers built in the oil boom of the 1970s were due for mandatory repair work. And as most were passing the 'front door', shuttling between the Gulf oil producers and Japan, Singapore was the logical place for the work to be carried out. With a reputation for a quick turnaround time, ship repair accounts for most of the marine industry's output. Singapore claims to have the largest repair capacity in the world, with a dry and floating dock capacity of three million dead-weight tons. Employing some 22,000 people, the marine industry in 1993 contributed 3.2 per cent of the country's GDP.[18]

Nevertheless, 1994 was a poor year, and most yards reported lower earnings. For the first time in years, there were empty docks, primarily due to the fact that shipowners reacted to lower freight rates by keeping repairs to the minimum and delaying orders of new ships. Industry analysts doubted there would be any significant recovery before the second half of 1996.[19] Nevertheless, yards continue to feel confident. Some of the biggest yards, including Keppel, are investing in additional capacity in anticipation of another batch of the world's oil tankers coming their way for repair over the next few years. Keppel Group Chairman Sim Koe Boon, for one, is confident that as Asia's demand for oil rises, so will the need for repairs and new tankers. 'We are preparing for the next wave. The main challenge is to remain competitive.'[20]

There is no doubt that the yards are competitive at present, but there are some challenges that need to be met, principally rising labour costs and as well as a labour shortage, the development of rival yards in neighbouring countries and the appreciating Singapore dollar. In anticipation of an upturn in ship repair, the government decided in 1994 to increase the labour supply from a ratio of one local worker against two foreign workers to three to one. Because of a shortage of domestic labour, a large proportion of shipyard employees come from India, Malaysia, Indonesia and China.

But while upgrading productivity and competitiveness is one of the government's chief aims, it also hobbles the yards financially by imposing a foreign worker level of $200 for every skilled man they take on, and $385 for every unskilled one. The government also actively encourages shipyards to upgrade skills by introducing training programmes, but the financial burden of these largely falls on the employers' shoulders. For yards like Keppel, therefore, an alternative strategy is to go where the workers are rather than bringing them to Singapore.

But ship building and repair is only one facet of the Keppel Group's international business interests. It has a US$90 million Vietnam Investment Fund, involving institutional investors from Europe, Japan, Hong Kong and Australia, which is involved in the property and hotel sectors of the Indochina state, as well as engineering and shipyards. At the time of writing, it had launched a new fund, planning to raise between US$20 and $30 million from investors world-wide, for various projects in Myanmar along similar lines to those in Vietnam. Through its property arm, Straits Steamship Land Ltd, Keppel is developing a 450-room, five-star hotel in Yangon (formerly Rangoon), and plans to invest in a service apartment project in the capital together with a 300-room international class hotel in Mandalay. It has also talked of launching a US$100 million China fund to explore investment opportunities in Suzhou, Shenzhen, Shanghai and Guangzhou.[21]

CHINA FIRST

By the beginning of 1995, it was self-evident that the two most significant Singapore-related investment drives involved China and India.

As already noted, Singapore is currently the fifth largest investor in China following Hong Kong, Taiwan, Japan and the United States. Singaporean firms put US$1.32 billion into China in the first half of 1994. The number of projects funded totalled 3,834 up from 1,751 in 1993.[22] Singaporean commercial investment in China started in 1981, with a new wave rising after the two countries established diplomatic relations in October 1990. It is mainly in medium-sized cities with thriving economies and little competition. They include Suzhou and Wuxi in Jiangsu Province, Qingdao and Yantai in Shandong, Xiamen in Southeast Fujian province, Dalian in north-eastern Liaoning Province, Chengdu and Chongqing in south-western Sichuan. Singapore has built industrial parks in Suzhou, Wuxi, Chengdu and Chongqing.

While directing small and medium-sized enterprises to remote provinces such as Yunan and Sichuan in the Southwest and Henan and Hubei in central China, the Government has advised multinationals to gain a foothold in Shanghai and Beijing. Of the total Singapore investment, 80 per cent is in real estate projects, including industrial parks, office buildings, apartments, hotels and commercial centres. But as China opens further, Singapore companies are shifting their focus into setting up factories to produce textiles, electronics, chemicals and other products, and building berths and ports for shipping.[23]

Bilateral trade reached S$7.5 billion in 1994 – almost 10 per cent higher than the previous year. When the two countries established diplomatic ties it was $5.2 billion. Oil and related products account for nearly 40 per cent of China's exports to Singapore, but this is now matched by electrical appliances and machinery, which is rapidly expanding.

The most ambitious project in China to be undertaken by Singapore entrepreneurs, in close partnership with the two governments, is the development of the Singapore-Suzhou Township which, when completed in the next century, will cover 70 sq.km. and cost over $30 billion. It entails the transfer by the Singapore government of its expertise in economic and public administration to the Chinese authorities, while a consortium of Singapore companies led by Keppel Corp. undertakes the physical development of the town.

The entire township will be developed in three phases – the first covering 10 hectares – and will include industrial, commercial, residential and recreational facilities as part of an integrated development that will eventually support a population of 600,000 and provide employment for 360,000. The Chinese government has approved the registration of the joint-ventre company which will develop the commercial side of the township. The software transfer from Singapore initially focused on urban management, economic development and financial management. Other areas of public administration that may eventually be included are labour management, personnel management in the public sector, business law and social amenities.[24]

The China-Singapore Suzhou Industrial Park Development Pte Ltd, with a registered capital of US$50 million, is a 65:35 partnership between the Singapore consortium and its Chinese counterpart. The consortium of 19 Singapore companies includes Straits Steamship Land, Liang Court, Lum Chang, Wing Tai, Centrepoint Properties and City Developments. There are 11 companies from Suzhou and Jiangsu Province also involved.

There will be ready-built factories of two, four and six storeys which manufacturers can lease or buy in a start-up area of two sq.km. Investors can also opt to build their own factories on prepared land parcels. At the time of writing, 14 international investors had snapped up 82 per cent of the industrial land available in the start-up area on 50-year leases, with an investment of $1.3 billion.[25] The range of industrial activities planned for the start-up area include the manufacture of semiconductors, precision plastic component parts, healthcare products, canned juice and drinks, precision tool and die, food processing, a brewery, residential development and transportation.

The largest investor, South Korea's Samsung Electronics, with a projected injection of more than US$500 million, is taking up 33 hectares of land in the township. Its initial investment will be in a semi-conductor plant. The long-term plan is to build a self-contained industrial complex to develop and produce electrical and electronic goods such as semiconductors, electric motors, condensers and finished home appliances. New Zealand brewery Lion Nathan is the second largest investor, taking up 15 hectares. The company will build a brewery with an ultimate capacity of 400,000 tonnes a year. Investment is expected to exceed US$352 million.

Three American companies which have taken space are semiconductor maker Advanced Micro Devices (AMD) which will invest US$29 million, healthcare company Becton Dickinson (US$25 million) and electronic parts maker Littlefuse Far East Ltd, which intends to construct a US$2 million facility but with plans to double it after three years. From Japan, drinks manufacturer Pokka plans to build a US$15 million factory. All were to begin operation in 1996.

In yet another fillip for the Suzhou town development, the consortia secured an agreement with the Jiangsu provincial government to incorporate a chemical park covering several square kilometres, although this will be in a phase three site and will need central government approval. Singapore has already convinced several American European chemical companies of the advantage of setting up operations in Suzhou.

Another interesting development is taking place not far away in the city of Wuxi. As a leader in technology-based industry and an active player in Singapore's external economy regionalization drive, Singapore Technologies Industrial Corporation (STIC) decided to enter the Chinese market through the tried and tested route of infrastructure development. Based on the Batam Industrial Park model, STIC is leading a joint venture between a Singapore consortium (including Jurong Environmental Engineering, Sembawang Industrial, Tamesek Holdings and the KMP Group) and the local government in Wuxi to develop a 'world class industrial park'.

Wuxi represents one of the more attractive cities for industrial development in China. Easily accessible 130 kilometres from Shanghai with a population of 4.3 million, it is one of the fastest growing cities in China. Its industrial base is well developed with more than 14,000 industrial enterprises ranging from machinery and electronics to textile. To date, foreign-funded projects total US$6.4 billion with 1,280 fully foreign-owned enterprises, equity joint ventures and contracted ventures.

Envisioned as a high-technology industrial area, Wuxi-Singapore Industrial Park (WSIP) seeks to attract manufacturers from industries such as micro-electronics, computer peripherals, telecommunications equipment and products, medical and pharmaceutical products, precision engineering, electro-optical devices, aerospace and automotive components and parts, consumer household electronics and other related and supporting industries. Among the early arrivals were the Japanese companies Alps, Murata and Sumitomo.

The park will be developed in phases to a final size of 1,000 hectares. The first factories in Phase 1, comprising 100 hectares, were due for completion before the end of 1995. There will be a range of four-storey factories each covering a floor area of 10,000 sq.m. and standard two-storey factories, each with a floor area of 5,000 sq.m. The development will have its own power and water supply, direct telecommunications access to 160 countries world-wide, and sewerage treatment plant; it will also provide a full range of amenities for the workers, including dormitories, medical and childcare centres, canteen/cafeteria, shops and sports and recreational facilities. Plans have been made for a commercial development located in the prime commercial district of Wuxi city to complement the industrial facilities provided at the park. It will house a business hotel, service apartments, retail outlets, entertainment facilities as well as an international school.[26]

INDIA NEXT

Singapore, according to the EDB, now ranks as the eighth largest investor in India. By late 1994, total investments totalled 199 projects involving an investment of $101 million, focusing on aquaculture, food products, computer peripherals and electronic components. Total bilateral trade in 1994 surpassed $3 billion, more than 20 per cent up on the previous year. There was an across-the-board rise in exports of most products particularly computers, electronic components and telecommunications equipment. Singapore's non-oil imports, such as diamonds, plastic products, textiles and electronic components, also expanded, by 10 per cent, to $1.1 billion.

The single most attractive reason for investing in India, according to some companies in Singapore, is a large domestic market that has been well established for years and comprises a middle class of between 100 and 300 million people, along with a potentially large export market. The low cost of production was another key factor, as well as a centre government now considered to be pro-business and willing to open up the previously tightly-controlled industrial sector.

For 1995, three Singapore government agencies planned a coordinated drive to build on the rapidly expanding trade and investment The EDB,TDB and Tourist Promotion Board agreed to:

- Encourage Indian companies to internationalize by setting up trading and operational headquarters in Singapore;
- Promote Singapore's investments in India in areas like real estate, infrastructure, tourism-related ventures and export-oriented industrial projects.
- Encourage and develop Singapore-India collaboration in third country markets and projects.

The Singaporean approach to India involves cooperation with local interests, particularly state governments, in the creation of industrial and high-tech science parks. Much of the effort is being channelled through Parameswara Holdings Ltd, an investment company established and led by the Singapore Indian Chamber of Commerce, named after a fifteenth century prince who fled to Singapore from attacking Siamese and later founded Malacca in what is now Malaysia. Formed in May 1993, PHL has since emerged as a fully-fledged public limited company with a successful public offering of $25 million worth of shares in 1994. Its chairman is Suppiah Dhanabalan, former Trade and Industry Minister.

PHL has a 10 per cent stake in the Singapore consortium which is building a $250 million Information Technology Park in Bangalore along with Singapore Technologies Industrial Corporation, Jurong Town Corporation and Temasek Holdings, plus public listed L & M Group Investments, Sembawang Construction and RSP Architect. It has since begun feasibility studies on another large industrial park, for more general use, in Haryana state just south of Delhi. PHL already has a stake in another Singapore consortium which is developing a five-acre commercial building complex in Burgaon, Haryana, with Unitech, an Indian public-listed company. PHL Company Secretary George Abraham, who is also secretary of the SICC, said the project was one of many being considered. Karnataka State, in which Bangalkore is situated, is already hoping to build on the existing projects there to encourage another $1 billion in investment via Singapore for tourism-related facilities, including an international convention centre.

In mid-1995, this was followed by an announcement that the state-owned Singapore Technologies Construction Pte. Ltd. had been given the design and management role for what was described as the region's first 'intelligent city' to be built in the West Bengal capital Calcutta. The 40-acre development will have two 22-storey 'intellicentres' (computer integrated office buildings) at its core, surrounded by 'intellihomes' along the same lines.

A source closely involved in the initial Singapore developments in India[27] said: 'We realized that among the easiest projects we could get into would be for infrastructure development. This involves the creation of industrial parks, with which we have a lot of experience, similarly in commercial property – but, more importantly in the context of developing countries, the main-tenance of commercial properties. We also thought of looking at three- or four-star hotels, and areas likes roads, highways and ports. We decided that we would want to get into industrial parks and commercial property as the first priority.

'But in all these, the problem we have is with land. First, there is the question of title; because you never know whether you really own the title because someone can come along later and say that his great grandfather was given it by the sultan or local king. They also have a legal system unlike China and Vietnam. It's based on the British legal system, but then it can take a long time to go through the courts and your investment gets blocked up in the meantime. The second problem that we found is the question of payment, because India has a parallel economy, and so a lot of land deals involve payments that are official and unofficial. So people want part of their land payments unofficially so they don't have to declare it for tax purposes. And as foreign investors we cannot get involved in this.

'So the easiest way out is to have a third party provide the land. And if you are going into industrial parks and commercial properties it would ideally be the state government. And then you could have a large Indian company as one of the partners because they can be relied on and know how to manage the local system.

'In Bangalore, we are part of a Singapore consortium of six companies, some large government ones with the expertise in building of parks etc., in cooperation with the Karnataka State Industrial Development Board and the Tata, one of the best known Indian industrial groupings. Singapore has 40 per cent and PHL has 10 per cent of that which means four per cent of the whole project. What this means is that we function like a reinsurance company in being able to spread our risk with larger companies and we are comfortable that this project will succeed.

'We then went into commercial office property in Gurgaon, Haryana State. We used another large Indian company called Unitech, one of the biggest builders, and we have a consortium of Singapore companies including PHL which again has taken 10 per cent. Here again, as regards the safety of the company, we are secure in the knowledge that any problems concerning land in India will be sorted out. The third one is an industrial park which is also in Gurgaon. This uses the same triangular approach of Haryana State, Unitech and Singapore consortium. One of the advantages of having the state government involved is that you have long-term commitment on land; they will sort out the problem of squatters etc. And you also have the government helping you with policies and problems that may arise in the implementation because they are a stakeholder in the project.

'The other advantage is that we can use the EDB and TDB in negotiations with the state government to make the whole project gel much faster. The Bangalore project was put together in less than a year and for the Haryana one a memorandum of understanding was ready in only three months. So, I think that if you want to get into large projects in India it would make sense to go in as a team, to work with large Indian companies, or if its in manufacturing with medium-sized companies, and adopt the PHL approach.

'There is no real reason why we or anyone else should be geographically limited, however, for India is a big country and different states offer different advantages. Bombay, for example has a very large industrial base. Haryana is different – plenty of land, close to Delhi so easy to hobnob with policy-makers – although that really isn't necessary because once central government lays down the investment policy, the state government is free to work on guidelines. Punjab has excellent medium-sized companies that make sporting goods, bicycles and automotive parts. In the south, Coimbatore, which used to be called the Manchester of the East because all the textile mills are located there; as a result of that they have built up an expertise in precision engineering industries. They are supplying components and parts to automotive companies in India. They supply parts to refrigeration equipment makers.

'The states are trying to market themselves for different opportunities. I think one thing that people are beginning to realise is that unlike other developing nations India is emerging *now* only because it chose to open up now. Unlike other emerging nations they already have an industrial base. It's just that because they were a closed economy, their industry has stagnated at a certain point. What is needed is an upgrading of existing industries; an upgrading of quality standards and improvements in areas like packaging and international marketing sophistication to help put their products into the international market. The domestic market has been such a good consumer that they have never really bothered to look at the external market. But now with the competition they will start looking at it. So there are a lot of areas for Western companies not just in selling to the domestic market but also export activities. You should have companies in manufacturing with export potential.'

But this does not provide a clear rationale as to why Western companies should seek joint ventures with their Singaporean counterparts to go into India. Another senior source within the Singapore Indian community, who spoke only on the understanding he was not identified, provided a clearer rationale:[28]

'I think you begin from the premise that a number of countries who are very big on trade and investment elsewhere in the world have a great deal of suspicion about Indian business conditions, primarily because for more than four decades India has been a closed economy to all intents and purposes. The European and the American businessman is unable to come to terms with the way business is done in India. They don't have enough Indians in their own population to help them understand how to get round things in India. Singapore has always had the advantage of having Indians from its early days and also maintaining links with India, because Singapore's South Indian community in particular tends to keep in touch with home – Madras and Tamil Nadu.

'So, because we understand the Indian mentality, because we share it, it is easier for us to talk and do business with the Indians and they understand us as well. They are more comfortable with us for two reasons. One is that we are Indians or have a significant section of Indians in the Singapore population, and secondly the Indian businessman thinks that if anyone is straight it is the Singapore businessman. I am sure that in their eyes some of us are naïve. But they probably feel more comfortable dealing with us than an American big boy, or a someone who is a MNC from Europe, because there is always the fear that an American or European is not used to coming in on the basis that they take a minority stake. They are used to running things.

'So, despite its liberalization and despite the fact that everything has opened up, the Indians are concerned that these guys are going to eat them up. Whereas the Singaporeans go in with the attitude that "look, if you have opportunities let's work together. You have labour, we have money. You have land, we have the expertise. We don't want to take advantage even if we could. Because the economic relationship that we have runs in tandem with our political relationship and if you hurt one the other gets affected". So, in a small country like ours everything is carefully managed and in a way that's good because it encourages confidence among Indian businessmen and politicians about people from Singapore.

'Therefore, the advantage of going into India via Singapore is that there is a great deal of respect and comfort for businessmen coming from Singapore. If you start on that footing things can only get better. But if you go into a proposed deal where there is mutual suspicion you might falter because of the economic imperatives: you want their technology, you want their know-how, so you go into it and then you find that there is trouble down the line, It's happened. For example, Coca Cola went in after so many years and they joined forces with a local company which had a substantial share of the Indian soft drinks market. Now they are fighting each other and it's sad. There were wrong assumptions on both sides, but it really comes down to the fact that you cannot expect a company like Coca Cola to go in and remain a passive minority partner.

'One has to understand that in India the contract is not a big deal. They don't work like the Westerners do in that you must have signed deals and, not only that, you must honour them. In India, it is the exception rather that the rule that lawyers are brought in to seal deals and ensure the documents are properly drawn up, to watch for the full stops and commas. In-house lawyers will draft something that is more like a memorandum of understanding. It's signed and then after the event there are so many loopholes and so many issues unaddressed. It's no use saying India has a marvellous legal system. It has a common law system but there are grave practical difficulties in the way of getting access to that system and I really think they should look at an international arbitration system to operate in parallel for the business community.

'Apart from the cultural affinity, and comfort level generated between our two countries, because of the political relationship, there is also the perception from India's standpoint that Singapore offers certain political advantages to India. It's a very sensitive area. India has its economic and political agenda. It wants to get close to some of the ASEAN countries. It makes sense. I'm saying that because (1) of the strength of the political relationship, and because (2) both sides are very eager, India more than Singapore, wants to send out a signal "that you can do business with us and that if you have problems we will address them". Given that context, today and in the immediate future, if you come through Singapore, chances are that if you have problems your problems will be solved faster, then problems faced by a company from another country where there the relationship isn't so settled yet.

'But very soon, if this relationship continues to improve we will reach a steady state, and then India will look towards other countries to nurture a new political relationship and then give them concessions that they might not give us any more. So, it's really a question of timing. In today's context, Singapore is a very good bet if you want to do business with India.

'We are not targeting America or Britain, because they have a history of economic relationships, particularly Britain. We are really looking at countries in this region. Western Europe, countries there who have had no relationship with India either politically, culturally or historically. And Japan. Japan has not moved into India in a big way and everyone is asking why. They have done a few deals in cars [Suzuki helps build the Maruti with a Suzuki engine] but they have not gone that one step further. Although there isn't any distrust in the relationship, politically or economically, the reason is people say that the Japanese have not come to terms with the Indian mentality. Perhaps they are used to having an environment that lends itself to certainty. In China, if the governor says I want this to be done, chances are it will be done. In India, if he says I want it done, you have to go through so many processes for it to be done. Everyone with his own interests. I don't think the Japanese are comfortable with this.

'So, it's very much up to India to change the system and I think it's asking too much to expect them to change it overnight. It will take a long time. Best, then, to go in with a Singapore company which has already established a relationship and who knows how to work out problems. The Japanese have confidence in Singapore partners and if the partners say "I'm confident about India", they will piggyback. And once they are comfortable with India themselves then they will probably take off on their own.

'We cannot look too far down the road. We have to look at short- to medium-term and make the most of it. If the Japanese went in with us, they'd be manufacturing the low- to medium-technology stuff, but the high tech will still stay in Singapore. So if we have a five- to 10-year fruitful relationship and then we have to look for new ways to make money and that's what Singapore has always done.'

CHAPTER NOTES

1. Interview in Singapore 16/1/95
2. Briefing Paper from the British High Commission Commercial Section. Sept.1994.
3. Telephone interview in Singapore, January 1995.
4. 'S'pore firms, NZ group in tie-up for Chinese cement deals', *Straits Times* 12/1/95
5. 'Bridging the culture gap between West and East,' *Financial Times*, 30/8/94.
6. 'Add a new dimension to regionalization with MNCs' by Narendra Aggarwal, *Straits Times* 16/1/95
7. 'Kuo-Toyota venture gets nod for Viet car factory', *Straits Times* 15/2/95.

8. Strategic Policies & Businesses in Singapore: A Manager's Reference. Tan, H.C. McGraw Hill Book Co., 1995, p60.

9. Ibid., p61.

10. Final Report Of The Committee to Promote Enterprise Overseas. Ministry of Finance. Singapore National Printers Pte Ltd, August 1993, p43.

11. The LIUP partners local enterprises with MNCs or large local companies. The latter adopts a number of local suppliers and assists them in upgrading. EDB finances the cost of a full-time LIUP manager appointed by the MNC or local company to work with the adoptee. The 'parent' organizations include Singapore Telecom, Port of Singapore Authority, Commercial and Industrial Security Corporation and Jurong Town Corporation.

12. Final Report Of The Committee to Promote Enterprise Overseas, pp8-9.

13. Strategic Policies & Businesses in Singapore: A Manager's Reference, p16.

14. Ibid., p17.

15. Final Report Of The Committee to Promote Enterprise Overseas, p31.

16. Ibid., pp32-3.

17. Singapore Enterprise, February 1995.

18. 'Shipyards aim to keep busy', *Financial Times* 24/2/95.

19. 'Stormy weather last year for shipyards, say analysts', *Straits Times* 15/2/95.

20. See note 17.

21. 'Keppel to raise up to $44m for projects in Myanmar', *Straits Times* 16/2/95 and 'Keppel group sets up fund to undertake Myanmar projects,' *Business Times*, same date.

22. *International Business News*, Beijing. 26/1/95.

23. Xinhua News Agency 22/1/95.

24. *Singapore Investment News*, EDB, June 1994.

25. 'The making of an integrated township', *Economic Bulletin*, October 1994. Singapore International Chamber of Commerce.

26. 'The Wuxi-Singapore Industrial Park', *Economic Bulletin*, October 1994.

27. Interview in Singapore 26/1/95.

28. Ditto.

5 Foreign Investment in Singapore

IMPACT OF INVESTMENT

DIRECT FOREIGN INVESTMENT has contributed greatly to the growth and transformation of Singapore's manufacturing sector, where output expanded an average 10 per cent between 1960 and 1990. Wholly and majority-owned foreign firms, though comprising only one-fifth of total establishments, account for a disproportionate share of gross output, value added, employment, direct exports and capital spending in manufacturing. There has been little displacement of growth from local enterprises since foreign firms have mostly moved into new industries which are heavily export-oriented.[1]

Foreign investment transformed Singapore's formerly small industrial sector, moving in the 1960s into petroleum refining, metals, and food and beverages (mostly for the domestic market), in the 1970s into basic petrochemical production and into labour-intensive export industries such as consumer and component electronics, textiles and garments, and shipbuilding and repairing, and in the 1980s into more skill- and capital-intensive industries such as industrial electronics, computers and computer peripherals, high value-added petroleum products and industrial machinery. Foreign firms and foreign-local joint ventures have accounted for 80 to 90 per cent of direct exports from Singapore's manufacturing sector since 1970, a factor partly responsible for catapulting Singapore into the ranks of the top 20 trading nations of the world in the 1980s.[2]

Its dependence on foreign investment in manufacturing is much higher than the East Asian Newly Industrialized Countries (NICs) of Hong Kong, South Korea and Taiwan. Unlike the latter pair, whose early industrialization depended on import substitution based on a sizeable domestic market, Singapore had no such market to absorb entrepreneurial learning costs. Unlike Hong Kong, which received a critical core of industrial entrepreneurs from mainland China during its early phase of industrialization, Singapore had no parallel pool of industrial entrepreneurs. Its Chinese and Indian businessmen were mainly traders who, essentially, possessed a very short investment horizon.

Industrialization in Singapore has to be export-oriented because of the small domestic market. Markets in nearby countries were heavily protected as these countries were embarking on import substitution industrialization. Producing manufactures for the global market was a much more difficult task than producing for the domestic market.

'Singapore was in a great hurry to industrialize, to restructure the economy away from entrepot trade and to combat large-scale unemployment. But it did not have the wherewithal to unbundle the direct foreign investment package, and to obtain the capital, technology, and managerial and marketing expertise independently and efficiently. For such an infant industrial economy anxious to leap into international markets, a heavy dependence on MNCs with their well-established marketing networks was unavoidable. In the initial stage, the foreign investment inflows also helped to establish Singapore's economic and political security. Singapore's investment policy had to be more liberal than most host countries so as to attract the export-oriented MNCs. Singapore preferred direct foreign investment as a means of securing foreign resources to promote domestic economic development, while other countries such as South Korea, preferred foreign borrowing.[3]

Export orientation is more difficult than import substitution since the former requires industries to be internationally competitive right from infancy. The official perception in the early 1960s was that it would be a long and tedious process to transform small domestic commercial traders into export-oriented industrial entrepreneurs. Export manufacturing could be more readily achieved by relying on direct foreign investment, particularly on MNCs with their in-situ global networks.[4]

For a small city-state like Singapore, market protection does not make much economic sense. Thus, except for a brief period of import substitution in the early 1960s, the government has never sought to impose quota restrictions on imports. Protective tariffs have also been few. The ability to import machinery and intermediate imputs at world prices has been an important factor in export competitiveness. The policy priority has always been on fostering competitiveness, through ensuring political, social and economic stability, through provision of efficient supporting infrastructure and factor supplies, and through use of investment incentives.

ATTRACTIVE FACTORS

In a land-scarce island like Singapore, industrial estates lower a foreign firms' search costs for suitable locations and project costs associated with land acquisition, and enable the quick start-up of commercial production; the last factor is considered an important consideration by foreign investors in electronics, an industry characterized by rapid technological changes, which will be discussed in Chapter Seven.

Singapore also provides an efficient network of public utilities, telecommunications and transportation. 'When statutory board charges and fees were perceived by the Economic Committee in 1986 to be "excessive" and contributing to escalation of business co sts and loss of competitiveness, a widespread corrective reduction of rates followed. Severe wage restraint was also implemented along with cuts in employees contributions to the Central Provident Fund and the Skills Development Fund.'[5]

Tax incentives were first introduced in 1959 and have been

liberally extended to promote industrialization, with incentives for industrial expansion, export promotion, industrial upgrading and research and development objectives. Incentives were also gradually introduced to a wide range of service activities. To encourage manufacturers to export, the export enterprise incentive was introduced in 1967 to provide for a 90 per cent tax concession on export profits for three-to-five years. Double tax deduction schemes were introduced for expenses incurred in overseas trade fairs and trade missions and for other overseas market development activities. To promote the use of foreign technology, approved activities were made eligible for exemption from withholding tax on interest and royalties.

The implementation of economic restructuring in 1979 led to tax incentives for promoting investments in more technologically sophisticated industries and to emphasise R & D, including double deduction from taxable income for up to five years for approved expenditures, accelerated depreciation allowances and full or partial exemption of withholding taxes on payments to non-residents for royalties, technical assistance fees or R & D contributions.

Selective tax and other incentives were also introduced during the 1980s to encourage the establishment of trading, technical and consultancy services, and the development of Singapore as the regional headquarters for foreign enterprises operating in Southeast and East Asia. For approved warehousing, technical or engineering services, with specified minimum fixed investment in warehousing buildings and productive equipment, tax concessions on corporate income tax has been provided. For trading companies which export Singapore manufactures and other domestic produce, a similar concession is provided on export profits.[6] These will be analysed in more detail later.

Foreign manufacturing firms have stimulated and often nurtured the creation of local suppliers who have increased their range and improved their quality, competitiveness and price over the years, so much so that they have eventually been able to export directly on their own account. One such example is Singatronics, a locally-owned listed company which began as a sub-contractor to foreign manufacturers based in Singapore and now exports industrial electronics products itself to the world market. Foreign manufacturing firms have generated spin-offs in the form of local employees, who acquire expertise and experience while working for a multinational and then leave to establish their own businesses, often supplying their former employers.[7]

While individual companies continue to flock to the island, one interesting new trend is the emergence of national trade and industry centres set up by foreign governments to help their own enterprises, particularly the small and medium-sized ones, take advantage of what has long been on offer for the MNCs. Typical was the German Centre for Industry and Trade (GCIT) which opened in April 1995 in the industrial suburb of Jurong East.

'Mr Joachim Ihrcke, GCIT's managing director, told the *Straits Times* that 75 companies had already signed up for facilities at the $50 million centre, which hopes to help German SMEs make inroads into booming South-east Asian markets. The centre will provide a targeted 100 companies with more than 20,000 sq.m. of space for office, production, storage and exhibition needs. Advisers will be on hand to help tenants establish contacts and negotiate contracts. The complex comprises two four-storey building wings linked by a five-storey central block, with a restaurant and five roof-top tennis courts.'[8]

This followed a more modest $3 million French Business Centre, opened in February 1995, to '. . . accommodate up to 48 small and medium-sized companies and offering them a package of office space and business services costing about $3,300 a month. Its four share holders are the French Business Association, the Paris Chamber of Commerce and Industry, the Association of Chambers of Commerce and the United Chambers of Commerce.'[9]

OPEN ECONOMY

Essentially, as already indicated, Singapore is a free port and an open economy. The Economic Development Board prohibits or severely limits foreign participation in only a small number of sensitive sectors, such as arms manufacturing, airlines, mass transit, press and broadcasting, public utilities, finance and property. Local retail banking is limited to those foreign banks with full licenses and the Monetary Authority of Singapore has issued no new ones since 1970. Insurance and brokerage firms are required to apply for a license and no new insurance licenses have been issued for several years. Foreign law firms are allowed to establish offices in Singapore on a selective basis, but they cannot practice local law or set up joint operations with Singaporean law firms to practice local law.

The parastatal Telecommunications Authority of Singapore was given a 15-year monopoly beginning 1992 on all 'basic telecommunications services', except cellular services in which it has a five-year monopoly. Although the Telecommunications Authority of Singapore is expected to continue to restrict sales of value-added networks by broadly defining the scope of 'basic services', gradual liberalization of telecommunications policy is likely to continue. An example of a recent step in this direction was the elimination of volume-sensitive charges on the sale of leased-line data services to third parties. The Singapore government began selling Singapore Telecom shares to the public in the last quarter of 1993.

Although the government in the 1990s began opening up membership on the Stock Exchange of Singapore (SES) to foreign firms, to date, only seven have been admitted The number is expected to increase, however, as the SES has drawn up guidelines to encourage MNCs and their Singapore operations to list shares on the exchange in any internationally accepted currency except the Singapore dollar.

Singapore has import duties on only a small number of items. Notably among these are duties of 45 per cent on automobile imports, designed to alleviate traffic problems on the crowded island. In addition, there are substantial import duties on tobacco products, alcoholic beverages and petroleum products, and minor tariffs on a few items including furniture and garments.

Various government agencies maintain regulatory or adminis-trative control over manufacture and/or sale of certain products in Singapore. For instance, the Public Utilities Board exercises control over all fittings and pipes for water services; the Ministry of Environment regulates materials used in sanitary plumbing and drainage systems; the Singapore Fire Service controls fire doors, fire dampers, emergency power supply equipment and portable fire extinguishers. In addition, certain types of telecommunications equipment are subject to approval by the Telecommunications Authority of Singapore.[10]

TAX CONCESSIONS

Tax concessions such as tax holidays and reduced tax rates play a key role in shaping the pace and direction of industrial development. They are used both for promotion of new investments in preferred industries and services and for encouraging existing companies to upgrade through mechanization or automation and through the introduction of new products and services. The EDB, the Trade Development Board and the Ministry of Finance administer a wide range of incentives with no differentiation between foreign and domestic capital. These are as follows:[11]

Capital Investment. A trade or business can claim accelerated depreciation allowance at the rate of 33.3 per cent per annum using the straight-line basis on machinery and equipment. This rate substitutes for the normal initial and annual allowance rates. Expenditure on furniture and fittings and vehicles (other than those designed principally to carry people) can also be depreciated at the accelerated rate. Commercial and residential buildings do not qualify for depreciation allowance and industrial bui ldings are not entitled to accelerated depreciation allowance.

Pioneer Industries. To be eligible, a company must manufacture a product which the government considers to have favourable development prospects. Generally, products with a high technological content are favoured. There is no restriction on foreign ownership for the qualifying pioneer company. An approved company is granted a five- to ten-year tax holiday. Exemption is on the amount of profit after deduction of depreciation allowances. In cases of exceptionally high capital investment, depreciation allowances need not be deducted in arriving at exempt pioneer profits. Losses incurred before the commencement of the pioneer period are treated as pre-operating expenses, which are not available for carry-forward. Losses incurred during the tax relief period can be offset only against income from the pioneer trade, but the unabsorbed amount on expiration of the pioneer period can be offset against income in the post-pioneer period. Unless approval is obtained from the EDB, a pioneer company is prohibited from carrying on other activities. There is no tax on dividends paid out of profits earned during the tax exemption period and such dividends, other than preferred stock (preference) dividends, remain tax exempt in the hands of shareholders. How this exemption affects the liability of overseas recipients in their country of residence depends on the terms of any tax treaty with that country. The tax exemption applies only to the income from the manufacture and sale of the pioneer product. Other income, such as interest and dividends, derived from Singapore by the pioneer enterprise is taxed at 27 per cent. Where such investment income is earned from offshore sources, it is not taxed until it is received in Singapore.

Post-pioneer.   This incentive allows the profits earned after the pioneer period to be assessed for a period up to 10 years at a rate as low as 10 per cent. Profits earned after the expiration of the incentive period are regarded as arising from new business and are taxed at 27 per cent.

Pioneer service company.   The pioneer incentive is also extended to service companies to promote Singapore as a centre for the development and export of high-quality technical services such as: 1. Engineering and technical services including laborat ory, consultancy and research and development activities; 2. Computer-based information and other computer-related services; 3. Development or production of any industrial design; 4. Services and activities that relate to the provision of entertainment, leisure and recreation; 5. Publishing; 6. Educational services; 7. Medical services; 8. Services and activities related to agricultural technology; 9. Services and activities related to the provision of automated warehousing facilities; 10. Services related to the organization or management of exhibitions and conferences; 11. Financial services; 12. Business consultancy, management and professional service; 13. Services and activities related to countertrade, including barter, counter-purchase, and compensation or buy-back; 14. Services and activities related to international trade; 15. Venture capital fund activity; 16. Operation or management of any mass rapid-transit system.

The incentive exempts the income of a pioneer service company from income tax for a period of between five and 10 years. Tax losses and depreciation are treated in the same way as for pioneer industries. Dividends can also be paid tax free by pioneer serv ice companies to shareholders, other than preference shareholders.

Expansion of established enterprises.   An approved enterprise that incurs expenses of more than $10 million on productive equipment in expanding its plant for the manufacture or increased output of an approved product is granted tax relief for up to 10 years from the date on which the new equipment starts to operate. The relief applies only to the increase in income arising from the plant expansion. Depreciation allowances must be deducted in arriving at the exempt expansion profits. Dividends paid out of the exempt expansion income are treated in the same way as those for exempt pioneer profits.

Expanding service company. Where a pioneer service company intends to substantially increase its volume of activity, it may apply for the expanding service company incentive after the expiration of its pioneer period, and this will provide further tax relief for up to 10 years on incremental income from the expanded activity. The method of calculating tax relief, the treatment of losses, tax depreciation, and the position regarding dividends are the same as those for the expansion of established enterprises incentive.

Investment allowance. This is given to stimulate investment in new production equipment that will result in high productivity in terms of labour utilization and generate higher value-added activities: for example, automation and mechanization. The investment allowance is an alternative to the pioneer incentive and export incentives for approved manufacturing and related service companies is to be discussed. The list of qualifying activities includes manufacturing, engineering and technical services, research and development, construction, reducing the consumption of potable water, computer-based information and other computer-related services, development or production of any industrial design, services and activities that relate to the provision of entertainment, leisure and recreation, publishing, medical services, educational services, activities and services related to automated warehousing facilities, agrotechnology, organization and management of exhibitions and conferences, financial services, business consultancy and management and professional services, international trade, venture capital fund activity, services for the promotion of tourism (other than a hotel) in Singapore, and textile and garment makers.

The specified percentage and the amount of fixed capital expenditure on which it is based are at the discretion of the Trade and Industry Minister. The allowances are granted over a period of up to five years (10 for tourism promotion) and any balance not used up in the period can be carried forward until fully absorbed. Dividends paid out of tax-exempt profits as a result of the investment allowance are tax free for other than preference shareholders, and the allowance does not interfere with the claim for normal or accelerated depreciation allowances.

Approved foreign loan.   This takes the form of exempting from withholding tax the interest paid to non-residents on a foreign loan of not less than $200,000 for the purchase of productive equipment. To qualify, an application must be made to the EDB to designate the loan as an approved foreign loan. Approval for this incentive is granted only where the tax authorities are satisfied the exemption would not increase the tax liability of the foreign lender in the home country.

Approved royalties.   A company engaged in any industry that pays or desires to pay royalties, technical assistance fees or contributions to research and development costs can apply to the Trade and Industry Minister for approval. This approval will have three consequences: (1) Withholding tax is payable at a reduced rate instead of the normal rate of 27 per cent. (2) Where the Trade and Industry Minister considers that the national interest would be served, the approved payments will be totally or partially exempt from withholding tax. (3) Where foreign recipients of such payments convert them into equity in Singapore manufacturing companies, such payments are also exempt from withholding tax. The relief or exemptions apply only where they would not result in an increase in liability in the non-resident's country of residence.

Research and development organizations.   Various tax incentives are given to R & D organizations, manufacturing companies and selected industries such as financial services, computer software, information services, agrotechnology services, laboratory and testing services, and medical research services to encourage them to use Singapore as their base. The incentives include a tax deduction for R & D expenses that are not usually tax deductible, a double deduction for tax deductible R & D expenses on approved projects, and tax depreciation allowances on R & D buildings.

Investment in new technology companies.   This takes the form of a limited group loss relief. Any loss incurred and depreciation allowances utilized by an approved technology company during the first three years may be offset against the taxable income of the holding company to a maximum of 50 per cent of the paid-up capital of the approved technology company. To be eligible, the holding company must be incorporated and resident in Singapore and must be at least 50 per cent owned by Singapore citizens or permanent residents.

Venture capital and overseas investments. These permit the deduction of investment losses (i.e. losses incurred on the sale of shares in a company or on liquidation of the company) against taxable income if they are incurred by any of the following circumstances: 1. By a Singapore citizen or permanent resident, or a holding company in investing in a venture capital company. In the latter case, the holding company should be incorporated and resident in Singapore and at least 50 per cent owned by Singapore citizens or permanent residents. 2. By a holding company in investing in a technology company which in turn holds an investment in an overseas company that is developing or using new technology for a product, process or service. 3. By a holding company in investing in an 'overseas investment company', the latter being a Singapore company that invests in an overseas company or to gain access to an overseas market for its holding company. There is no loss relief if the shares are held for less than two years or if they are sold after eight years from the date the venture capital company, technology company or 'overseas investment company' is approved for this incentive. The relief is not available to the transferee of such shares.

Singapore-registered ships. Exemption from Singapore tax is granted on income derived by a shipping enterprise from the operation or chartering of seagoing Singapore-registered ships. The shipping enterprise may be foreign-owned, but Singapore-registered ships are usually owned by Singapore companies.

Approved international shipping enterprise. To encourage major international shipowners to locate in Singapore, an international shipping enterprise, if approved, will be given tax exemption for an initial period of up to 10 years on profits from operating non-Singapore-registered vessels outside Singapore and dividends from approved shipping subsidiaries. To be eligible, a company should be resident in Singapore, own and operate a significant fleet of ships with at least 10 per cent or a minimum of one ship registered under the Singapore flag, incur directly attributable business spending in Singapore of at least $4 million a year, and support and make 'significant use' of Singapore's trade infrastructure, such as banking, financial, business trading, arbitration, and other ancillary services.

Warehousing and servicing. A warehousing and servicing incentive was introduced in 1978 to promote Singapore as a centre of such activities. This provides for tax exemption on 50 per cent of the incremental export earnings of eligible goods and services. To qualify, a company must invest at least $2 million in fixed assets. The period of tax exemption is 10 years, and it may be continually extended for further periods of up to five years.

Art and antique dealers and auction houses. Approved dealers are taxed at a concessionary rate of 10 per cent on income derived from transacting on behalf of non-residents with approved auction houses. This incentive is given for an initial five years, but can be extended for a further five-year period. Well-established auction houses that conduct substantial auctioning activities in Singapore and local private museum operators can obtain the pioneer service company incentive for five years with a possible five-year extension.

EXPORT TAX INCENTIVES

An approved enterprise engaged in deep-seat fishing or in manufacturing any approved product, either wholly or partly for export, is granted an exemption in respect of 90 per cent of the increased export profits over a fixed base. In the case of an enterprise that has been exporting an approved product, the fixed base is the average of the annual export profits for the three years preceding the date of application for an enterprise export certificate. In other cases, the fixed base is determined by the Trade and Industry Minister.

For a non-pioneer enterprise, the exemption period is five years. For a pioneer enterprise, the exemption extends for three years after the expiration of the pioneer period. In very special cases, exemption may be granted for 15 years. The position with regard to dividends paid out of exempt export profits is the same as those paid out of exempt pioneer profits already discussed. Few export enterprises have been approved in recent years although the legislation for the incentive remains in force.

The export incentive is granted to manufacturing companies, to selected services and to overseas projects for companies or individuals who are neither resident nor have a permanent establishment in Singapore. The qualifying services are technical services such as construction, distribution, design and engineering; consultancy, management, supervisory or advisory services relating to any technical matter or to any trade or business; fabrication of machinery and equipment and procurement of materials, components and equipment; data processing, programming, computer software development, telecommunications, and other computer services; professional services including accounting, legal, medical and architectural services; educational and training services. The export incentive takes the form of a tax holiday for five years on 90 per cent of the increased export service income over a fixed base. The qualifying income is determined in a similar manner to that for the export profits incentive.

To encourage international trading houses to set up their regional base in Singapore, approved traders are granted a concessionary 10 per cent rate of tax on offshore income from trading in approved commodities, which include agricultural, industrial and mineral commodities, bulk edible products, building materials and machinery components. The tax concession is given for an initial period of five years. Qualities desired are an international trading company with a world-wide network and good track record, incurring directly attributable business spending in Singapore of at least $2 million a year, employing at least three experienced international traders and contributing to training for trading expertise in Singapore, with an annual turnover in the Republic of at least $200 million, making significant use of Singapore's banking, financial and other ancillary services and supporting and making use of the country's trade infrastructure. The income covered by the incentive includes profits from trading and commissions from brokerage in physical commodities, profits from trading in approved futures exchanges and foreign exchange gains incidental to the transactions listed above.

Similarly, to encourage energy-trading activities, approved oil traders are granted a concessionary 10 per cent rate of tax on income derived from activities such as trading in physicals and futures and brokerage commissions in the former. Income from trading and brokerage in paper barrels are also taxed at 10 per cent, provided such activities are incidental to and support the trading and brokerage of physical barrels. To qualify, a company should have similar characteristics to those already outlined for trading firms, although the annual turnover in Singapore should be at least US$100 million and the directly attributable business spending at least $500,000. In addition, the company should have 'substantial funds', contribute to the success of the oil futures market, make a commitment to use Singapore as a centre of arbitration in case of disputes in its international trade, and make a commitment to make full use of the banking and ancillary services in Singapore. The products covered include crude oil, gasoline, kerosene, naphtha, gas or diesel oil, heating oil, fuel oil, low sulphur waxy residue, LNG, LPG, gasoline or fuel oil components, aviation fuel, paraffin wax and sulphur.

Approved companies engaging in counter-trade activities are exempt from tax on profits for an initial period of five years. Counter-trade activities include barter, counter-purchase and buy-back transactions. To qualify for this TDB-administered incentive, at least one leg of each transaction, whether financial or the physical movement of goods, must be routed through Singapore.

An approved international consultancy company is exempt from tax for five years on 50 per cent of its incremental income from providing specified consultancy services in connection with approved overseas projects. The consultancy revenue from these projects must exceed $1 million a year. Qualifying for the benefit are advisory services relating to any technical, construction and engineering matter, design and engineering services, fabrication of machinery and equipment, procurement of materials and equipment, management and supervision of the installation or construction of any project, data processing, programming and other computer services.

A new incentive has been set up to encourage large international trading companies to seek and develop new overseas markets for Singapore-made goods and produce or to engage in offshore trade in non-traditional commodities. It provides for tax exemption on 50 per cent of the incremental income derived from export sales of qualifying goods for five years. Double deduction is given for approved expenses incurred in promoting the export of goods manufactured in Singapore and the export of services. The categories approved expenses include trade fairs, exhibitions, trade missions, the maintenance of overseas trade offices, export-market development, advertising, feasibility studies, product certification and packaging for export.

EXPORT NON-TAX INCENTIVES

The Monetary Authority of Singapore operates an export bills rediscounting scheme which enables banks to rediscount certain eligible export and re-export bills with the Authority at a preferential rate, currently 3.75 per cent per annum. The maximum commission receivable by the negotiating bank under the scheme is 1.5 per cent per annum. Effectively, the concessionary rate of interest payable to the Authority by the negotiating bank is to be passed on to the exporter.

The Export Credit Insurance Corporation of Singapore (ECICS), in which the government has a 50 per cent shareholding through Temasek Holdings, provides insurance coverage to a Singapore exporter against non-payment by the buyer caused by political upheavals in the buyer's country. ECICS has also introduced a bankers' guarantee scheme to cover short-, medium- and long-term credit needs for local exporters. It also has a subsidiary engaged in bond and guarantee underwriting. ECICS is a full member of the International Union of Credit and Investment Insurers.

Broadly, the export credit insurance facilities can be grouped into two categories – comprehensive and specific. The distinction between the two lies in the nature of the goods and services to be insured and the length of credit involved. Comprehensive policies are generally for exporters engaged in the export and re-export of goods and services which are repetitive in nature and where the credits are normally for not longer than six months. Specific policies are more suitable for exports of capital and semi-capital goods which are non-repetitive in nature and involve credits in excess of one year. The risks insured against can be classified into two categories:

• **Commercial risks:** buyer's insolvency, buyer's failure to pay within six months after the due date for goods delivered to and accepted by him, and buyer's failure or refusal to accept goods even though these are according to specifications.

• **Non-commercial risks:** blockage or delay in the transfer of payment outside the control of the insured and buyer; imposition of import restrictions outside their control; cancellation of valid import licences outside their control; cancellation or non-renewal of an export licence or the imposition of an export restriction (applicable to contracts cover only); war between the buyer's country and Singapore or war, revolution or other similar disturbances in the buyer's country; failure or refusal to pay, in cases where ECICS agrees that the buyer is an overseas government or that the contract has been guaranteed by an overseas government and redress is impossible.

The policies, whether comprehensive or specific, do not cover any loss arising from the insured party's own negligence or default or his failure to comply with the stated terms and conditions. They also do not cover foreign exchange loss or loss arising from a collecting bank's or agent's failure. Nor do they cover risks which are normally commercially insurable, such as marine and fire risks.

As a supplement to its comprehensive policy, ECICS offers three main types of guarantees:

• **Letter of Assignment,** a form of conditional guarantee enabling the policyholder to transfer his right to claim proceeds under his policy to his bank. There are two types of LAs. Under LA Part IV, ECICS' payment to the bank will be conditional only on the buyer's failure to pay; it will not be conditional on the policyholder's observance of the terms and conditions of the insurance policy. However, if the policyholder fails to fulfil his sales contract, due either to a quality dispute or collusion, then ECICS has no liability. On the other hand, the corporation's payment to the bank under LA Part III will take into consideration the policyholder's observance of the policy in addition to his compliance of the sales contract.

• **Unconditional Guarantee to Bank** assures the bank of payment by the ECICS under all circumstances. This means that once a transaction is guaranteed, the bank can make a demand for payment by the corporation regardless of whether the cause of it was default by the buyer or policyholder. The guarantee applies to individual shipments and the percentage of indemnity is up to 85 per cent of the face value of the bill or the net discounted value of the bill, whichever is the lesser.

• **Pre-shipment Credit Guarantee** is issued to banks in respect of pre-shipment advances made to exporters for purchasing, manufacturing and packing goods for export against confirmed orders. The guarantee period is up to 90 days with a flat premium rate. When shipment is effected, the guarantee can be converted to either a letter of assignment or an unconditional guarantee to the bank.[12]

INDUSTRY NON-TAX INCENTIVES

There are a wide range of non-tax incentives available to investors, most of them administered by the Economic Development Board.[13]

• **Capital Assistance Scheme** provides long-term fixed rate loans for up to 70 per cent of the costs of productive assets to investors in the manufacturing and service industries. The scheme is normally applicable to projects of technological or economic benefit to Singapore. The EDB also has an Equity Participation Scheme which provides capital assistance to potential investors through an equity share in the investment. This is not intended to be permanent, but only to provide initial support and confidence to the investor, and would not normally exceed 30 per cent of the total paid-up capital. A $100 million Venture Capital Fund administered by the Board aims to assist local companies in acquiring new technology or diversifying into new technology areas to support local entrepreneurship and innovation. Investments may be based in Singapore or overseas. The EDB runs a Venture Capital Club bringing local entrepreneurs and potential investors together.

• **Local Enterprise Finance Scheme** is a low-cost, fixed interest rate financing programme designed to encourage small and medium-sized local enterprises in upgrading and expanding their operations. Loans are available to companies engaged in manufacturing or related support activities and service companies employing not more than 50 workers, both of which must have at least 30 per cent local equity and fixed productive assets such as factory building and equipment of not more than $12 million. The loans may be used to establish a viable new business, modernise and automate plant and machinery, expand existing manufacturing capacity and diversify into other product lines. Financing is available for up to 90 per cent of industrial facilities and machinery and equipment. The interest on one-year domestic factoring loans is six per cent, while that for equipment and factory loans is six per cent for up to four years and 6.75 per cent for four to 10-year loans. There is a separate scheme for overseas operations, LEFS(O), with loans for industrial facilities and equipment incurring a six per cent interest up to four years and 6.75 per cent from four to 10 years. The rate for ex port factoring is three per cent.

• **Local Enterprise Technical Assistance Scheme** aims to encourage and assist small and medium-sized companies in seeking external expertise to improve their operations. The EDB will reimburse up to 70 per cent of the costs for engaging an external expert for an approved short-term assignment, which must be for the purpose of improving business operations or imparting further technological skills. The eligibility criteria for this scheme are the same as those for the LEFS except that the ceiling on fixed productive assets is $8 million.

• **Market Development Assistance Scheme** assists local companies by delaying the initial costs of their export development efforts, such as setting up overseas marketing offices, improving product and package designs, overseas marketing trips, participating in trade fairs and missions, producing promotional brochures and bidding for overseas contracts. The scheme provides grants on a reimbursement basis. The products or services should have at least 25 per cent Singapore content. Eligible companies must manufacture and/or export goods or services to independent customers and not to their overseas parent or affiliates.

• **Business Development Scheme** aims to encourage and assist small and medium-sized enterprises to develop business opportunities, particularly in international markets. The scheme is available to companies engaged in manufacturing or related support activities and service companies with not more than 50 employees, at least 30 per cent local equity and productive assets of not more than $12 million. Grants are available of up to 70 per cent of the costs of studies or overseas trips to explore new technology or markets, establish new business contacts, pursue joint-venture arrangements, and participate in approved business development workshops and seminars.

• **Product and Process Development Assistance Scheme**. Under the EDB's Product and Process Development Assistance Scheme, an expansion of an earlier scheme available only for product development, dollar-for-dollar grants are provided to assist companies with at least 30 per cent local equity to develop new or improve existing products and processes. Eligible local companies are those with a satisfactory track record and sufficient resources to develop and commercialize their products or processes. The government and the company bear equally the direct costs of the project. Eligible costs include those for manpower, utilities, materials, prototyping, consultancy fees, and a proportion of essential additional equipment. The scheme, which is aimed at encouraging local product design and development capability and building up indigenous technological know-how, includes support for technical and marketing feasibility studies. The PPDAS grant will provide 50 per cent support for qualifying process development up to a maximum of $1 million.

• The **Research and Development Assistance Scheme**, administered by the National Science Technology Board, provides grants for Singapore-registered companies conducting R & D of technological significance. Each grant covers from 30 to 70 per cent of the direct costs of the project, which includes the cost of manpower, equipment, materials and utilities. For projects that will result in a commercially viable product or process, a token royalty of 0.5 to three per cent of revenue derived from it is paid to the Board, as well as a portion of the license fees.

• The **Research Incentive Scheme for Companies** provides financial grants to enable companies to develop in-house R & D capabilities and facilities in Singapore in strategic-technology areas. Grants can be used to fund up to 50 per cent of the incremental total research costs for up to five years, including manpower, equipment, training and material costs.

• The **Manpower Development Assistance Scheme** provides various financial assistance programmes to help companies achieve their R & D training needs. The programmes cover academic and on-the-job training in technology areas and the management of technology. Financial assistance is also provided for the recruitment of top international R & D manpower.

• A **Software Development Assistance Scheme** is designed to encourage local companies in the business of information technology to initiate and develop innovative and high-quality software products. Grants are available up to 50 per cent of the develop ment costs in software product design, development and enhancement.

• The EDB's **Initiatives in New Technologies (INTECH) Scheme** encourages investment and manpower development in the application of new technology, industrial R & D, professional know-how and design and development of new products, processes and services so as to establish new capabilities within a company or an industry. INTECH provides assistance through grants to cover 30 to 50 per cent of the costs of undertaking desirable projects. Both manpower and infrastructural costs are covered. For highly sophisticated projects with a substantial economic impact, a higher level of support of up to 90 per cent of the manpower costs and up to 100 per cent of the equipment and building costs may be considered. The level of activity and use of technology are examined critically to assess the contribution towards increased capability in Singapore in that field of technology with the extent of support tied to the extent of contribution.

• The **Skills Development Fund** provides incentive grants for the training of persons in employment and the retraining of retrenched or redundant workers through the Training Grant Scheme. For in-house technical and vocational training courses, a grant of $12 per trainee per hour is offered. Trainees on overseas courses attract a payment of $80 a day up to a maximum of 12 weeks. Between 30 and 70 per cent of the costs of public courses, including those by external consultants, are covered subject to a maximum of $10 per trainee per hour.

• There are various enterprise development incentives available for companies with at least 30 per cent local equity. Under the **Total Business Planning Programme**, grants are given to help companies defray part of the costs of engaging a consultant to formulate a business plan. The maximum grant is 50 per cent of the direct costs, including the costs of engaging the same consultant on a retainer basis to help implement the plan. The grant may be increased to 70 per cent for projects with potential spin-offs for the industry.

• A **Business Collaboration Programme** is aimed at fostering cooperation among local companies to achieve synergy and benefit from economies of scale. The grants awarded under this programme can be used to engage consultants to develop concepts, conduct feasibility studies and draw up action plans, as well as to help implement them.

• Various incentives are also on offer to encourage manufacturers to automate. Under the **Automation Feasibility Study. Scheme**, consultants from the Automation Applications Centre study the operations of the company and identify areas where automation is feasible. The company may then approach the Centre, or any other automation consultant, to look at the recommendations of the feasibility study – which costs $1000 – and implement the automation project. For multinational companies with in-house automation expertise in the parent company, a grant of 70 per cent of the qualifying cost is available if experts from the parent company are used to identify areas for automation in the Singapore operations. The maximum grant is $50,000. Qualifying costs include the salaries of the experts for the duration of the feasibility study, which should normally be about two weeks and no more than four, return airfares and hotel accommodation costs were applicable. A copy of the feasibility study report must be submitted within a month of completion. Under the INTECH scheme, training grants are given to help companies training automation engineers and technicians either locally or overseas. The grants cover 70 per cent of the approved training cost, which include salaries, course fees, airfares and cost of living allowances.

• The **Automation Leasing Scheme** aims to encourage and assist companies in Singapore to introduce and apply robots and related automation equipment and systems. It provides low-cost financing through a company called Robot Leasing & Consultancy Pte L td. The robots or other automation equipment or machinery may be obtained through finance lease, hire purchase instalment or mortgage loan arrangements. The amount of financing is subject to a maximum of $3 million, repayable over three to seven years. Interest rates are 3.5 per cent for small and medium-size enterprises and 4.5 per cent to foreign and other larger local enterprises. Approved automation equipment that results in substantial labour saving and improved productivity may qualify for Extended Automation Leasing, which offers interest rates respectively of two and three per cent. An Investment Allowance

Incentive gives a deduction against taxable income of a specified proportion of capital expenditure over and above the normal deductions. To encourage investment, a 50 per cent investment allowance is granted to companies that implement automation projects resulting in substantial labour reduction and productivity improvements.

• A **Design For Automation Scheme** is available to all Singapore companies to design their own products to make them suitable for automated manufacturing. The product need not be a new one, but must be manufactured in Singapore. There should be significant redesigning and a potential for improvements in the production process. If other considerations such as aesthetics and functionality are involved, only the portion directly related to the design for automation qualifies for grants of up to 70 per cent of the approved costs, which include consultancy fees, salaries of technical personnel involved in the project, and airfares and overseas living allowances when necessary. The maximum grant for a single project is $200,000. Generally, a project should not take longer than six months to complete. A report on the findings and proposed action plans must be submitted within three months of the end of the project.

CHAPTER NOTES

1. Foreign Direct Investment & Industrialization in Malaysia, Singapore, Taiwan and Thailand. Lim, Y.C. and Pang E.F. Development Centre of the OECD, 1991, p91.
2. Ibid.
3. *Policy Options for the Singapore Economy.* Lim, C.Y. and others, National University of Singapore. McGraw-Hill Book Co., 1988, p252.
4. Ibid., p255.
5. Ibid., p256
6. Ibid., p260.
7. Foreign Direct Investment and Industrialization in Malaysia, Singapore, p92.
8. *Straits Times* 23/1/95.
9. *Straits Times* 25/1/95
10. *Doing Business in Singapore 1994 Guide for US Exporters*, prepared by the U.S. and Foreign Commercial Service, American Embassy.
11. Drawn from a variety of sources including publications of the bodies concerned and 'Doing Business in Singapore', Price Waterhouse, 1992, and 1993 supplement.
12. *The Investors Guide to Singapore*. Singapore International Chamber of Commerce, pp42-3.
13. See note 11.

6 Industrial Profile

PROMOTED ACTIVITIES

THE FOLLOWING activities are promoted by the Singapore government for possible inward investment: oil trading and oil futures, management and engineering services for offshore supply base; chemical and plastics product development, technical servicing and processing of high value-added products with direct export potential, manufacture of ABS resins, acrylic acid, styrene monomer, phenol and hydrocarbon solvents; manufacture of food products and food intermediaries for regional and world markets, new food product development; manufacture of drugs and health care equipment, biotechnology research and development; high value-added electronic component design and manufacturing, such as IC design and wafer fabrication, design and manufacture of industrial electronic products, such as computer systems and subassemblies, computer peripherals and communications equipment, systems; systems design, engineering software development and installation and technical support for laser and optical instrumentation systems; design and manufacture of specialised industrial equipment such as variable speed drivers, programmable controllers, industrial circuit breakers and uninterrupted power supplies; developing linkages for existing capabilities in ship repair/building and rig construction, developing more capabilities in emerging marine-related businesses such as underwater operations; manufacture of aircraft engine parts and components, repair and overhaul services; manufacture of automotive components with new market potential; manufacture of industrial equipment such as food-processing machinery, packaging machinery and semiconductor assembly equipment; development of automation technology and equipment and collaboration between local and foreign companies in this sector; manufacture of sophisticated precision engineering products such as powdered metallurgical products, microwave ICs, micropositors, linear and rotary tables, measurement and sensing devices, and drives and transmissions; film, video and music production, theme parks and entertainment centres, publishing, advertising, exhibitions and visual and performing arts.[1]

CASE HISTORY: PETROCHEMICALS

Apart from electronics, which will be dealt with in the next chapter, petrochemicals has a very high industrial profile. The petroleum industry accounted for two per cent of the island's GDP in 1993, while employing only 0.3 per cent of the total labour force. It currently accounts for more than 12 per cent of total exports.[2] New investments will ensure these figures continue to expand in the next few years.

Product storage was a major petroleum-related activity from the colonial days, and Singapore retains its position as the world's leading bunkerage centre, with a current oil storage capacity of 75 million barrels.[3] The petrochemical industry, however, came on stream only in the 1960s when Singapore became a major producer of hydrocarbon solvents. The Singapore Petrochemical Complex, ASEAN's first, was launched in 1977 by a group of Japanese, European and US companies. Construction of the $2 billion complex on Pulau Ayer Merbau started in 1980 and commercial production began in 1984. It consists of a naphtha/LPG cracker and downstream plans manufacturing polyolefins, glycols, MTBE, acetylene black and others. The cracker has since been upgraded to a production capacity of 428,000 tonnes per annum of ethylene.

All these plants are owned by eight companies or groups of companies, some of which are related through a network of common shareholders. A scouting study for expanding the complex and making more valuable products started in 1990 and eventually culminated in the official announcement in March 1994 that a second complex would be built to double the present cracker and polyolefins capacities and introduce new capacities for the manufacture of styrene, polyurethane intermediates and propylene glycols on Pulau Sereya. It is scheduled to start up during the second quarter of 1997 at a total cost of about $3.4 billion. In addition to the developments Pulau Ayer Merbau and Pulau Sereya, other major projects have been implemented in Singapore. Examples of these are Mobil's aromatics plant, Atochems polystyrene plant and Dupont's manufacturing complex in Pulau Sakra.

Another American company, Caltex, also has a large presence in Singapore which it has built up since arriving first in 1936. In fact, it has made the republic the headquarters of its worldwide trading activities, and revenue from this operation accounted for 60 per cent of the company's global income in 1993. It announced plans to double its investments to $1.5 billion by the end of 1995, and is studying the possibility of making Singapore its head-quarters for a wide range of regional activities and services.[4]

Singapore's biggest-ever foreign investment project is taking shape on a group of islands some three kilometres offshore, where the second petrochemical complex referred to earlier, is being built by a group of local and international partners including Royal Dutch/Shell, Phillips Petroleum and Sumitomo Chemical. Ground was broken in December 1994 for the development, which will allow the downstream producers involved to enter higher value-added sectors as well as markedly boost their own overall volumes.

The government is closely involved, as always. It is contributing $6 billion for a proposed 35-year land reclamation to link the facilities on the islands while providing space for further expansion which it believes the next century will require. The seven islands just south-west of the financial district will eventually become one – Jurong Island – and their present 1,000 hectare area will treble. 'This means filling in an ocean acreage nearly four times that which was needed to build Japan's new Kansai Airport in Osaka

Bay.'[5] The first phase, a causeway linking Pulau Seraya, Pulau Ayer Merbau, Pulau Aya Chawan and Pulau Sakra was opened in early 1994. Eventually, three road links will be built to the mainland.

The development is going ahead at a time when the industry has squeezed every drop out of their current capacity. Petrochemical Corporation of Singapore (PCS), the upstream producer in which the Singapore government has a 30 per cent stake, has upgraded its ageing plant to raise ethylene output from the original 300,000 tonnes per annum to 450,000 tonnes. When its new naptha cracker comes on stream in the second quarter of 1997, it will deliver another 428,000 tonnes a year. Its propylene capacity, in turn, will almost double from the present 225,000 tonnes. 'PCS, jointly run by Shell and a Sumitomo-led Japanese consortium, will continue to sell nearly all its output to its downstream partners – an unusual integrated arrangement which means that each of the new installations must begin operation at the same time, or benefits will be lost. A capital-intensive-industry such as this cannot afford to run below capacity for long, and as a closed complex "we have to work in a synchronized manner," says Takayuki Okada, PCS managing director.'[6]

The Singapore petrochemical industry has been built on the premise that regional demand for plastic resins will grow rapidly. Having a market sufficiently big enough for the complex to compete internationally is a necessary but not sufficient reason for success. There have to be other factors that give Singapore an edge over major competitors. It is situated on the crossroads of shipping lanes in the region and has exploited its favourable location to become the logistic hub of the region. Consequently, raw materials for the products from the petrochemical industry can be transported efficiently from Singapore. Equally important, the industry benefits from being sited near five refineries in Singapore, complemented by a sizeable trade in feedstocks such as naphtha.

The petrochemical industry boosted output by a record 20.3 per cent in 1994.[7] This partly reflected a contribution from new plants unrelated to the Jurong Island development, such as the aromatics complex opened by Mobile in March of that year. The EDB believes new investment commitments should remain strong for several years, but are 'unlikely to be sustainable at this level in the long term.'[8] The key factor is regional consumption.

The expansion of the Singapore petrochemical complex is taking place at a time when regional demand is certainly growing, with estimates that the increased requirements in Asia-Pacific will be twice the rate of the developed world. However, many countries in the region are themselves either building up or proposing to build petrochemical plants. Malaysia commissioned its first cracker in late 1993, which exploits Malaysia's rich hydrocarbon resources. Thailand's first petrochemical complex became operational in 1989 and a second is presently being commissioned. Over in Indonesia, the first cracker was due for start-up in mid-1995.

By 1997, about 17 new ethylene crackers are expected to be started up, adding 4.8 million tons per annum of ethylene capacity. Five of these will be in ASEAN, seven mostly small ones in China, three in India, and one each in Japan and Taiwan. Some of these plants will have volumes for export markets and hence will compete with the Singapore complex. However, most experts expect regional capacity to trail behind that of demand for some time yet. The comfort for the Singapore complex is that there will still be enough markets in the region for its products but there will be more competitors for the same markets. Singapore will also have to adopt to a new pattern of imports as traditional markets build their own plants and new markets emerge. It is likely that it will become more dependent on fewer but larger countries for its exports than in the last 10 years.

Mr Okada of PCS says the partners in Jurong Island had factored in the arrival of all the new capacity before deciding that they should go ahead with the project, especially in few of the rapidly growing demand from China and India (the latter already taking 15 per cent of Singapore's output at present).

Plastics producers see particular promise in China, for everything from bags to injection moulding parts to bottles for drinking water and for daily consumer products such as detergents, shampoos and cosmetics. As infrastructure in China and elsewhere develops, plastic pipes will be needed for water, sewage, gas, as well as large storage drums. PCS makes linear polyethylene from which all these can be made. It is doubling capacity to 400,000 tonnes per annum.

Despite the general industry optimism, there are a few worries – notably the increasing costs of operations. In Singapore, an operator costs twice as much now than he did 10 years ago. Land rental is almost five times what it was in early 1980s. While it is true that costs in other countries in the region have gone up too and that overall Singapore may still have an edge over other countries, the difference has narrowed as others improve their infrastructures.[9]

PROMISING SECTORS

Based on research by the commercial departments of several foreign embassies,[10] the following sectors have been identified as the most promising for future growth:

Industrial Chemicals

The chemical industry of Singapore consists of more than 200 companies engaged in the production and trading of petrochemicals, speciality, fine chemicals, industrial chemicals and pharmaceuticals. Generally, companies in the industry have diversified their operations to include R & D and technical support services. Singapore has become not only an important base for industrial chemicals to the region, but an attractive technical support base as well. Singapore imported US$2,348 million worth of industrial chemicals in 1983, but it re-exports substantial amounts of its imports to Malaysia, Japan, Thailand, Korea and the Philippines. Overall, the output of the chemical industry is about US$10 billion, but an additional $2 billion is expected over the next few years as new plants belonging to Dupont, General Electric, Shell and Esso come into production.

Aircraft and Parts

The aerospace sector continues to be one of Singapore's major industries. In 1992, output of the sector rose by eight per cent to US$731 million and was projected to reach $1.1 billion by 1995. Singapore is evolving into a world-class aero-component manufacturing and overhaul centre for the world market. The aircraft component overhaul and manufacturing industry has grown steadily at 10 per cent annually since the late 1980s and is expected to continue growing at an accelerated pace well into the 21st century. Singapore Airlines expanded rapidly over the past two decades and expects to continue the growth to meet increased passenger demand in the Asia-Pacific region and beyond.

Airport and Ground Support equipment

Changi Airport is Southeast Asia's major hub airport, linking 108 cities through more than 2,100 flights by 58 airlines each week. Singapore's goal is to become the leading air hub in the entire Asia-Pacific region by the end of the century. With two terminals and two runways, Changi is capable of handling 24 million passengers a year. Physical planning for Terminal 3 and planning for the reclamation of land for Terminal 4 and a third runway have begun. As a result, demand for ground support equipment will increase. To meet expected cargo growth, Changi's cargo capacity was expanded to 1.3 million tons in 1985.

Electrical Power Systems

The electrical power generation market can be broadly divided into two categories: high capacity generators and medium/low-capacity generating sets. The Europeans and Japanese dominate the high-capacity, public utility market, while the Americans have done well in the medium/low capacity area. Estimates place Singapore's annual growth of electrical power demand at about seven per cent. Plans are underway to upgrade and build new power plants, including a 4,800 megawatt facility to be completed by 2005. Imports exceeded US$2.45 billion in 1993, with a substantial proportion re-exported to Malaysia, Japan, Hong Kong, Korea, Thailand and Taiwan.

Telecommunications Equipment

Singapore places great emphasis on the development and maintenance of a sophisticated and advanced telecommunications industry, and with one of the world's most advanced information communication infrastructures it has achieved much of its ambition to become a regional and international hub. In the five years from 1994, US$2.2 billion has been earmarked for capital investment and will cover, among other things, technologies such as intelligent networks, broadband ISDN and optical fibre links to all homes and offices. The 1993 import figure exceeded US$4 billion, with a large re-export market to Malaysia, the United States, Hong Kong, Thailand and Japan.

Audio/Visual Equipment

The buoyant video industry is supported by the robust demand for corporate and product advertising on television. In recent years, commercials, corporate projects and documentaries have also flourished on a much larger scale. The potentially viable areas to be exploited include telemovies, sitcoms and game shows. As clients increasingly require better-quality productions, companies have responded by upgrading facilities and investing in state-of-the art equipment. There is considerable market potential for suppliers of digitally equipped editing suites. In addition, Singapore's music industry is expanding rapidly, while local recording studios, recording engineers, technicians and musicians are among the best in Southeast Asia.

Industrial Process Controls

Manufacturing will continue to be the mainstay of the Singapore economy. Increases in demand will come from the petroleum, petrochemical, polymers, chemicals and food processing industries as their technology and facilities are constantly being upgraded. The market in 1993 finally broke through $1 billion, with a substantial volume of re-exports to Malaysia, Thailand, China, Taiwan and Indonesia.

Robotics

To overcome its acute labour shortage and increase productivity, Singapore is actively encouraging automation. The Economic Development Board has various financial and tax incentive programmes to encourage this goal. There is wide managerial acceptance of automation, both in terms of hard capital purchases and soft business re-engineering to create an 'automation culture', leading industry analysts to project 10 to 15 per cent market growth for the rest of the century.

Machine Tools and Metalworking Equipment

Metalworking equipment suppliers form a major segment of the Singaporean support industries. The market is dominated by Japanese and German firms in the higher-end tooling, and have taken a long term view by setting up technical institutes and support centres of their own. There is a substantial local market, further enhanced by a high volume of re-exports to Malaysia, Thailand, Korea and Japan.

Automotive Parts and Services Equipment

In an effort to control road congestion, the government tightly controls vehice registrations. But despite the high costs of vehicle ownership and a vast array of extremely high duties and taxes, demand exceeds supply since many Singaporeans have the means to purchase cars and car ownership is considered a status symbol. Therefore, continued growth in demand for vehicle repair and body work is anticipated by analysts. Due to minimal demand for remanufactured parts, the market demand for new replacement parts is excellent. Singaporeans also tend to maintain their cars well, creating strong demand for car care products and accessories such as rust protection systems, sealants, lubricants and car mats. There is a current market of about $600 million a year. Singapore is also the main distribution centre for automotive parts for all of Southeast Asia.

One example is Mercedes Benz, which invested $50 million to set up a new Regional Parts Centre for commercial vehicles in view of rapidly rising sales in Asia, to be expanded eventually to cover passenger cars. The company said the centre would support the manufacture of the company's new small truck MB-700 the commercial production of which was due to start in 1995 with initial output of 5,000 a year. The parts centre was scheduled to open by the end of 1995 and ultimately will stock 15,000 parts and components from 140 suppliers.[11]

Drugs and Pharmaceuticals

Singapore's national expenditure on drugs increased by more than 50 per cent in the 1990s. The island is also a key offshore manufacturing and support base for several multinational pharmaceutical corporations with markets in Malaysia, Brunei, Thailand, the Philippines, Indonesia, Korea, Taiwan, Pakistan, Sri Lanka and Vietnam. The National Biotechnology Master Plan, launched in 1990, emphasised the development of research on rational drug design and screening and vaccines, laying the ground for a strengthened R & D base here. The Master Plan is also a five-pronged strategy to develop the country's biotechnology industry, with a start-up budget of $40 million channelled into developing technology, infrastructure, manpower, industry alliance and public education. The pharmaceutical and healthcare industries, food technology and biological sciences are among the niches identified for development.

Construction Equipment

Singapore's construction industry has posted excellent growth rates in recent years, reporting earnings in excess of US$6 billion in 1993. The government is the main impetus with commitments to major projects such as the mammoth 10-year US$9.4 billion public housing upgrading and retrofitting programme and several major infrastructure projects including hospitals, schools, business parks as well as road construction and upgrading, airport development, public utilities distribution network upgrading and various land reclamation projects.

Air-Conditioning and Refrigeration Equipment

Steady growth is predicted through 1995 in both the household and institutional markets. The hotel industry continues to expand. residential housing is also experiencing a boom period, with a big demand due to the public housing upgrading and retrofitting programme already referred to. Furthermore, new housing estates will require shopping centres and restaurants, increasing the demand for institutional refrigeration equipment. As with most other sectors, there is strong re-export demand mainly to Hong Kong, Malaysia, Sri Lanka, Brunei and Thailand.

Food processing and Packaging Equipment

Demand for automated food processing and packaging equipment will continue to grow as Singapore food producers look for ways to solve their acute labour shortage and to increase productivity. The food processing market currently exceeds US$2 billion in annual output value, and is expanding rapidly, especially with a big market in neighbouring countries to compete for.

Printing and Graphic Arts Equipment

There are approaching 400 Singaporean and foreign printers whose annual exports in US dollars currently match their numbers (up from $301 million in 1991). There is a big demand for rotary presses and bookbinding equipment.

Franchising

Franchising is a very popular and explosive concept in Singapore, particularly in areas such as food, health and recreation services. American fast-food restaurants such as McDonalds, Burger King, Kentucky Fried Chicken and others have established more than 200 outlets on the tiny island. The government's efforts to foster entrepreneurial endeavours and to increase per capita output, combined with Singapore's high per capita income, have provided a wellspring of franchise opportunities. The government is seeking to facilitate this growth through the Economic Development Board and the Franchise Development Centre.

Made-in-Singapore franchises only started developing in the 1980s. The better-known ones are the NTUC Fairprice super-markets and the Econ Mini-Mart provision shop chain. Greater local interest in franchising was generated in 1993 when the government took steps to use this option to upgrade the domestic retail sector. Currently, local small and medium-sized retailers account for 17,500 or 97 per cent of all retail establishments on the island, employing 55,000 people or 76 per cent of the workforce in the retail sector. But the retail sector's value-added per worker is only $13,400, half that of foreign small retailers. Small and medium-sized retailers are also 52 per cent less productive than their manufacturing counterparts and 59 per cent less productive than their service counterparts.

Convinced that franchising is a highly viable option to boost productivity and competitiveness, the National Productivity Board set up a Franchise Development Centre (FDC) in April 1992. To date, it has helped to launch 28 franchises in 18 different trades such as confectionery, Chinese medicine and beauty care services. Its target is to set up 60 franchises by 1997 and it has identified 16 industries with potential for spawning local franchises, ranging from florists to vehicle repair.

The government is also creating four 'franchise streets' in Housing Development Board (HDB) housing estates – where the majority of Singaporeans live – in Toa Payoh, Chong Pang, Hong Hah and the West Coast area in the next few years. The idea is to showcase success stories in the industry.

The NPB's goal is to influence up to 20 per cent of Singapore's 10,000 HDB retailers to franchise their operations by the year 2000. Already, success stories are emerging. Franchise outlets of Base Ball and Medicine East have registered a doubling or more of sales compared to a year ago. Travelnet franchises have attained sales increases of more than 25 per cent and reduced staff turnover.

The recent emphasis by the government on regionalizing local businesses has rekindled interest in a scheme called FRANDAS or Franchise Development Assistance Scheme administered by the Trade Development Board, which aims to help export local franchises. The TDB has identified 60 companies in the retail, lifestyle, travel and food sectors that have regional potential. To date, the government has committed about $2 million to help 20 Singapore companies develop and expand through franchising abroad.[12]

CHAPTER NOTES

1. Doing Business in Singapore. Price Waterhouse, 1992 and 1993 supplement.
2. 'Petroleum: Fuelling the Motors of Profit', pp33-4, *Directions*, January/February issue, US Embassy, Singapore.
3. Ibid., p35.
4. Ibid., p34.
5. 'Basic capacity to be doubled', *Financial Times* 24/2/95.
6. Ibid.
7. Figures released by EDB.
8. EDB annual report.
9. 'The Petrochemical Industry: trends and Prospects,' by Roelf Venhuizen, Director of Chemicals of Shell Eastern Petroleum and Shell Eastern Chemicals. Economic Bulletin, SICC, December 1994.
10. Including the US Embassy, Australian and British High Commissions.
11. *Straits Times* 12/1/95.
12. British Business Association News, December 1994.

7 The Electronic Spark

ECONOMIC LIFELINE

SINGAPORE'S ECONOMIC SUCCESS story has gained much by the rapid development of the electronics industry, moving from the first television assembly plant established before the republic was created in 1965 to its present position as the world's largest exporter of disk drives. There is no exaggeration in saying that the sector is seen as Singapore's lifeline to continued prosperity.

A few figures will quickly confirm this. Growth averaged 24 per cent throughout the early years of the 1990s. The sector accounts for half of Singapore's total manufacturing output and a third of total employment.[1] According to business analysts Merrill Lynch, 41 per cent of value-added in the manufacturing sector in 1993 came from the electronics industry, which provided 55 per cent of its total domestic exports.[2]

While the high growth pattern was expected to continue until at least the middle of 1996 – on the back of strong regional demand for computers, semi-conductors and telecoms equipment, there are some who worry that the heavy dependence on such a narrow band of products, especially in a sector known to be highly volatile, and sensitive to exchange-rate pressures, is not good for long-term economic health. But the moment, this vulnerability does not seem a problem, Singapore, according to Merrill Lynch, being 'in the right place at the right time'.[3]

A study of the industry's brief history certainly shows that the island has had to endure something of a roller-coaster ride. Demand surges, new products are developed and employment goes up; demand declines, or prices drop due to market saturation, and factories close down or move some of their operations elsewhere. Some of them have gone to Batam, such as AT & T. In December 1994, it laid off 600 of its workers, halving the staff at one of its Singapore telephone handset plants and relocating production in the BIP (see Chapter Three). Mitsubishi of Japan followed soon after, shutting down a television and a car audio plant and moving the entire operation to Malaysia.

Only a few weeks before, 900 employees, out of a work force of 5000, of the French Multinational Thomson Consumer Electronics lost their jobs when the company closed down its colour television manufacturing plant and divided production between new factories in Batam and Bangkok. Rising costs in Singapore, where TCE has operated since 1969, were the main reason for the move. 'Mr Didier Trutt, a general manager of Thomson in Asia, said the television manufacturing industry operated under severe cost pressures. "Expanding our manufacturing operations in Thailand and Indonesia, while strengthening our support functions at the regional headquarters in Singapore, makes good economic sense".'[4]

The concern on the jobs front is evident in the publicity given to company reassurances such as 'Philips has no plans to retrench any of its 6,000 employees in S'pore', the headline over a newspaper which began: 'Unlike three other MNCs based here, Dutch giant Philips has no plans to retrench any of its 6,000 employees here, according to Philips Electronics president J.D.Trimmer. There was little chance of this happening, what with the plants here showing the highest sales growth among Philips worldwide operations, he said.'[5] And a day later another banner headline declared: 'No plans for Western Digital to relocate'. The story began: 'Disk-drive maker Western Digital (S)

Pte Ltd has no plans to relocate any of its local operations to the region, a senior company official said yesterday. Amidst increasing worries about the possible 'hollowing out' of manufacturing activities here, Mr Jim Steger, Western Digital's Asian operations managing director said the US company, which recently opened a plant in Malaysia, would be here for the long haul.'[6]

Fortunately for the national unemployment rate, many of the workers unfortunate enough to be laid off have been able to move into new jobs as other companies expanded their operations. But there are an increasing number of older workers whom the government fears will not be able to respond as readily to the constant process of retraining and upgrading required. And there is less elasticity than before in the job market, with many of the new investments being made in higher value-added production where much of the work can be done by computers and robots.

A portent of things to come was the opening in January 1995 of a $7 million fully-automated plant to produce controls for industrial robots, the first such facility outside Japan and the United States. 'Fanuc GE Automation's plant can make 30,000 programmable logic controllers a year, the bulk of which are to be exported. Of the total investment half went towards the building of the factory, and the other half to outfitting the fully-automated plant which has only three operators.'[7]

The factory relocations and creation of plants run almost entirely by machines are symptoms of what Singapore officials see as a 'natural progression' up the value-added ladder, but one that needs to be carefully planned and controlled if the manufacturing side is not to witness a 'hollowing out'. There is a big effort underway, therefore, to transform Singapore into a hub of high-tech electronics and a centre for research and development in Asia. A number of R & D institutes have been established. Hewlett Packard, for example, has a R & D centre for all its mobile printers, personal information products and networking software. Apple Corporation has set up a facility to develop software for an Asian language recognition system for personal computers.[8] Sony Corporation has opened its first integrated circuit design centre in Asia outside of Japan.[9]

Thomson Consumer Electronics, one of the National Science and Technology Board's top 12 R & D spenders, perfectly illustrates the changing climate for electronics in Singapore. Its television plant closed down in late 1994, laying off 900 workers. Mr Guy Urschel, Vice President of TCE's video group, said the closure was a 'do or die' choice as labour costs were too high. But the French multinational has had a video product development laboratory in Singapore since 1968. 'It has no plans for moving; indeed, it wants more software engineers. It employs a staff of 119, including 70 engineers, of whom only five per cent are expatriates. Its designs are used in all Thomson brands worldwide. Video products make up 21 per cent of the firm's revenue, second only to televisions with 48 per cent. Other Thomson labs here include one for television and another for audio and communications, employing a total of 200 engineers. In 1994, TCE spent over $45 million on its Singapore R & D operations.'[10]

A further indication of official thinking on electronics was provided by Lim Swee Say, Managing Director of the Economic Development Board, during a factory opening ceremony in January 1995. The government, he said, '...will introduce more front-end activities such as integrated circuit design and wafer fabrication. Back-end activities such as IC assembly and testing, which form the backbone of the industry, will also be strengthened'.[11]

These developments will be examined in more detail later in the chapter. But, for the moment, it will be helpful to go back to the start and trace the development of the Singapore electronics industry from its humble origins about 30 years ago when two local firms began assembling black-and-white television sets for a tariff-protected domestic market under license from Japanese consumer electronics firms.

1970s INVESTMENT SURGE

The industry was transformed in 1967 when, in response to competitive industry pressures and Singapore government policies to promote foreign investment, the American electronics multi-national Texas Instruments set up an offshore sourcing semiconductor plant to perform labour-intensive assembly for export. Within a few years, virtually every major American manufacturer had a similar plant on the island which quickly became the largest exporter of semiconductors in the world.

By the early 1970s, they had been joined by the Japanese, Europeans and other American firms mainly engaged in producing electronics components and consumer products for export to the world market. European and Japanese companies in particular were attracted by GSP (Generalized System of Privileges) trade promotion benefits which allowed their Singapore-made products to enter industrial-country markets (including the US after 1976) duty-free. The electronics industry became the largest employer in Singapore, with two consumer electronics firms – General Electric of the US and Philips of the Netherlands – becoming the two largest private sector employers with 11 and seven plants and 12,000 and 8,000 workers respectively by the early 1980s. [12]

Production costs rose and the host policy environment changed for the industry by the late 1970s, due to a tightening labour market and a government switch from a low-wage to a high-wage policy as part of a proclaimed 'Second Industrial Revolution' which began in 1979. Education, skill and experience levels had also risen to the point where Singapore could now accommodate higher-skill industries, and electronics firms had already begun capital-substitution in the late 1970s as labour costs rose and new products and technologies developed. A major industry shift occurred in the early 1980s, as semiconductor firms ceased expanding their labour-intensive assembly operations in Singapore, which fell to third place behind Malaysia and the Philippines in the ranks of the world's leading exporters of this product.

Semiconductors were replaced by computers and computer peripherals as the dominant segment of Singapore's electronics industry. American disk-drive companies, which were much less labour-intensive and had much higher value-added than semiconductors, other components or consumer products, established themselves in Singapore beginning in 1980. Within a few years, Singapore became the world's leading supplier of disk-drives. By 1987, it accounted for 77 per cent of the global output of Winchester (hard) disk-drives and 60 per cent of the US market.

Although the electronics industry as a whole averaged a 25 per cent annual growth rate in output, and a 15 per cent annual growth in value-added from 1981, it experienced a severe shake-out in 1985. This was due both to international industry developments – a drop in world demand for personal computers, in particular, and a loss of global market share to the Japanese by US and European multinationals heavily represented in Singapore – and to domestic factors – rapidly rising overall costs of production and a loss of international competitiveness to other NIEs and developing countries, especially in consumer electronics. There were large-scale layoffs by several multinationals. General Electric, for example, pulled out of the consumer electronics business altogether, closing its plants in this division in the United States and in Singapore and laying off more than half its employees in the republic. Philips also laid off some of its workers, but did not close entire divisions. However, both companies actually increased their capital investments in Singapore, in other, more profitable high-tech divisions, for example, GE's avionics division. Their position as Singapore's largest private employers was at the same time usurped by Seagate Technologies, which by 1988 employed more than 10,000 workers.

Singapore's rise to international prominence in the disk-drive industry has been phenomenal. Growth in hard-disk output averaged 80 per cent a year throughout the 1980s, and by the end of the decade they accounted for almost one-tenth of Singapore's domestic exports. Initially, all were shipped to the United States, as all the manufacturers were from that country. But with the growth of personal computer manufacture in Asia, the bulk of the output began to go to the region from 1988 onwards.

Virtually all the major drive manufacturers in the world – Seagate (the largest), Micropolis, Miniscribe, Maxtor, Conner, Control Data and Unisys – are present in Singapore. Labour shortages have forced some of the early-comers to relocate their simpler activities to neighbouring countries while bringing in newer, higher-value-added products. Thus, for example, Seagate moved most of its 5.25 inch 20 megabyte hard disk-drive production to Thailand, while shifting to Singapore all its production of newer 3.5-inch drives. The company then began R & D activities at the Singapore Science Park, where its local engineers worked on a compact disc read-only memory (CD-ROM) project.

The easy availability locally of parts and materials also helped attract the drive companies, either through Singaporean firms, foreign sub-contractors who decided it was worthwhile moving in or additional factories set up by the main manufacturers themselves. Thus, in addition to its disk-drive assembly and testing operations, Seagate supplied half of its total printed-circuit board needs from two additional factories in Singapore (though this capacity has now been shifted to Malaysia and Thailand). Maxtor set up two separate factories to supply components for its two disk-drive factories.

In 1988, a surge in world demand pushed all the disk-drive companies in Singapore to increase their capacity. In the same year, in order to double total output, Maxtor moved all its 5.25-inch drives and all its lower-end 3.5-inch drives from the United States to Singapore, and also set up a R & D centre. Miniscribe doubled its capacity and added a third factory building, with an eventual employee total reaching 4,600 by the end of the year. Micropolis and Western Digital tripled their capacity, and Control Data set up a second factory within a few months of opening its first, with two more to follow soon after. Conner, which ships 80 per cent of its Singapore-made 3.5-inch drives to Compaq Computer in Texas, its largest customer and major shareholder, set up a third Singapore plant which meant that the republic monopolized four-fifths of its global output. The boom also lured back National Micronetics, a magnetic head manufacturer which moved to Manila in 1985 but returned in 1988 with a highly automated plant.

With the extended capacity, a slowdown in world personal computer demand in late 1988, resulted in a short-lived slump for the Singapore-based US disk-drive industry. Seagate, whose slowness in shifting from 5.25 to 3.5-inch drives aggravated its sales decline, laid off 800 non-production workers, about eight per cent of its Singapore workforce, in November 1988, but within a few months was aggressively hiring new production workers. Micropolis introduced a shorter work-week while Miniscribe also laid off workers. However, Conner expanded even during the downturn. By April 1989 the industry had largely recovered.

Besides disk-drives, Singapore also became the world's largest producer of computer-tape drives used to store computer data and provide back-up for disk-drives in personal computers, work-stations, microcomputers and mainframes. The world leader, Archive Corporation of California, which claimed to produce 45 per cent of the global supply of quarter-inch tape-drives, produced almost all of them in two Singapore factories. By 1990, it had doubled its investment, with three factories and an R & D unit. Two other California tape-drive manufacturers – Cipher Data and CMS Enhancement also moved in.[13]

SEMICONDUCTORS FLOURISH

The rise in computer peripheral manufacture, however, was not at the expense of other sectors of electronics, since semiconductors, components and consumer electronics continued to thrive. In the semiconductor industry, there were 19 manufacturers in 1988, with more than 50 others in the supporting industries. Semiconductor output rose from $2.3 billion in 1992 to $4.2 billion in 1994.[14] New investors in automated chip manufacture include NEC Corporation from Japan, the world's largest maker of semiconductors, and North American Philips. Both were attracted to Singapore by the presence of major customers who manufacture electronic equipment locally or in the neighbouring region, where demand was growing rapidly.

In 1988, SGS-Thomson Microelectronics, a French-Italian joint venture, spent $60 million to upgrade its fully-integrated wafer fabrication plant in Singapore to make more advanced MOS semiconductors, and an additional $20 million to expand its assembly and testing facility. In 1989, it announced another $180 million increase in investment in semiconductor manufacture in Singapore in an effort to propel the company from its 12th-place ranking among world semiconductor producers into the top ten.

SGS-Thomson Microelectronics set up a plant in Singapore in 1969, when many other multinational companies preferred to invest in Europe and the United States. Since then, it has rapidly increased its presence, including the setting up of the high-tech wafer fabrication plant in 1984, the first of its kind outside Japan. From its regional headquarters in Singapore, its operations have now expanded to cover the design, manufacture, marketing and sales of its products throughout the Asia-Pacific. In 1993, the company's sales in the region totalled US$460 million, representing only 3.3 per cent share of the Asia-Pacific market but 23 per cent of the company's total sales. In 1994, sales expanded to US$650 million. The company has invested a total of US$400 million in two plants in Singapore and one in Muar, Malaysia. Its operations in Muar and Toa Payoh account for some 65 per cent of SGS-Thomson's back-end output, while the wafer fabrication plant at Ang Mo Kio accounts for 30 per cent of the company's total production. An Asia Pacific Design Centre and Applications Laboratory is also based in Singapore.

Siemens of Germany, Europe's largest electronics company which already assembled 80 per cent of its plastic-moulded integrated circuits in Singapore plant, meanwhile, invested another $70 million to make its plant its biggest integrated circuit assembly and test facility in the world and main global manufacturing base for integrated circuits.

Besides expanding, semiconductor production also began diversifying and upgrading. Semiconductor companies decided to do more product and process development locally, with several setting up R & D centres. Eight multinationals – AT&T, Microelectronics, SGS-Thomson, Chartered Telmos, Hewlett-Packard, National Semiconductor, Texas Instruments, Silicon Compilation Technology and Silicon Systems – had commercially integrated circuit design centres in Singapore by the late 1980s.

The consumer electronics sector was plunged in the doldrums by the recession of the mid-1980s, but soon began to pick up again. The Dutch multinational Philips reversed a decision to halve its planned $300 million investments in its five factories in Singapore and began steadily expanding local operations in 1987. Production of some consumer products was even relocated from the Netherlands and Taiwan. Thomson, meanwhile, built a major new plant to manufacture video cassette-recorders for export to the United States and Europe.

In the same year, Matsushita Electronics of Japan expanded its Singapore output of audio products, while lesser-known Japanese manufacturers of audio equipment and components such as Foster and Kenwood also relocated to Singapore to escape the high yen. Among other products, Kenwood began making compact disc players. Toshiba added compact disc players and digital audio tape (DAT) machines to its profitable colour television output on the island – a move mirrored by Sanyo, which had four plants on the island and in 1987 shifted output of low value-added audio products to Malaysia. Another Japanese company, Asahi Electronics, shifted production of its Phonemate answering machines from Japan to Singapore, for eventual export to the United States.

In the industrial electronics sector, besides computers (e.g. Apple, Unisys, Nixdorf, Digital Equipment Corporation) and peripherals (disk-drives and monitors) there was increased foreign investment in the manufacture of such products as telecommunications equipment (e.g. AT&T and Ericsson), facsimile machines (Matsushita) and process control systems (Yokogawa). General Motors invested another US$70 million in its Delco Electronics division in Singapore – its only Asian plant, producing 13 per cent of Delco's global output – to expand production of automotive electronics products.

Suppliers to the electronics industry which also moved to the island at this time included firms in other sectors, such as glass, engineering and chemicals. For example, the Japanese industrial plastics manufacturer Sumitomo Bakelite built a plant to manufacture epoxy moulding compounds used by chip makers to encase integrated circuits. The company already had two joint ventures in Singapore making printed circuit boards and embossed carrier tapes for surface mounted devices. Hitachi Chemicals, producer of multilayer printed circuit boards built a second factory and introduced new technology. Matsushita, the largest Japanese investor in Singapore with eight local subsidiaries making a variety of consumer and industrial electronics products – and, like Seagate employing more than 10,000 people – began manufacturing high-precision automatic inserting equipment for printed-circuit-board manufacture.[15]

When the Singapore government began offering new tax breaks to encourage multinationals to establish regional operating headquarters (OHQ) – for which the qualifications included basing their regional R & D, distribution, service network and financial system in Singapore – a number of electronics companies, including Data General and Hewlett Packard, Nixdorf Computers, Philips, Matsushita, Sanyo and Sony quickly obtained approval.

In the case of Sony, its Singapore headquarters covered the multinational's entire operations in the Asia-Pacific region outside Japan. Singapore became the global distribution centre and regional hub coordinating Sony's eight plants in Thailand, Malaysia. South Korea and Taiwan, providing warehousing, packing and shipping for parts and products going all over the world, undertaking procurement and providing support services to train and helping suppliers improve their quality.

Separate from this OHQ arrangement, Sony also opened its first precision engineering centre overseas. The highly automated centre, employing mainly skilled craftsmen, technicians and engineers, supplies high-precision parts and components to the company's overseas plants for audio, video and office automation products, serves as a training centre for personnel from Sony's other Asian plants, and includes special projects such as a software R & D laboratory. In the case of Philips, Singapore provides servicing and support facilities for its television manufacturing plants in countries such as Pakistan, Malaysia, the Philippines, Indonesia and China.[16]

It followed this up in early 1995 with the establishment of a $1.1 million design centre for integrated circuits, its seventh such facility along with four in Japan and one in each in the United States and Britain. Initially, the centre has been engaged in designing ICs for consumer audio products made by a Sony factory in Thailand. The President of Sony's semiconductor company, Dr Sieichi Watanabe, indicated that within two years the centre would expand into other types of ICs, including those for video, television, hard disk-drive and telecommunications products.[17]

CASE STUDY: RACAL

Racal Electronics (S) Pte Ltd, part of Britain's Racal Group, appears to be the only foreign company that can claim to have been a long-established participant in the developments just described. In 1955, it celebrated its 26th anniversary as a limited company, having started life as a representative office two years before that. And throughout that time, it has been a regional type of operation. The Singapore office, with few exceptions, handles Southeast Asian business for most of the companies in the Racal Group, particularly telecommunications business. One exception is the military communications division which, for political reasons, deals direct with the island's two closest neighbours, Indonesia and Malaysia, as well as Brunei.

Apart from the electronics operation, Singapore is also the base for Racal Survey, which provides high-accuracy positioning systems for off-shore oil rigs. A subsidiary of Racal Energy bought a Singaporean manufacturer of underwater remotely-operated vehicles for £24 million in 1994 to complement the oil rig business. There is also a small operation, Racal Health and Safety, which provides breathing apparatus, oxygen generators and other safety equipment to industrial users, and which operates independently.

Duncan Fisken, Director and General Manager of Racal electronics says:[18] 'In the early days, Racal was the biggest supplier of green boxes [man-pack radios] to the military and it's still very big business for us. Over the years, we have built up a strong regional presence. We have quite important markets in Indonesia, Malaysia, Thailand in the field of commercial voice and data, particularly areas like communications security for banking networks. Racal is about number one in the world in providing link security between ATM machines and bank mainframe computers [to protect your PIN number when you put your plastic bank card in the slot] and electronic fund transfer point of sales security systems.

'Singapore, I would imagine, was chosen 28 years ago for strategic reasons – probably for much the same reasons they would choose it now – bang in the middle for communications, and the place to be; infrastructure being better developed than elsewhere, although Malaysia is catching up fast.'

At the time of the interview, the executive had only been with Racal for a year. But he has worked in Singapore since 1979, first working for an AEG Telefunken subsidiary, and then buying out that company, which he ran until selling it and joining Racal.

'We've seen a lot of changes in the electronics business, away from what many people would still have as their perception of Southeast Asia as a cheap place for labour. In some places it is, in Singapore it certainly isn't. Singapore's costs are getting too high, too expensive to be in at that end of the business because there isn't enough value-added. The EDB, TDB, and MTI are continually urging people to upgrade and add more value to their process.

'We are very much in the value-added business because of the system engineering content and the support that our products require. Southeast Asia is probably going to be the biggest market for the foreseeable future and I would suggest it will challenge China in the next few years because Indonesia and Thailand are making very rapid strides towards privatization in their telecoms sector. In many ways, Malaysia is further down the track than Singapore, which is quite unusual. Singapore usually gets there first and the rest follow along, but in the telecoms sector Malaysia is ahead in privatizing networks in service provision.

'As a leading supplier in the world of financial systems security, we have had a very big market share in Southeast Asia and believe that with the rapid development of communications infrastructure in places like Indonesia and Thailand, and with the roll-out in Malaysia of ISDN services on a country-wide basis, those three countries will catch up very quickly with Singapore in terms of sophistication of the products and services offered by the banks. We are establishing a dedicated security division here in Singapore in which we will encapsulate a very high level of technical expertise to provide support in the region for our customers in that business.

'Singapore will remain the hub, although investment in training and support and possible joint ventures in other countries in the region can never be ruled out. I am personally very committed to taking as much advantage as possible of the EDB's regionalization incentives [discussed in the last chapter] over the next few years. We are certainly planning our strategy to take us to business headquarters [BHQ] status in due course. Whether or not we go further to OHQ [Operational Headquarters] remains to be seen.'

Racal does not have a manufacturing presence in Singapore, nor anywhere in Southeast Asia. But Fisken indicated the company was looking at the possibility of migrating manufacturing away from its American sites to the region. 'There are some product lines the American plants are indicating they may discontinue, even though there is still a market in this region for them. Low-speed modems is one such example. We would be looking at possibly two sites for relocation. One would be the Batam/Bintan technology park development and the other would be in China to take advantage of the Singapore government's bilateral agreements with the Chinese, where we would be seen to be a British company investing in China but would be a Singapore company investing there, and would enjoy not only the protection of the Singapore government can offer us but also the financial benefits they are prepared to give us for doing it.

'We have an open mind about other products we might manufacture. But Singapore is not one of the places where we would be looking to do that. The costs are just too great to justify that sort of operation. It's quite labour intensive. The boards themselves can be manufactured using automated processes, but the final assembly still requires human beings.'

Racal Electronics (S) Pte Ltd, with 35 staff, supplies and supports voice- and data-communication systems. It has distributors throughout the region who may take shipment direct from factories in Britain and America, but in many cases the products transit through the Singapore facility because they may have to be worked upon, especially if they are to be integrated into a system. The distributors in Indonesia and Malaysia are technically competent, having bee trained in Singapore. But for new products and more complex systems, the Singapore office would provide a technical support team.

Asked about the future of the electronics industry in Singapore, Fisken replies: 'There has been a constant shift away from the low end of manufacturing and now even the high end... the disk-drive guys, for example, are under pressure. I am not convinced that there is a future for electronics manufacturing in Singapore unless the processes are largely automated.

'I see the future for electronics in Singapore in the manufacturing sector to probably be right at the very top, cutting edge of technology, in terms of wafer manufacture, chip manufacture, chip foundries. Singapore does not have the labour resources to support labour-intensive operations. But they certainly have the skill base and the level of education required to draw on large pools of engineers to run those very, very sophisticated assembly-type operations; design operations, with people like Grumman, Silicon Graphics, InterGraph, Mentorgraphics, which are all involved in Singapore in more or less the software CAD-CAM-type arena, with quite extensive support operations. I believe it is pointing to probably the highest end of the component manufacturing business.

'But, of course, there is quite threat from Malaysia now. There are a lot of semiconductor operations in Penang. Malaysia has free-trade zones established for them in Kuala Lumpur as well. So Singapore cannot afford to be too blasé about it. Over the last year we have seen big companies retrenching because it's not cost-effective any more. They are left with a choice of either migrating their manufacturing as it is to somewhere else like Thailand or Vietnam, or to upgrade and automate their operations here.'

CASE STUDY: SIEMENS

'Mr Hartmut Lueck, Managing Director of Siemens' semiconductor plant in Singapore, has the sort of problem many of the world's industrialists dream about. His factory is working round the clock, every day of the year, yet it still cannot produce enough to satisfy demand. Siemens first established an electronics factory in Singapore in 1970. Now it employs 1,600 people at a new components plant capable of turning out more than 300 million semiconductors a year. Singapore serves as the base for Siemens' components sales in the Asia-Pacific region.

'Like many other companies, Siemens is increasingly focusing on the region as the area of future large-scale sales growth. In October 1994, all of its directors flew to Singapore for the first board meeting to be held outside Germany in the company's 147-year history. For Siemens as a whole, the Asia-Pacific countries represent one of the world's most promising growth regions. The group's business there has been growing at double-digit percentage rates and is expected in a few years to be as large as that of the United States, accounting for some 15 per cent of turnover.

'The group's order volume in East and Southeast Asia rose by 50 per cent to US$3.5 billion in the financial year to end-September 1993, while sales from its Singapore operations reached nearly DM800 million – a rise of more than 50 per cent on the 1992 figure. By late 1994, sales for the year [had] already exceeded DM1 billion, fuelled by growth in the region's telecommunications industry, particularly in China.

'Mr Lueck feels his company has some advantages over competitors. Siemens started its Singapore factory in the 1970s, in order to benefit from the island republic's low wages. "Though wages have risen here, they are still low compared with Germany or the US and are an important factor in our operations. But the character of the semiconductor industry is changing. Now cost is not so crucial. The most important thing is innovation and being first – then you can name your own price. You can also then achieve cost advantages through volume and quickly recoup your costs – in order to invest in the next cycle of the industry."

'Accumulated investment in Singapore by Siemens is put at DM450 million. Siemens also has two other regional plants, both in neighbouring Malaysia, which together employ nearly 4000 people. Aided by a Singapore government grant, Siemens is opening an integrated circuit design centre linked to a similar facility at its headquarters in Munich. When Munich sleeps, the design centre can take over. Technological advances in the semiconductor industry are rapid: every three or four years a new generation of chips comes along which is far more powerful than its predecessor. "By working round the clock, the R & D and innovation cycles are shortened," says Mr Lueck.

'The wafers from which the chips are cut are flown in from Europe. Finished chips used to go back to Germany for testing, but now that is done in Singapore and Malaysia. Siemens Singapore does have problems, however. Labour shortages and job-hopping are top of the list. About 30 per cent of the workers at the Singapore plant travel each day from Malaysia. For its top engineers Siemens has had to hold recruitment drives in the US and elsewhere to lure talented Singaporeans back home.'[19]

NEW INVESTMENT

At the time of writing, the mood in the electronics industry is upbeat. In the second half of 1994 and at the beginning of 1995, there was a flurry of announcements of new investments by some of the major players. To capture some of the flavour of this, the next few paragraphs will detail some of the most important developments.

Philips Singapore, in conjunction with the opening of its $15 million Asia-Pacific Centre for Manufacturing Technology, unveiled the centre's first R & D project – Flexline, a fully automated assembly line that can handle different sizes of components as well as different products. The system was due to be introduced worldwide during 1995. The research centre was partly financed by a $5 million grant from the National Science and Technology Board under its Research Incentive Scheme for Companies. Philips is one of the few companies in Singapore doing basic research. The centre will carry out research and development work in various areas of intelligent manufacturing and also provide technical support to Philips factories and their in-house R & D departments in Singapore and the region.

Asahi Techno Vision (S) Pte Ltd opened its second pioneer

status colour tv glass panel manufacturing plant in Tuas, adjacent to its existing plant which started operation in 1989. The company is wholly owned by Asahi Glass of Japan, the largest colour tv glass bulb maker in the world. The $300 million plant has three process lines and a larger production capacity of 13 million items per year. With an initial investment of over $300 million in the first plant, and subsequent investment on the production line expansion over the past five years, accumulated total investment is about $700 million, with a combined total annual production capacity of 23 million pieces. The new plant will be capable of producing larger sizes such as 25 and 29-inch and above, as well as higher technology products such as wide screen, high definition, and highly specified screens for CRT monitors. It will be a highly automated operation.

Sony Corporation invested $22 million through a subsidiary, Singapore Precision Engineering Centre (SPEC), to produce high technology electron-guns, a key precision component for cathode-ray tubes (CRTs), which helps to produce sharp images for CTVs. This is Sony's first production of electron-guns outside Japan with a projected production of three million units annually in the initial stage. The President of Sony's components division, Mr Yoshiyuki Kaneda, said the move to transfer technology was due to the high value of the Yen, a need to build products closer to the market and to manage risk. Production of the electron-guns started in late October 1994 at SPEC's plant in Tuas. The electron-guns will be used for CTVs made in Malaysia, Thailand, Japan and other countries. Mr M. Sekiya, SPEC's Managing Director, said that the production would be increased to eight million units within two years. The bulk of the production will go to Sony Display Device Singapore which makes CRTs, while the rest will go to Sony's plants in the US and Europe.[20]

Production began with the manufacture of a gun for 14-inch colour televisions. Sony Display Services (S) Pte Ltd, which makes picture tubes for Sony Trinitron colour TVs, will take the bulk of the initial output. 'Kaneda said SPEC's experience in ultra-fine processing assembly and automated assembly technologies made it the ideal choice for the production of electron-guns. He said: "The accumulated know-how of both facilities will be invaluable in developing and producing the world's most advanced and cost-effective electron-guns and in localising know-how and technology for wide-screen CTV and HDTV related parts, production methods, and die-casts.'' Sony decided to expand its production of electron-guns here because Asia heads the increased demand for colour televisions. SPEC has 470 skilled workers and an annual sales turnover of $500. It has invested a total of $246 million in Singapore to date.'[21]

Disk-drive maker Seagate Technology Inc. decided to construct a multi-million dollar design, development and manufacturing facility in Singapore as part of an expansion strategy for its high volume manufacturing operations in the Asia-Pacific region. Investment in the new one million sq.ft. facility is approximately $200 million. The company had already invested $600 million over a 12-year period in facilities to produce three-quarters of its global output of disk-drives. With the completion of the new building, scheduled in mid-1996, the company planned to consolidate the operations of all its three facilities in Singapore under one roof. Currently, the company's PCB assembly plant is at Senoko, its disk-drive manufacturing plant at Tuas, and its headquarters and main disk-drive operations at Kallang. Company officials said the move would reduce factory space by 200,000 sq.ft. and save millions of dollars in factory rentals, but employment would remain unchanged at 13,000. 'Manufacturing operations at the new building will include some of the most advanced automated process technologies for the production of Seagate's full line of 1.8-,2.5-,3.5- and 5,25-inch data storage devices.'[22]

A similar consolidation was carried out by Apple Computer. It was investing $55 million over a two-year period to build a second factory at its manufacturing site in the 'new town' of Ang Mo Kio to bring its various activities, previously scattered across the island, under one roof. This brought Apple's total commitments in Singapore to more than £235 million. The new complex houses regional service functions such as physical logistics, system integration, service logistics and demand fulfilment, in addition to manufacturing, R & D, sales and marketing, and warehousing operations. 'Fred Forsyth, Apple Inc.'s Senior Vice President for World-wide Operations, said: "Singapore manufacturing has played an integral role in the introduction of both the PowerMacs and our latest additions to the PowerBook family. We are building these systems here in Singapore for distribution world-wide".'[23]

'More Quantum disk-drives are expected to be shipped from

Singapore to the Asia-Pacific following the opening of new facilities by Quantum Corporation and Matsushita-Kotobuki Electronics (MKE) of Japan. Both Quantum Asia-Pacific Logistics Centre, previously at Tagore Lane, and MKE's manufacturing subsidiary, Kotobuki Electronics Industries Singapore, are now located in a new building in Jurong. The two facilities complement each other. Kotobuki Electronics began producing Quantum's 3.5 inch hard disc-drives in Singapore in April 1994 with a staff of 600. The finished drives are configured at the Quantum facility according to the specifications of its OEM customers. "The co-location of both facilities means lower operational costs and shorter time-to-volume production. We work closely together from design through to the mass production stage," said Mr Young K. Sohn, President and Managing director of Quantum Asia-Pacific.'[24]

'US-based National Semiconductor Corporation, which opened its $12 million plant extension in Toa Payoh, said it will invest another $190 million over the next five years for further upgrading of its technology and equipment. This is to help its plant build additional capacity for its future-generation products, said Wan Choong Hoe, managing director of National Semiconductor Manufacturer Singapore. National Semiconductor makes a variety of semiconductor products for personal computing and telecommunications and automotive industries. The new three-storey factory extension will increase the plant's current output of 140 million chips a year by 25 per cent. Over the next five years, production capacity will increase threefold. But this won't lead to any more jobs on top of the existing 1,800. Established in 1968, the Toa Payoh plant is one of the group's eight manufacturing sites in the world and is the largest assembly and test facility for its high-end communications and computing group products, currently contributing US$800 million to the $2.3 billion global revenues. Major customers include the Singapore operations of Apple Computer, Compaq, AT&T, General Motors Quantum, Maktor, Seagate and Micropolis. The plant also supplies to multinational companies in the US and Europe.'[25]

'Gul Technologies began manufacturing multi-layer printed circuit boards in Singapore in October 1988. In 1989, its first full year of operation, it had sales of $28.6 million. In 1994, sales were $68 million, compared to $56.2 million in 1993. The company places top priority on keeping ahead of its competitors. This is reflected in its plans to spend another $10 million in 1995/6 to manufacture high-density multi-layer PCBs and to develop advanced interconnect systems, which enable end-manufacturers to reduce the size of a product while increasing its functions, reliability and system speed. The company, which has invested $35 million so far, aims to build PCBs with 3 mils lines and spaces by 1995/6, reducing to 1.5 mils in later years. It is now able to make PCBs up to 12 layers with 5 mils lines and spaces, a product in which it has few competitors. A big breakthrough came in 1991, when Gul Technologies formed a joint venture with Teledyne to use Teledyne's rigid flex assembly process known as "Regal Flex" to make PCBs which have flexible sections, allowing them to be folded three dimensionally. Such PCBs can be configured into volume-efficient multi-planar shapes, opening up new possibilities for products that are smaller and more compact in size.

'Because no other company is making PCBs with rigid-flex technology in Asia other than Japan, Gul Technologies has found a niche which has boosted sales significantly. The company was a captive manufacturer of PCBs for Data General before its senior managers succeeded in a management buyout in 1988. Gul Technologies customers now include multinational companies such as Apple Computer, Baxter Healthcare, Ericsson, Ford, Motorola and Seagate. The markets it serves range from computers to medical equipment, telecommunications equipment and electronics. On the company's plans to go regional, President Jerry Rodriques said: "We will consider manufacturing in Malaysia and elsewhere in the region if it is more cost-effective to do so, but given the high-technology base we have here and the good infrastructure, we want to maintain our Singapore plant as the centre for added-value technology".'[26]

FUTURE CONCERNS

Thus, for the moment at least, Singapore is doing well out of electronics. But it cannot afford to relax. As already noted, it is heavily dependent on a highly volatile industry governed by cycles of rising and slumping demand. The government, for example, is keen to reduce the leading position of disk-drives, the manufacture of which is highly cyclical and which currently accounts for 22 per cent of total value in the electronics sector. It wants to see expansion of the semiconductor industry, and particularly wants to see multinationals investing in wafer technology. As the foregoing section indicates, some of this is beginning to happen.

One problem, however, is a distinct shortage of electronic engineers on the domestic market. Many of the engineers now working in the republic are recruited from China, India and the United States. This is a challenge the Singapore education system has yet to fully meet.

With so many global giants crowding into the market, local electronics companies have had to struggle to gain a niche. Various government-funded R & D institutes have been set up to assist local companies to develop competitive technologies, in such areas as highly complex miniature disk-drive parts. But these companies tend to be very product-specific and, therefore, vulnerable to any changes in the business health of their prime customers.

Creative Technologies is often cited by the government as an example of a Singaporean success story, and it has done well in securing for itself an estimated 65 per cent share of the global market for soundboards, but it is almost completely dependent on this one product. Faced with the prospect of eroding profit margins, Creative Technologies has now begun addressing this issue by looking at ways to develop a broader product mix.

Those likely to suffer most as the industry moves into more capital-intensive products are the local sub-contractors for the multinationals. Over the past 10 or 20 years most of these companies have not needed to focus on marketing by virtue of their activity as assemblers for well-known brandnames. Now, they are vulnerable to structural changes taking place in the industry. 'It has evolved to such a stage that having the right technology alone does not guarantee success. You need the marketing and a lot of smaller companies do not have that experience,' says David Toh, investment analyst for Barings Securities.[27]

With the technology constantly changing and product cycles becoming shorter, electronics manufacturers have to constantly upgrade to lower costs and stay competitive. This tends to lead to a 'price war' on international markets, as the major companies seek to undercut each other to widen their market share, leading to pressure on their sub-contractors to lower their prices and, usually, reduce their already tight profit margins.

Nevertheless, more local companies are learning how to survive. Many have gained enough confidence to set up overseas when their main customer decides to relocate out of cost considerations. A number of sub-contractors have moved to Penang, for example, to continue working alongside their MNC clients.

The EDB has recognized this trend through its Manufacturing 2000 and Local Enterprise 2000 programmes designed to provide a multi-agency administered package of financial and other initiatives to help local companies cope with change and hopefully build them up into the 'industry leaders of tomorrow', to quote from the board's 1994 Yearbook. It cited a few examples of companies who have responded to the challenge:

'Omni Mold has expanded its large mold manufacturing capacity to meet the outsourcing trend [of MNCs], whilst Santech Corporation is teaming up with a Japanese partner to manufacture miniaturized plastic components for use in disk-drives, cameras and consumer electronic products. Shinluck is backward integrating into the manufacture of surface mount stencils by teaming up with a UK technology partner, Tecan. Through this venture, Tecan will be transferring its full photochemical machining capabilities which will allow Shinluck to meet the increasing needs for high precision metal parts in miniaturization.

'In the electronics supporting industries, companies are responding to miniaturization trends through developing capabilities in high-density interconnect products including chip-on-board, fine-pitch printed circuit-board assembly, multi-chip module and tape-automated bonding. Applying its strong MNC linkage, the Local Industry Upgrading Programme enabled local companies to acquire new capabilities. A collaborative project to manufacture insert-moulded parts was successfully concluded between Mold Technic, a local company, and Capsonic of the US. These critical developments support new and better investments under our M2000 strategy. Others include multi-layer PCBs, surface treatment, composite moulding, liquid crystal displays and the manufacture of key modules such as mechadeck and VCR drums.'

CHAPTER NOTES

1. 'Electronics climbs up value-added ladder' by Manuela Saragosa. *Financial Times* 24/2/95.
2. 'Singapore electronics to see strong growth,' Asia-Pacific Telecoms Analyst, 1/8/94.
3. Ibid.
4. 'Singapore to lose tv plant,' *Financial Times* 10/11/94.
5. *Straits Times* 10/1/95.
6. *Straits Times* 11/1/95.
7. *Straits Times* 24/1/95.
8. 'Electronics climbs up value-added ladder' FT 24/2/95.
9. *Business Times* and *Straits Times* 14/2/95.
10. *Straits Times* 26/1/95.
11. 'National Semiconductor to invest another $190m in S'pore', *Straits Times* 11/1/95.
12. Foreign Direct Investment & Industrialization in Malaysia, Singapore, Taiwan and Thailand. Lim, Y.C. and Pang, E.F. Development Centre of the OECD, 1991, p123.
13. Ibid., pp124-6.
14. See note 7.
15. Foreign Direct Investment & Industrialization in Malaysia, Singapore, Taiwan and Thailand., pp127-8.
16. Ibid., p129.
17. *Straits Times* 14/2/95.
18. Interview in Singapore 26/1/95.
19. 'Siemens Dream Factory in Singapore' by Kieran Cooke, *Financial Times* 12/10/94.
20. The Economic Bulletin, Singapore International Chamber of Commerce, Nov.1994.
21. *Singapore Investment News*, EDB, Sept. 1994.
22. Ibid.
23. Ibid., August 1994.
24. Ibid., June 1994.
25. 'National Semiconductor to invest another $190m in S'pore', *Straits Times* 11/1/95.
26. *Singapore Investment News*, EDB, June. 1994.
27. Quoted in the *Financial Times* 24/2/95.

8 The Intelligent Island

DIGITAL ECONOMY

SINGAPORE is well on the way to becoming the world's first digital economy, where information of any kind whether sound, films, television of data is deconstructed into the 1s and 0s of computer code before being dispatched simultaneously across the world down telephone lines or broadcast through the air.

The city-state is not only ambitious to lead the rest of the world in the application of information technology but is well on the way to implementing the vision of being an Intelligent Island by the year 2000. It started with the telephone system which was the first in the world to become completely digitized so that all telephones are now push button. In the centre of town, shoppers have the dubious security of hardly ever being out of sight of a mobile phone being pressed to someone's ear. Singapore also claims to have more pagers to keep in contact with each other.

Cash is going the same way too. You can already pay for your bus ticket by inserting a plastic card into a machine on the bus which will deduct it from the current account of your savings bank or download it automatically from a deposit account if your normal account is empty. Soon smart cards of this kind will be used for all transactions.

Buildings are being put on a digitized grid to speed up land transactions and construction. 'Intelligent' buildings are being designed with the capacity (or 'bandwidth') not only to receive all that the information revolution can throw at it in the form of multimedia newspapers and live video conferences, but also with the brains to control the economic provision of water, electricity and waste disposal.

Six schools have been chosen to pioneer the 'borderless' classroom. Lee Kwok Cheong of the National Computer Board explains: 'We want to make Singapore a learning nation where people continuously learn and upgrade themselves, but don't necessarily do it by going to the classroom'. Instead, pupils could be at home researching, for example, Shakespeare from databases all over the world using special software to search for the particular context required. Lectures at overseas universities could be seen or heard live in between communicating with your teacher or tutor electronically.

Computerization of school budgets, timetables and performance tables is reckoned to have saved several million pounds thereby freeing teachers to do other things. Research is being done into how children can do homework on their personal computers and send it through a modem to the school's computer. In the case of multiple–choice questions the computer would mark the paper and provide comments on the strengths and weaknesses of pupils, based on analysis of the patterns discerned in the answering of the questions. Schools and universities are also starting to be linked up to the Internet, the worldwide network of information sources used by an estimated 25 million people.

This will be backed up by a library of the future to make books and source material from domestic libraries (themselves linked to libraries overseas) available instantaneously to users of computers at home coupled with home delivery of books or faxed copies of pages which cannot be accessed remotely. Users will be able to subscribe to a service which alerts them to new material on their special interests as it comes into the library. In this way, the government will receive a much higher return on its investment in libraries as their contents are made available to a much larger base of users.

The revolution is also moving into the high street. Singatouch, a multimedia public information system will eventually be in place across the island through kiosks sited in public places. By placing a finger on the relevant part of the colour screen (to 'call up' the appropriate words and images) people will be able, for example, not only to find out the best combinations of buses and trains to get to the cinema, see a video preview, and then call up on the screen the theatre's seating plan, paying for the seats with a smartcard.

The proposed National Information Infrastructure (NII) – which aims to wire up every home in the state by 2005 with optical fibres of almost unlimited carrying capacity – offers other achievable scenarios. In medicine, patients will be able to stay at home but linked to the hospital by a bedside terminal monitoring their progress and transmitting the results to the hospital online. Electronic road pricing will be used to control congestion, dynamic road signs will automatically warn drivers of road conditions ahead and smart bus stops will display the expected arrival of the next bus.

What is being planned now for consumers has already been largely achieved in the corporate sector. Singapore's port is totally automated. Vessels, monitored by satellite, can enter all their documentation from computer screens directly into the port's computer which instantly checks them using artificial intelligence while simultaneously passing the results on to Customs and Excise for speedy compilation of the country's trade figures. This project, called TradeNet has a counterpart in LawNet, which speeds up access to legal and corporate documents. These will be discussed in more detail later.

This is very much in the Singapore tradition. 'Just as previous generations lived by adding value to products coming along the main trade routes (by, for instance, refuelling ships and of offloading cargo to its final destination) so the new Singapore is in the business of "knowledge arbitrage". By seizing a leading role in the application of information technology, the country hopes to process "knowledge" products in order to sell them profitably to the fast-expanding economies of the Pacific Basin.'[1]

'We see technology as allowing us to enlarge our economic space, overcoming our country's small size,' says NCB Chief Executive Koh Kheng Hwa. 'Using technology will enable us to compete better in the first division of nations [because] we have resource and manpower constraints, and our costs are rising.'[2]

This ties in with the regionalization issue discussed in Chapter Four, offering an enhanced electronic means to achieve 'remote management' where companies locate only their higher value-added functions in Singapore. The idea is that executives based there will be able more precisely to monitor their manufacturing operations sited elsewhere in the region without leaving their office. Complex tasks such as product planning, involving design, production and marketing staff, could be conducted down the line.

NATIONAL IT PLAN

This is not a new development. Singapore created its first National Information Technology Plan in 1985, which consisted of six 'building blocks':

(1)**Manpower** – develop a group of IT professionals to enable industries to exploit the new technology fully.

(2)**IT culture** – efforts to be made to overcome resistance to change. IT to be taught more extensively in schools.

(3)**Information communication infrastructure** – Singapore must continue to improve its telecommunication infrastructure.

(4)**IT application** – new users, especially the small enterprises, must be provided assistance to overcome their resistance to IT.

(5)**Industry** - every encouragement must be given to promote the development of IT industry in Singapore.

(6)**Culture for creativity and entrepreneurship** – develop a local capacity in applied research in IT.[3]

In 1991, the National Computer Board initiated the IT2000 Study to examine how information technology could create new competitive advantages for Singapore. There were 11 sectoral study groups: construction and real estate, education and training, financial services, government, healthcare, IT industry, manufacturing, media, publishing and information services, retail, wholesale and distribution, tourist and leisure services, transportation. The study group recommended that Singapore should:

• Take advantage of the continuing improvement in IT by planning for an information infrastructure and experimenting with advanced applications so as to have a headstart.

• Capitalize on B-ISDN and wireless networks to create new information services to improve business competitiveness and in the fields of education, culture and entertainment, to improve the quality of life.

• Aggressively exploit tested and standardized technology (e.g. internetworking, electronic data interchange (EDI), interactive distance learning, product scanning) on a national scale.

• Take advantage of its friendly ties with the three industry leaders (US, Japan and Europe to forge international strategic alliances to create new growth opportunities for its own information industry.[4]

The final report said that, 'In our vision, some 15 years from now, Singapore, the Intelligent Island, will be among the first countries in the world with an advanced nation-wide information infrastructure. It will interconnect computers in virtually every home, office, school and factory. The computer will evolve into an information appliance, combining the functions of the telephone, computer, television and more. It will provide a wide range of communication modes and access to services.

'Text, sound, pictures, video, documents, designs and other forms of media can be transferred and shared through this broadband information infrastructure made up of fibre-optic cables reaching to all homes and offices, and a pervasive wireless network working in tandem, the information infrastructure will also permeate our physical infrastructure making mobile telecommuting possible and our homes, work places, airport, seaport and surface transportation systems "smarter".

'Too small to rely only on its own resources, Singapore has always plugged into the global networks. More Singapore companies are spreading their wings overseas. Networking with other countries will generate mutual benefits and greater prosperity for all, as is being shown through the Growth Triangle, The NII has an important role in this strategic economic thrust. It will help turn Singapore into a highly efficient switching centre for goods, services, capital, information and people.

'IT can help make geographical distances transparent to companies with globally-distributed operations. With high bandwidth communication, companies will be encouraged to base more high value-added functions like product design, research and development, regional marketing and technical support in Singapore. For example, a company's designers and marketers will be able to collaborate on product planning even though they may be an ocean apart and not able to meet. The NII's support for interchange of multimedia information, videoconferencing and remote management will make Singapore an outstanding site for the coordination of business.

'With high bandwidth communication many knowledge and information-intensive services can be provided from a remote location. Our distance learning system could be projected overseas to turn Singapore into a regional education and corporate training centre. Similarly, our medical specialists, architects, engineers and other experts could provide consultancy services to counterparts in other countries, without having to do much travelling. This extended reach will make Singapore a more attractive base for world-class experts.

'Furthermore, the NII will create an electronic marketplace for information, media and entertainment products and services. This will in turn help to strengthen our information and creative services industry into a major economic sector with abundant growth opportunities. With the early exploitation of advanced IT through the development of information gateways, Singapore could eventually become an exporter of value-added information services to other countries. Although our information product capacity will be limited by the size of our intellectual resources, the opportunity to add value by integrating and packaging information produced by other countries is only limited by our creativity.

'The NII will support the electronic exchange of data and sharing of our information to make our air and sea ports most efficient in moving goods and providing convenience for passengers. An important step towards building a smart airport would be the development of an integrated airport information network. This would enable the electronic exchange of common operational data among the many stakeholders, including airlines, the Civil Aviation Authority of Singapore (CAAS), ground handling agents and the public, Timely and reliable information on aircraft, passengers and cargo handling would improve planning, increase productivity and enhance quality of services. IT will also play an expanding role in maintaining and enhancing the competitiveness of our port. A Maritime Information System will be able to streamline information flow among the shipping, trading and freight forwarding.[5]

To create the necessary climate of collaboration between IT R & D institutes and the industry, a scaled-down NII called Collabrium was created. This provides the testbed where new applications are tried out before widespread adoption. According to the National Computer Board, its main functions are the '. . . collaboration of technology development, experimentation of concepts, showcasing of innovative applications, and deployment of infrastructure and application services [. . . .] such as smart school, smart home and smart office'.

PRACTICAL APPLICATIONS

To test the NII architecture, five prototype applications – 'telemedicine, construction and real estate network, remote technical support, information services and concurrent engineering' – were demonstrated to industry leaders and the R & D community in 1 993. Applications under development at the time of writing include the SINGATOUCH information kiosks already been mentioned, LIBRARY 2000, a project to electronically link all public-funded libraries and allow users to access a variety of multimedia information databases from their homes and offices as well as libraries, and CORONET, a network linking all the organizations in the construction and real-estate industry. By re-engineering the business processes, Coronet aims to achieve an improvement in turnaround time, productivity and quality. The network's three initial application areas are submission of development and building applications for government approval, procurement of goods and services for construction projects and information access to support business operations. The NCB is also helping teachers develop multimedia courseware for classroom use. Teachers from Raffles Girls Secondary School, for example, have produced useful innovative courseware in mathematics, literature, Chinese and chemistry.

In April 1994, the Public Works Department began a three-month trial run of the proposed electronic road pricing (ERP) system to be implemented in 1997. This is an unmanned high-tech version of the manual Area Licensing Scheme (ALS) long in force which requires drivers to buy a daily or monthly license for display on their windscreens in order to be able enter the congested Central Business District.[6] It detects a vehicle passing under the restricted zone gantry and makes a deduction from a stored-value card attached to the vehicle's windscreen. The components tested included the detectors buried in the road for sensing the passage of vehicles. Another component is the antennae to be mounted on gantry posts to operate the deduction of the payment from the stored-value card. The system was tested under different working conditions and tests included varying vehicle speeds and using different types of vehicles. If stored-value cards are absent in the vehicle or have insufficient value, the system should trigger cameras mounted on the gantry to photograph the registration plates of the vehicles as they pass by. The full-scale system is due to be introduced in stages from 1997.

In order to lead by example, the government launched a Civil Service Computerization Programme (CSCP). All government departments have been computerized. As a result, it is claimed, procedures have been simplified and faster processing time has resulted in shorter waiting time. For example, business registration at the Registry of Companies and Businesses has been shortened from four weeks to only one hour. Instead of submitting paper forms over the counter, companies can transmit these forms electronically from their computers to the relevant government computers. Government permits, approvals and certificates will be sent to the companies through the same computer connections.

Users can access a wide range of information in the databases. For example, companies can do on-line enquiries of selected government records via computer instead of queuing up in person at the department counters. On-line public enquiries on land title deeds and business registrations are now available. Corporate users can also obtain government econometric data to aid their strategic planning through better understanding of the business environment.

Access to databases is also made possible through Teleview, a service of Singapore Telecom providing both broadcast and telephone lines transmission of information to business and home terminals to access such services as telebanking, teleshopping, business communications, directory services, brokerage services, interactive on-line education and travel information.

With the introduction of IRIS (Inland Revenue Information Service), taxpayers can dial up and get tax information. NCB and the Inland Revenue Authority of Singapore have also launched InTax, a software programme that computes tax relief figures and tax payable.

CSCP also introduced SIGMA (Singapore Government Management Accounting System) to the Ministry of Health to help keep track of all direct and indirect costs of its activities and thus enable it to determine more equitable charges in hospitals and clinics. At the Ministry of Finance, a Budget Executive Support System gives senior officials a macro view of the budget for better decision-making and more effective budget allocation.

Other applications already in use include TRADENET, a nation-wide EDI system which allows the various parties from the public and private sectors to interchange trade documents and information in the conduct of international trade including import-export approvals, reducing the cost and turnaround time for the preparation, transmission and processing of documents and information. By the end of 1994, some 12,000 companies were linked up to 20 government ministries and agencies by the system. The government estimates that with around 95 per cent of goods shipment now handled electronically the saving to all users totals $1 billion a year.

Users can access trade-related databases such as trade statistics, trading regulations, controlled items lists, dangerous goods lists, flight schedules and movement information, shipping schedules and other general airport or seaport information. Singapore's trading community and port authorities are able to exchange trade documents and information electronically with their overseas counterparts through access to international trade networks and databases.

TradeNet's connection with GEIS (General Electric Information Services), for example, allows world-wide interchange of business information on financial management and report systems, securities trading, exposure and risk management for international banks, sales and marketing, global electronic messaging services and equipment management systems. TradeNet subscribers can use their existing computer systems to transmit or receive electronic documents from users of GEIS which include 4,000 American and 1,500 international clients. They are also linked up to Fujitsu's Enhanced Information and Communication System, FENICS, and the French air transport network SITA, which enables 300 member companies in 170 countries to transact business electronically with their overseas counterparts in air transport.

And then there is LAWNET, the network for the legal community introduced in 1990, whose database contains more than 400 Acts of Parliament. Search can be done and displayed in seconds. In 1992, new services were added, including: a case law, subsidiary legislation, LOTBASE, a landlot information database of the Registry of Land Titles, BIZNET, a database on companies and businesses in the Registry of Companies and Businesses, a bankruptcy search system which contains information on bankruptcy notices and petitions, and a Supreme Court Notices system containing law notices and other hearing lists on an electronic bulletin board.[7]

But LawNet was only just the start in the computerization of the Singapore legal system. 'Perry Mason probably would not approve. Rumpole of the Bailey would hate it. Singapore recently unveiled its latest high-technology creation – the so called court of the future, dominated by computers and video conferencing, rather than files and shuffling clerks. Singapore is trying to computerize most aspects of government business. Now its technicians from the National Computer Board have moved into the courtroom. Though Singapore no longer has a jury system, its justice system still resembles the old colonial British model, with judges taking endless notes in longhand, lawyers shuffling mountainous files, assistants carrying weighty legal tomes. 'The first thing we want to try and do is to use technology to organize paperwork and procedures in court,' says Joseph Teo of the NCB. 'Everything would be digitized and fed on to the judge's computer. The court system would become paperless and there would be instantaneous transcription of proceedings.'

'Teo is one of a handful of NCB technicians behind a scheme called Court Vision 21, billed as the most ambitious court computerization plan under way in Asia. "In time, we want to try and move into virtual courts – which would allow people the freedom to transact court matters from offices and home," says Teo. [He] demonstrates how a robbery trial might take place in the years to come. The prosecution would be able to present its case on a large television screen through using a series of icons describing how and when the robbery took place. The icons could be animated and there would be sound. And, for example, a witness would give his or her statement via a video conferencing link with Hong Kong.

'IBM and other companies have helped NCB come up with the equipment to make the court of the future work. A range of "litigation support software" is used to allow the judge – who need not necessarily be in court – to call up on his personal computer both evidence and exhibits through a variety of multimedia tools. The court has access to other computer aids: SING – Sentencing Information Guide System – allows instant storage and retrieval of documents in the form of text, video, image and voice. In a jury system, members could, while making their decision, have instant access to voice testimony, exhibits or specific areas of the prosecution or defence cases presented. All past court decisions will also be available through LawNet.

'The system has several advantages. It would be likely to speed up court proceedings dramatically. Juveniles would no longer have to go through the trauma of going to court – they could give evidence from their homes. Singapore is already implementing computer-based systems for hearing applications for bail, eliminating the time and money it takes to bring a prisoner to court. The system, however, asks a great deal of lawyers and judges. They would not only have to be experts on the law, they would have to become computer technicians as well. The court of the future might speed up the legal system. But digital justice could make the judicial system seem very inhuman and distant. It could also make going to court more expensive. In many countries the judiciary worries that the person with the most expensive lawyer has too many advantages. In the court of the future, a defendant might find he or she not only needs a good lawyer but also that a good multimedia presenter could be a great asset.'[8]

No such controversy surrounds PORTNET, the Port of Singapore Authority's electronic data communication system introduced in 1989, allowing port users with a computer to access PSA's database for vessel, cargo, container and shipping information. and also enable them to apply for berths, tugs and pilots. This electronic link allows 24-hour paperless shipping documentation for import, export and transhipment cargo containers. Users can also gain access to TradeNet. They can make inward, outward and transhipment declarations to the various governing authorities like the Trade Development Board, Customs and Excise. PortNet also provides information on several foreign ports such as Le Havre in France, Hamburg and Bremen in Germany, Seattle in the United States, various ports in New South Wales, Australia, as well as Hong Kong and Penang in Malaysia.

ALL-WIRED ISLAND

Tampines lies in the North-east of the island. It is a newly-developed area of endless pink and cream slabs of public housing, no different outwardly than any other of estates scattered across the island. It is, however, about as far as one can get physically from the commercial hub of Singapore without falling into the sea. At first sight, therefore, not the sort of place one would expect to be on the cutting edge of high technology.

But Tampines is the testing ground for bringing the benefits of IT into the daily lives of Singapore. Its newly-opened public library bristles with personal computers linked to CD-ROM drives, and a clutch of young people sit at booths manipulating the on-screen displays. By mid-1995, families in the housing blocks were due to be the first in Singapore to receive cable television, its 30 channels the expected precursor to wider multimedia service into the home via optical fibre cable networks now being installed by Singapore Telecom. All high-rise residential and commercial buildings are to be linked to the proposed island-wide optical fibre cable network by the end of 1997. At the time of writing, all the major commercial buildings in the central business district and hotels along Orchard Road shopping belt had been linked up.

In mid-1994, Singapore Telecoms reported that optical fibre cables had been laid to 60 per cent of the high-rise buildings with main distribution frame rooms (housing the equipment to provide telecoms services to a building's occupants), and the total length of fibre lines in the network had reached at least 107,350 km.[9]

The partly-privatized company will gain a return on its investment by being allowed to offer additional services over the network beyond voice and data telephony. The ultimate scope of these is not yet clear, but is likely to find itself in competition in some areas from Singapore Cablevision (SCV), a consortium of three Singapore partners and the third largest US cable company, Continental Cablevision, which is investing about $500m in an island-wide cable television network taking coaxial feeders from the Telecom installations to complete the link into each home.[10]

The Singapore members are Singapore International Media (SIM), a subsidiary of the government-owned Tamasek Holdings, Singapore Technologies Venture (STV), a unit of government-linked Singapore Technologies Group, and Singapore Press Holdings (SPH), parent company for all the island's newspapers. The full network, involving some 700,000 homes, will not be in place for several years, so that SCV is likely to have a monopoly for some time to recoup its investment, although the government has indicated rivals might be permitted at some stage.[11]

The consortium began operations by offering three UHF channels over the air to subscribers supplied with a decoder. Its service marked the first break in the monopoly held by the State-owned Singapore Broadcasting Corporation. As will be discussed later, satellite dishes are banned for all except a few approved institutions such as banks and embassies as the government seeks to control the inflow of information and ideas from abroad.

IMPROVING TELEPHONE LINKS

On January 25, 1995, the island's main English newspaper, the *Straits Times*, carried a two-page advertisement which declared: 'ST Mobile Data, a member of the Singapore Technologies Group, today launches a new wireless service that will do for data communications what cellular has done for the traditional wired telephone: total freedom for data transmission at any time throughout Singapore. Designed to work over the airwaves of Singapore, the Mobile Data Network allows users to exchange electronic data between hand-held portable devices, vehicle-mounted terminals and host computers. The data that is transmitted may be transactions to update a database at head office, request stock market reports, get the status on a client's account or information on transportation-related services like taxis, airlines and shipping companies.'

This is the first private operator in the mobile data field, although Singapore Telecoms has had a service in place for some time.

Yong Lum Sung, ST Mobile Data's General Manager, explained that the new service would cater '...to companies with a requirement for exact and timely information transfer between corporate and field personnel'. Immediate applications include a Dispatch and Automatic Vehicle Location systems for taxi, truck and courier fleet management, and wireless credit-card verification and point-of-sale transactions. 'Just as notebook computers have allowed information processing to be carried out anywhere, wireless data communication technology as provided by [us] extends communication to the mobile worker, instead of relying on commercial wireline equipment', Mr Yong said.

In many cases existing voice and fax services might be inadequate and no longer cost-effective. Wireless data had lower transaction costs because it can send a greater amount of information in less time. 'The ST Mobile Data network operates in the 420MHz range with an air-interface data transfer rate of 8000 bits per second. Store-and-forward is a key feature. If a wireless terminal should temporarily lose contact with the network, any incoming messages for the user can be stored in a network mailbox. When contact with the network is re-established, all stored messages are immediately delivered to the user.'

According Mr Yong: 'Existing notebook computers and terminals are "empowered" with wireless communications through the use of a radio modem.' Every terminal and host connection will be given an address, called the access number, when the subscriber pays a one-time activation fee and a subsequent monthly charge for the service. A number of subscription options are available to the user. For example, a personal subscription allows a user access to the ST Mobile Data network from any one of a number of terminals. A password provides security. Also an electronic serial number which is hard-coded into each radio modem is validated by the network during connection greatly reducing the risk of fraudulent use.

Beyond the immediate confines of the island, Singapore continues to strive to improve its telecommunications links and range of services with other countries in Asia, again as part of the regionalization programme already discussed.

Singapore Telecom, in January 1995, announced it had linked up with three major telecom operators in the region to form a company providing a 'one stop shop' for MNCs in Southeast Asia.

Telekom Malaysia, Philippines Long Distance Telephone Company and PT Indosat of Indonesia will coordinate services with ST so that MNCs do not have to go through the tedious process of applying separately for telephone services in each country.

A ST spokesman said: 'Any company with a lot of interest in ASEAN countries can go to the local representative office of this joint-venture company and sign up. Each country provider will then install the telecommunications services that the company wants. Europe- and US-based MNCs will also be able to benefit from this arrangement.' According to the statement, the Communications Authority of Thailand and Jabatan Telekom Brunei were considering joining the non-exclusive alliance. The joint-venture company, headquartered in Singapore, will develop single-billing services for installation and maintenance work.[12]

This is not the only collaborative effort to make Singapore a regional telecommunications hub. Eunetcom, a joint venture between France Telecom and Deutsche Telecom, has established a presence on the island as part of what it calls '...a global network to provide advanced services to large international companies with worldwide subsidiaries'. Mr Hugues Ferreboeuf, vice-president of marketing for Eunetcom, said the Franco-German alliance will set up and operate 'private communication links on this network for MNCs with far-flung offices'. To do so, Eunetcom leases existing lines provided by various public telecommunications operators and provides custom-made services for the MNCs. These include electronic mail, specialised data transmission and multimedia capabilities. At the same time, Singapore will act as the starting point for Eunetcom's aggressive expansion into Asia.

According to a foreign telecoms analyst based in Singapore, this is likely to be an important growth area. 'British Telecoms has been in the region for a long time and has 25 hubs in Southeast Asia and Asia-Pacific for its GNS, global messaging and communications network service. By the end of 1995, it was aiming to have to have 126. They are headquartered in Singapore and a lot of service providers are looking at it as the place to be to put your hub to sell band width in the region in the region. More companies going to outsourcing, entrusting their whole communications network management to a private company. Instead of having a communications manager on your staff, ensuring you have the right PABX, and the right ISDN service etc, you just sign a contract with a service provider like BT, or Racal Network Services. It's incredibly profitable.'

A further development is satellite-based regional mobile telephone services, which will emerge from a joint venture established in early 1995 between a three member consortium, comprising Singapore Telecom, Singapore Technologies and the US-based Hughes Aircraft Co., and the Telephone Organization of Thailand (TOT) and Communications Authority of Thailand (CAT). The Asia Mobile Telecommunications Project is expected to become operation in 1998, involving an investment of about US$600 million and providing an initial capacity of 16,000 lines. Thailand will spend an additional US$40 million on 'gateway' facilities in Bangkok and the northern city of Chiang Mai, followed by provinces in the south. Singapore Telecom estimates the system could attract two million users within a decade.

'China is viewed as the largest market for cellular use, followed by Indonesia, which has been experiencing rapid economic growth but lacks proper telecommunications infrastructure, especially along common borders. Singapore Telecom said the satellite-based project would be easier to manage than a global system since it aims to cover Asia only.

'In addition to facilitating private mobile telephone calls, the project would also offer public telephone service via satellite. Either card- or coin-operated public telephone booths will be installed at hotels, airports and in remote areas where normal fixed lines were inaccessible.[13]

Although the partly-privatized Singapore Telecom currently enjoys a near-monopoly of most domestic telecommunications services, its chairman, Koh Boon Hwee, insists it would be wrong to say it faced little or no competition. 'Our competition is every other commercial centre in the world, particularly Hong Kong in this region.' He regards domestic competition as 'inevitable', particularly with cellular phone services where new operators are to be licensed from 1997.

Half of the company's revenue currently comes from international calls, mostly generated by corporate clients. The Telecommunications Authority of Singapore is very aware of how easily this income could be siphoned off by the growing number of services that enable travellers to make international calls and have them billed to their home telephone, for example –

services that sell themselves heavily on the basis of cost savings. Thus, TAS is constantly assessing Singapore Telecom's tariffs in accordance with a basket of international phone prices which includes Hong Kong and other leading commercial centres.

THE MEDIA DILEMMA

What is clear from the foregoing is that Singapore wants to turn itself into a global media hub. But there is a problem – a major contradiction, in fact – which poses something of a dilemma for Singapore's leaders. The problem is that they remain deeply suspicious of outside influences and wish to keep the doors closed while throwing them wide open at the same time. 'We have to stay special and unique,' argues Brigadier General George Yeo, Singapore's Minister of Information and the Arts, and '...to achieve this, we need a kind of semi-permeable membrane to preserve our own bubble in Singapore.' Shades of Star Wars!

While Singapore does not plan literally to wrap itself in a cocoon, BG Yeo's remarks are very much a reflection of the dilemma the government feels it is facing. On one hand,. Singapore's planners see the economic necessity of being plugged into the global information network. Singapore has the technology and expertise to be the information entrepot of the dynamic southeast Asia region. Its people are among the most computer-proficient.[14] And, as Prime Minister Goh Chok Tong stresses, '...the future belongs to countries whose people make the most productive use of information, knowledge and technology. These are now the key factors for economic success not natural resources'.

On the other hand, the government is deeply concerned about losing control over information flows within Singapore. As already noted, satellite ownership is not allowed for the general public, although with dishes getting smaller all the time, it is debatable how much longer this form of cultural control will be feasible. The local media feel that it is in Singapore's long-term interests to faithfully reflect government policy. The importation of foreign newspapers and magazines, ranging from the *Far Eastern Economic Review* to *Cosmopolitan* is carefully controlled, and transgression of the government's rules on what is legitimate comment can result in even tighter restrictions – as Singapore's leaders have shown no hesitation in taking court action, usually involving substantial damage suits, against foreign media which they feel have impugned their integrity. Even newspapers from Malaysia are not allowed to circulate in Singapore.

But as the technology changes, censorship becomes more difficult. And the key strategy on which Singapore is relying to maintain its economic strength could prove to be a Trojan Horse, gnawing away at the foundations of its society.

Another battlefield is now looming between the forces of the free market for information and those of social paternalism as practised by the government. In 1994, it licensed an initial two service providers to supply connections for Singaporeans to Internet.

As one commentator noted: 'Whether the Internet, unregulated by any external power, can be controlled is debatable. It is non-commercial and contains merely the data which users anywhere see fit to put on it, including scanned pornographic images. While that is frowned upon by most users, the culture of the Net is libertarian and debate about political as well as sexual mores knows no bounds. All of this might be thought to be an anathema to a Singaporean administration which values social discipline above free speech.

'But the Net is also a business tool, and fewer foreign companies would these days locate on the island if they were deprived of electronic mail and information retrieval facilities. Professor Eddie Kuo, Dean of the School of Communications Studies at Nany ang Technological University, says the government remains anxious to protect the population from "decadent" Western influences. But there is a tension between that and an open economy for which, by definition, ". . . information is good, and the government will go all the way to make business people competitive and attract multinationals to Singapore".'[15]

As Microsoft Chairman Bill Gates put it, in an interview with the *Straits Times* during a visit to Singapore in January 1995: 'They [government leaders] are going to try to have their cake and eat it, too, because joining cyberspace is essential to the role they play as a major hub in global commerce. They want to be connected globally, but maintain local values. They will have to work out this co-existence of two colliding worlds.'[16]

Similarly author William Gibson, who coined the term

cyberspace, observed on his own visit to Singapore that the leadership '... expect that whole highways of data will flow into and through their city. Yet they also seem to expect that this won't affect them.' But what worried him most was that a state with the 'look and feel of a very large corporation' might continue to flourish by repressing free expression. 'They will have proven that information does not necessarily want to be free.'[17]

The government admits that where technology is concerned, it is fighting a losing battle. 'Censorship is becoming quite impossible to enforce at the individual level,' says Mr Yeo. 'Once digitized, an objectionable book, magazine or video can be sent through the telecommunication network. We can inspect magazines, books, tapes and discs but we cannot possibly screen every bit or byte that comes down the information highway.' Instead, says Mr Yeo, Singapore needs what he calls an immune system capable of fighting off the infection.

A code of what are seen as Asian values, emphasising the family and the primary role of the male, discipline and above all, the needs of society above those of the individual, is the pill the government wants Singaporeans to dutifully swallow to counteract foreign viruses. 'Asian values' was the main theme of a national day address in August 1994 by Goh Chok Tong. The maintenance of such values is seen as vital for Singapore's continued economic success. 'You may think decline is unimaginable,' said Mr Goh. 'But societies can go wrong very quickly.'

While the Singapore government remains deeply sensitive to outside criticism, Mr Goh has no hesitation in painting what he sees as moral decay and lawlessness in the West, most notably in the US and Britain. He warned Singaporeans not to fall prey to corrosive outside influences, such as welfarism, divorce, children being allowed to call their fathers by their first names. 'We must not unthinkingly drift into attitudes and manners which undermine the traditional politeness and deference Asian children have for their parents and elders.'[18]

Government officials say the obviously unacceptable sites on the information superhighway have been blocked off by the two licensed operators, which act as gatekeepers. But the nature of Internet is that other sites spring up. As Professor Kuo observes: 'Whether or not it should be censored is irrelevant. The fact is it can't. The question now is how to minimize the damage.' He believes, the authorities are engaged in a process of managed liberalization to accommodate the technological changes.

'Singapore is a global city,' he says. 'There's no going back.'

CHAPTER NOTES

1. 'The Colony strikes back', by Victor Keegan. *The Guardian* 12/12/94.
2. 'The all-wired island,' by Gordon Cramb. *Financial Times* 24/2/95.
3. *Strategic Policies & Businesses in Singapore: A Manager's Reference.* Huat, T.C.,McGraw-Hill Book Co., 1995, p110.
4. Ibid., pp112-3.
5. A Vision Of An Intelligent Island. IT2000 Report. National Computer Board.
6. Originally, this scheme only operated during the morning and evening rush hours, but has now been extended to cover the entire working day from Monday to Saturday lunchtime. Before high-tech began to take over, special traffic police monitors stood on the roadside at all entry points to note down the numbers of any vehicles not displaying a current license – not an easy task when there might be up to four lanes of traffic flying past. Violators face a fine of $70.
7. *Strategic Policies & Businesses in Singapore: A Manager's Reference,* pp121-5.
8. 'Electronics in the dock', by Kieran Cooke, *Financial Times* 18/11/94.
9. 'ST ahead on Fibre-To-The-Home Network Project', Asia Pacific Telecoms Analyst 1/8/94.
10. See note 2.
11. 'Consortium to invest in Singapore cable tv.' See note 9.
12. *Straits Times* 26/1/95.
13. 'S'pore firms in $870m mobile phone venture'. *Straits Times* 15/2/95.
14. In the mid-1980s, Singapore had only about a thousand computer professionals. Now it has 14000.
15. See note2.
16. Life Section of the *Straits Times* 22/1/95.
17. See note 2.
18. 'Singapore caught in media dilemma' by Kieran Cooke, *Financial Times,* 6/9/94.

9 Establishing A Presence

KEY POINTS

- Establishing a Singapore operation
- Key provisions of the Companies Act
- Incorporating a company in Singapore
- Establishing a branch
- Forming a joint venture
- Operating in the Riaus
- Types of companies permitted in Indonesia
- Changes in Indonesian tax laws
- Investing in Malaysia
- Malaysian incentives
- Malaysian legal requirements

SINGAPORE OPERATIONS

FOREIGN INVESTORS have four options in Singapore: a locally incorporated company, a branch office, a sole proprietorship (i.e. an unincorporated business) or a joint venture or partnership with a local corporate or non-corporate partner.

A number of preliminary points can be made. For foreign corporations, the option is usually between establishing a branch or a subsidiary company, and this choice will depend largely on the company's particular circumstances, the nature of the business and tax considerations. For example, both will pay the same amount of basic income tax – 27 per cent – but the company's liability will perhaps eased through a number of incentives not likely to be available for a branch; a company's liability is limited to its paid-up and uncalled capital, but this does not apply to a branch.

There is no requirement for funds to be imported or for local equity participation. There are no exchange controls nor other restrictions on the repatriation of funds.

Other than for banks and insurance companies, the minimum share capital is two shares. A minimum of two founding shareholders may later be reduced to one corporate shareholder. There must be at least two directors, one of whom must be resident in Singapore. For a foreign-owned business, a local manager personally responsible for the business must be appointed. For a branch, at least two agents resident in Singapore must be appointed.

Limited Company

A limited company may be either public or private. The fact that an enterprise is limited and/or private is indicated by its name either in English (e.g.Limited, Private Limited, Pte Ltd) or in Malay (Berhad, Sendirian Berhad, Sdn Bhd).

Under the Companies Act, a private company is one that restricts the right to transfer its shares, limits the number of shareholders, excluding employees and former employees, to not more than 50, and prohibits any invitation to the public either to subscribe for its shares or debentures or to deposit money with the company. A private company is an exempt company if it has no more than 20 shareholders and if no beneficial interest in its shares is held by any corporation. A local subsidiary of a foreign corporation, therefore, would not qualify. This category involves being relieved of certain obligations under the Companies Act, such as filing copies of its accounts with the Registrar of Companies, which would then be available for public inspection, and the prohibition of loans to directors and companies connected with the directors does not apply.

A public company is used where it is proposed to invite the public to subscribe to its shares or debentures or to place money on deposit with it, but it may also be used even if it is not proposed to call for public subscription. In addition to the normal registration requirements, a public company, before allotting shares or debentures, must file with the Registrar of Companies a prospectus in relation to its affairs, or a statement in lieu of prospectus if no public subscription is called for on incorporation.

If public subscription is called for, the minimum number of

shares stated in the prospectus must have been allotted, and the Registrar must be satisfied that the allotment and other provisions of the Companies Act have been complied with before certifying that the company is entitled to commence business or exercise any borrowing power. If no public subscription is called for, the Registrar must be satisfied that shares taken by the directors have been paid for.

Any two or more persons may, by subscribing at least one share each and complying with the formation procedures, incorporate a company under the Companies Act. Application is first made to the Registrar of Companies for reservation for two months of the proposed name of the company in order to ensure that the name is acceptable and available. Among the documents to be filed on incorporation is a memorandum of association (articles of incorporation) giving the name of the company, the objectives for which it was formed, its share capital, and other matters required by law to be stated therein. It is usual also to register the articles of association (by-laws) which comprise the regulations for the management of the company.

Only public accountants and lawyers are permitted to engage in the formation of companies. Professional fees and other costs usually range from $2,000 to $3,500 depending on how straightforward the formation is. In addition, a registration fee is paid at the time of filing the incorporation documents, determined on a sliding scale related to the authorized (nominal) share capital. This is $1,200 for nominal share capital not exceeding $100,000. From there to a million shares, the rate is $400 for every additional $100,000, and above one million, it is $4,800 for the first million, then $300 for every additional million, up to maximum fee of $35,000.

The legislation permits the issue of common (ordinary shares), preferred (preference shares) and redeemable preferred stock. These shares can have different voting rights except that in the case of a public company or a subsidiary of such a company, each equity share (any share that is not a preferred stock) will confer the right on a ballot of one vote and to one vote only for each dollar or part of a dollar paid on that share. Loans and debentures that carry conversion rights to common stock at a future date can be issued.

Branch Office

Before a foreign corporation establishes a place of business or commences to carry on business, it must file certain documents with the Registrar of Companies:

1. A copy of the certificate of incorporation or registration in the place of origin (or a document of similar effect) certified by an official holding an office corresponding to that of the Registrar of Companies in the country in which the foreign company is incorporated.   2. A copy of its charter or articles of incorporation and by-laws, or other instruments constituting or defining its constitution, certified by the above official, or a notary public or on oath by a director or secretary of the corporation.   3. A list and particulars of its directors.   4. Where there is a local board of directors, a memorandum stating the powers of the local directors, a memorandum stating the powers of the local directors.   5. A memorandum of appointment or power of attorney stating the names and addresses of two or more 'natural persons' resident in Singapore authorised to accept notices served on the corporation as its agents.   6. Notice of the corporation's registered office in Singapore.   7. A statutory declaration, in the prescribed form, made by the agents of the company confirming particulars relating to the corporation.

Any changes have to be reported promptly to the Registrar and appropriate fees paid. Any documents filed in an language other than English must be accompanied by an officially certified translation. On receiving its certificate of registration, a company must display this outside its registered office and any other place of business in Singapore and the information must be shown on its letterheads, billheads and other official publications. The Registrar may refuse to register a foreign corporation by a name considered undesirable.

Representative Office

A foreign company may establish a representative office in Singapore to undertake promotional and liaison activities on behalf of its parent company. The office, however, directly or on behalf of its parent company, must not be engaged in business, conclude contracts, provide consultancy for a fee, undertake transhipment of goods or open or negotiate letters of credit. Approval to open a representative office comes from the Trade

Development Board. The application must be accompanied by the annual reports and audited accounts of the latest three years (for new application) and certificate of incorporation of the parent company. For renewal, which is to be made annually, the application needs to be accompanied by the latest annual report and audited accounts.

All supporting documents must be in English or officially translated English versions. The TDB will consider the application for registration of a representative office whose parent company is in the trading, manufacturing, services and logistics/shipping sectors. All applications to establish foreign government trade centres or representative offices, including those by foreign provincial/state governments should also be made to the TDB.

Sole Proprietorships

Sole proprietorships and partnerships are registered under the Business Registration Act rather than the Companies Act. There is no requirement for annual accounts to be filed, but the registration has to be renewed annually. Any number of people up to a maximum of 20 may enter into a partnership.

LEGAL REQUIREMENTS

Incorporated companies in Singapore are required to keep accounting and other records for seven years. They are also required to prepare a profit-and-loss account and a balance sheet accompanied by the directors' reports every year. The annual accounts must be filed with the Registrar of Companies. Statutory registers of the company's directors, secretary and shareholders are required.

Foreign company's branches are not required to hold their accounting records of their Singapore operations in Singapore. However, they must have a register of the branch's resident Singapore shareholders. They must also file their annual financial accounts in the form required by their countries of origin, together with a statutory declaration and the audited branch account with the Registrar of Companies.

All companies must appoint registered auditors who will report annually to shareholders. For branches of a foreign company, the financial statements must be audited by persons qualified to act as auditors in the country of origin. Company directors must report the activities and results of the company during the year, movement and status of reserves, share issues, name of directors and their interests in the company's and related companies' shares and some account matters. Misstatement or omission of facts by directors are serious offences with severe penalties.

The various types of direct taxes in Singapore are company tax, personal income tax, property tax, estate duty, stamp duty and Skills Development Fund levy. There is at present no capital gains or turnover tax. The government, however, is gradually moving the emphasis towards indirect taxation and as a first step introduced a three per cent Government Sales Tax (GST) in 1994. There are various tax incentives which have already been discussed in detail in Chapter Five on foreign investment. The Singapore tax structure is discussed in more detail in the appendices.

The manufacture of certain goods may be prohibited under the Control of Manufacture Act. Goods that cannot be manufactured for sale or for any other commercial purpose without proper registration include pig and sponge iron, steel ingots, billets, blooms and slabs, and rolled steel and drawn steel products; beer and stout; cigars; fire crackers; refrigerators and air conditioners; cigarettes and matches; and chewing gum.

Import duties apply to three broad classes of products: intoxicating liquor, tobacco and petroleum products. Protective duties are imposed on certain consumer products such as clothing, non-essential foodstuffs and motor vehicles. Most goods can be imported without special license, but there must be inward declarations for them. Trade of any description with Iraq is banned, and import licences are required for all goods originating in or consigned from Albania, People's Republic of China, Laos, People's Republic of Mongolia, which are subject to an import cess of 0.2 to 0.5 per cent of their CIF value. Rice imports from all countries is licensed. The import of certain goods such as lighters or toys in the shape of a pistol or revolver, toy currency notes and coins, and fire crackers is prohibited. Raw materials for industrial enterprises may be imported duty free on application to the Customs and Excise Department, but it will be found that many of them are not dutiable in any case.

There are no export duties, but all shipments must be covered by outward declaration forms. Export control applies to certain goods like second-hand motor vehicles, rubber and timber, and there are quantitative restrictions on textile and garment shipments to some developed countries, primarily in Europe and North America. Granite and sand are subject to export licensing.

As a major transhipment port and warehousing and distribution centre, Singapore has more than adequate storage facilities. The Port of Singapore Authority (PSA) operates five cargo terminals covering more than two million square metres of open and covered warehousing space inside and outside its various free-trade zones. There are five free-trade zones for seaborne cargo and one for air cargo. These provide facilities for the storage and re-export of dutiable and controlled goods. While in the zones goods may be repacked or processed without having to comply with customs documentation and other formalities and without incurring customs duty. Seaborne cargo for transhipment or re-export enjoys free storage for 28 days. The PSA has its own security police force and fire service.

SETTING UP IN RIAU[1]

In general, regulations governing foreign investments in the Riaus are the same as those applicable to other Indonesian provinces. In May 1989, the government opened more industries for foreign investors, leaving only nine categories which are completely closed to foreigners. The nine protected industries, plus another 65 businesses which are open to foreign investors subject to certain conditions, are compiled as the country's restricted or Investment Negative List, which is constantly reviewed as the government endeavours to create a more open market economy. The investment restrictions on foreigners also apply to Batam which was designated as an industrial bonded zone since 1978. However, some of the more stringent rules governing foreign investment were modified for Batam to attract foreign investments. It is understood that Batam's more liberalized foreign rules implemented in 1989 may be extended to Bintan and other parts of Riau at a later stage, on a case-by-case basis, as part of the Growth Triangle plan. Further relaxation of rules governing foreigners is expected as Indonesia gears up to take part in the joint implementation of the proposed ASEAN Free Trade master plan in the next five years.

Foreigners may wholly own their operations in Batam, with divestments of five per cent equity to Indonesians after five years. This compares to the general divestment rule set by the government in 1987. The general rule requiring foreigners to relinquish majority shareholding to locals within 15 years may be relaxed for investments in other parts of Riau on a case-by-case basis. Special tax incentives and exemptions from import duties and other domestic tariffs like sales tax are available in Batam only. Indonesians need only pay 100,000 Rupiahs in exit fee for each disembarkation from Batam instead of the normal 250,000 Rupiah fee payable in the rest of Indonesia.

Generally, foreigners are encouraged to form joint-venture companies with Indonesian partners. The minimum capital investment for foreigners is US$1 million which may be reduced to as low as US$250,000 in certain cases, for example in Batam when 100 per cent of the production is for export. Priority is also given to projects which generate plenty of jobs for Indonesians, or are export-oriented or which produce parts and components as supporting industries.

Before investors head for the Riaus, they should be aware of relevant Indonesian laws and investment regulations, as well as the special economic privileges accorded only to Batam which are not yet available to other parts of the province. It should also be noted that the development of Batam is under a separate jurisdiction from the Riau provincial government. The Indonesian government has set up three special agencies to oversee Batam's development, an enviable position not given to any of the other 13,700 or more islands throughout Indonesia.

The agencies are the Supervisory Body of the Batam Island Industrial Zone, the Batam Corporation – PT Persero Batam – and the Batam Industrial Development Authority (BIDA). The Supervisory Body supervises and provides BIDA with directives on industrial development and coordinates the policies of government institutions pertaining to the development of Batam. The Supervisory Body is composed of government ministers and other senior officials, and is directly responsible to the President. PT Persero Batam, a state-owned company, is responsible for controlling the movement of goods in and out of Batam, ensuring the payment of duties and levies, and managing various warehouse and other service facilities. The most prominent agency is BIDA which has been given almost a free hand to steer Batam's industrial development.

As mentioned in Chapter Three, the major industrial developments on Batam and Bintan maintain offices in Singapore which will handle all the administrative requirements of the Indonesian authorities. Nevertheless, one should be prepared to deal with the Indonesians directly and it makes sense to know exactly what the latter require.

Documents to be submitted with investment applications include a letter of intent, references, a summary of the nature and value of the proposed investment and a business plan indicating the amount of land, manpower, utilities, raw materials required and the types of technology to be used. Approvals are normally granted within a few months of the formal application, although projects listed on the Investment Priority List will be processed faster. Priority industries include those which are export-oriented, capital-intensive, non-pollutive and require little water resources. Investments in tourism, agribusiness, aquaculture, transhipping and logistic bases are also welcomed.

TYPES OF BUSINESS

The main types of businesses operating in Indonesia are:
• **Limited Liability Company (PT Company)**. These are governed by the Commercial Code which sets out basic regulations, incorporation and dissolution procedures and other matters relating to such companies. At least two founder shareholders are required for the formation of a PT company, with Indonesians generally appointed as Directors. Foreigners may be appointed to the Board of Directors for a Foreign Investment Company (PMA), which are normally joint ventures with foreign and local shareholders. The 'limited liability' or PT prefix is also used for these companies. An operating license is normally granted for an initial period of 30 years with renewal for another 30 years to be given provided there is no substantial change in the company's business as originally approved. PMA companies are governed by the Indonesian Commercial Code and Foreign Investment Law.

• **Representative Office**. Foreign companies may set up representative offices solely to provide support services on behalf of the head office, such as market research, promotions or acting as intermediaries. Licenses may be obtained from the Ministry of Trade or the Ministry of Public Works. The former issues licenses for buying, selling or manufacturing offices. Only buying representative offices may conclude contracts with Indonesian sellers. Foreign contractors and construction consulting companies have to apply to the Ministry of Public Works in order to set up representative offices to tender for contracts and to oversee their construction projects until completion.

• **Partnerships**. There are three main types:

MAATSCHAP – a simple partnership not requiring any formal registration, filing of documents or approval from the authorities. Governed by the Indonesian Civil Code, it is mainly suitable for lawyers, notaries, accountants and other professionals.

FIRMA – a basic partnership used by small trading and service enterprises. It is regulated by the Indonesian Commercial Code, with the partner ship agreement to be registered with the local court and published in the State Gazette.

COMMANDITAIRE VENNOOTSCHAP – a partnership governed by the Commercial Code and is often found in the trading and service sectors. The partners are either directly involved in the business or merely as contributors of funds. The former partners have the burden of unlimited liability, while the latter enjoy the protection of limited liability.

Foreigners are allowed to invest in existing Indonesian companies governed by the Domestic Capital Investment Law, by acquiring existing or newly issued shares provided certain conditions are satisfied. Verifications are generally required from a registered accountant or bank. The Indonesian companies being acquired must be engaged in activities open to foreign investment. the maximum foreign participation allowed is 25 per cent for companies requiring financial assistance or for upgrading technology, 49% where part of the company's products are for export, and 80% where all of the company's products are for export, to be divested to a maximum equity share of only 49% within 15 years to conform with the overall general rule for foreign investments.

• **Joint ventures**. The Indonesian partner usually takes a stake in the agreed equity and contributes in kind, in the form of land and manpower for the joint venture operations. Where an existing Indonesian partner does not have the funds to subsequently increase his share ownership as required by the divestment law, the foreign partner may offer the shares to other Indonesian parties such as banks, non-banking financial institutions or sell the shares to the Indonesian public via the capital market. Alternatively, the foreign company may ask BKPM to extend the prescribed time limit by another five years if the joint venture company is unable to meet the diversified needs.

In general, foreign partners are expected to provide most of the finance, technology and other specialist skills and machinery required by the joint venture. Capital injection may be in the form of equity or a mixture of equity and loans. Working capital may be funded from foreign or domestic banks in Indonesia. State-owned banks are not allowed to supply credit services PMA companies. Foreign investment (PMA) companies have to obtain their licenses from the Investment Co-ordinating Board, BKPM, which also compiles a list of potential Indonesian partners and provides general advisory services for foreign investors.

Details of Articles of Association, directors, shareholders, etc., have to be lodged with the Ministry of Industry within three months of incorporation. PMA companies are also expected to submit periodic reports to the Investment Co-ordinating Board, half-yearly at the end of June and December during the construction phase, and annually at the end of December with the commencement of operations. PMA companies must lodge annual audited financial statements with the Bank of Indonesia; in addition, PMA companies must submit quarterly and annual reports, signed by a registered public accountant, giving details of foreign currency loans.

The Indonesian Commercial Code obliges businesses to maintain proper accounting records. It also requires the books and records to be retained for 30 years. However, in practice, few businesses comply with this requirement.

Specialized industries such as banks, insurance companies and financial institutions have to comply with the regulations relating to their respective activities. There are no general laws nor regulations, such as the Companies Act, governing enterprises and businesses in Indonesia. All enterprises, however, are required to submit financial statements when filing their tax returns.These financial statements should either be audited by qualified independent auditors or by the tax officials themselves. Public-listed companies are also required to submit audited annual financial statements to the Jakarta Stock Exchange. In addition, foreign companies are required to file financial statements with Bank Indonesia, the BKPM and relevant government departments overseeing the various industries. Domestic companies which fall under the jurisdiction of BKPM also have to submit similar reports to the government board. Finally, foreign investment companies, PMAs, are required top report their progress in the implementation of their projects to BKPM using standard forms provided.

For tax purposes, all transactions records should be denominated in rupiah currency terms using the Indonesian language. A second language and currency, such as English and the US dollar, may be used by PMA companies in the oil and mining industries. Indonesian should, however, be used for all tax returns and other official documents.

All businesses are required to prepare a balance sheet within six months from the end of the financial year. A profit and loss or income statement is also prepared in practice by most businesses although this statement is only required from limited liability companies. Consolidated financial statements are not usually prepared by companies in Indonesia as they are not required to do so by law. But for tax purposes, a balance sheet and an income statement are required for each business entity, as accompanying documents to the annual tax documents to be filed within three months from the end of the fiscal year.

The directors of a limited liability company are required to submit a balance sheet and an income statement at an annual general meeting to shareholders within nine months from the end of the company's financial period. Books and records, plus a copy of the annual balance sheet, should be retained for 30 years. Copies of relevant correspondence must be stored for 10 years. The tax law requires all records to be retained for at least 10 years.

There is no general law or regulation stating the audit requirements of businesses in Indonesia. However, it is becoming increasingly common for various authorities to request for the submission of audited financial statements. As a result, it is generally necessary for foreign investors in Indonesia to have their financial records audited. Public companies, banks, financial institutions and insurance companies must also present audited annual financial statements to their respective regulatory bodies.

TAXATION MATTERS

The Indonesian government has introduced a series of special privileges, incentives and deregulations to attract investors to Batam. In addition to the investment incentives and investment guarantees that Indonesia offers to foreign investors, those in Batam also directly benefit from the island's status as a bonded zone: Goods entering Batam for re-export or for the purpose of processing for re-export are not subject to import duties. If exported goods are entirely made from materials sourced from outside Indonesia they are duty-free. Exports, or export components, sourced from within Indonesia are subject to either Value Added Tax (10%) or Luxury Sales Tax (10-30%).

Indonesia's income tax laws previously were complex and cumbersome. But considerable simplification was achieved by revisions announced to take effect from January 1,1995. Unlike some other countries, Indonesia has not as yet established a comprehensive system of tax incentives to attract investors and promote development of Riau.

All enterprises and employees in Riau are liable to tax in the same way as their counterparts in the rest of the country. Although Batam is a duty free zone, it is **not** an income tax-free haven. Thus, businessmen investing or doing business in Riau should be aware of the possible tax implications which may arise from revenues generated in Batam and others parts of the Raiu province. Withholding tax is another common area to be looked at when payments are made from profits derived in Indonesia. As for other kinds of taxes like customs duties and value added tax, some exemptions are available on Batam only.

Indonesia's Income Tax laws generally follow the 'deductible-taxable' principle. This means that if an item is allowed to be deductible for tax purposes for the payer, the same item will become taxable on the recipient; and vice versa. The most obvious example is employee benefits such as rent-free housing. The costs of such benefits are not deductible by the employer and therefore are thus not considered as taxable items on the employee. Taxpayers are treated either as residents or non-residents.

Current corporate tax rates are 15 per cent on the first 10 million Rupiah, 25 per cent on the next 40 million and 35 per cent above 50 million Rupiah. Taxpayers are generally able to deduct all expenses from gross income to the extent that they are incurred in the process of generating the income. expenses that are not deductible include benefit-in-kind, donations and reserves. There is no separate taxation on capital gains. All capital gains are taxed in the same way as income or profits and are simply added into the normal tax computations.

An overseas incorporated company operating in Indonesia through a permanent establishment will be taxed at the same rates as an Indonesian incorporated company. A final remittance tax of 20 per cent, which corresponds to the rate of withholding tax on dividend payments to non-residents, is charged on after-tax profits which are not subject to any treaty protection. There is a system of withholding tax on certain payments to resident and non-resident taxpayers. The rate of withholding tax on dividends, interests, royalties, technical and management fees is currently 20 per cent of gross payments if paid to non-residents. This can be reduced by relevant tax treaty provisions. A 15 per cent rate applies to similar payments to resident taxpayers and represents a payment on account of the recipient's final tax liability.

Value Added Tax is charged on domestic consumption at various levels from the manufacturer down to the wholesale trader, as well as on services rendered to end-users. The prevailing rate is 10 per cent. Special regulations apply to Batam only. Deliveries of taxable goods and services within Batam are not subject to VAT. But deliveries from Batam to the rest of Indonesia, and vice versa, are taxed at the full VAT rate. Deliveries from Batam to foreign countries are treated as exports and are therefore zero-rated. Imports into Batam are also not subject to VAT.

Other taxes levied in Indonesia include stamp duty, sales tax, on luxury goods and customs duty. Some reliefs apply to Batam and to certain assets approved by the BKPM.

The changes introduced at the beginning of 1995 by the Jakarta government were designed to simplify the requirements, but also make tax collection much easier.

The main change is the concept of 'permanent establishment' for foreign entities operating in Indonesia. Permanent establishment is a business presence defined in most tax regimes. Under Indonesian domestic law previously it was quite easy for a foreign company to be exposed to having a PE in Indonesia. The wording in the old law used to state that as long as a company had an intention to operate or regularly carry out business in Indonesia it technically had a PE.

Under the new law, the scope and definition of PE is somewhat narrowed to define how many days a company has to be in Indonesia before actually become exposed to PE regime. If a company sends employees to work and in total they remain for more than 60 days then the company will have a PE (previously there was no minimum).

In addition, under the old PE arrangement, a company was taxed on a world-wide basis. Now, the authorities have adopted an 'effectively-connected' concept which is not as wide. According to a Singapore-based analyst: 'Once you have a PE they will only look at that presence and effectively connect whatever income that presence causes you to earn and you will pay tax on that only.

'Once a company has a PE, it must file a return on its income and claim expenses related to the PE. Previously it was based on normal Indonesian tax computation where you could actually informally deduct expenses such as royalties charged by head office and management fees. Now, under new law, they have specifically limited the deduction of the PE. So it's not really good news. Royalties, management fees, other service fees if charged by head office, and interest, are not deductible. What is deductible is a deemed percentage of income. We don't know what a deemed percentage they will allow a deduction for. So this is not a good change for most foreign companies. They will taxed on a wider margin most likely.'

Another concept that needs to be studied is the 'Force of Attraction Rule': In the old days, once a business operation in Indonesia was declared a PE, the income of all its related companies, whether parent, sister or subsidiary was lumped together for taxation purposes if they engaged in any activities in Indonesia although not coming under the PE rule. From now on, only the company that has PE will be the focus of attention by the tax authorities.

Another provision in the domestic law relates to what is known as a 'Special Relationship' which covers transactions between related entities. An expert explains: 'Let's say an Indonesian subsidiary of a Singapore company, a 100 per cent subsidiary, pays a service fee to the Singapore parent. This payment will fall under the special relationship provision. Because these two entities are related, the tax authorities have the power to redetermine the transaction. They might deem it to be a siphoning profits out of Indonesia, so they will either limit the deduction in the subsidiary's books, or impose a withholding on the payment to the foreign company. They could even deem a margin way above the one in the books of the Indonesian company. But the special relationship was somewhat ill-defined before, and one of the changes under the new law is to provide a clearer definition.

'Another aspect of the special relationship is control by technology. In the new law they define what is control. Where it used to be controlled by share ownership, now there is a new definition saying that if you control by technology – technical assistance agreement – then you also deemed to have a special relationship as well, and this is going to have implications for companies who have franchise agreements or who make payments under service agreements etc.'

Indonesia operates a withholding tax system under which someone making a payment of say, 100 dollars, to another company, might only hand over, say, 80 dollars, with the rest going to the taxman. This applies in areas like dividends, interest, royalties, rental, and all services.

The legal changes involve two important areas. According to the tax analyst: 'One is that all kinds of services are subject to withholding tax in or outside of Indonesia. Previously, it was only for services performed in Indonesia. So this is a very big thing. It affects quite a lot of companies. It used to be that they could structure payments for offshore services and they were free of withholding tax because there was no mechanism to collect it. But with this change, the Indonesians have removed the words 'performed in Indonesia' so now it covers all.

'Another change is withholding on sale of assets and property. This is capital gains, actually. Previously, Indonesia had a capital gains tax, but if you were a non-resident realizing capital gains there was no mechanism to tax it. Having put this under the regulation now, it means that the buyer of the asset will withhold tax from payment to the seller. That will be a final payment. As a non-resident you are not required to file a return in Indonesia so whatever tax is withheld will be your final tax. You won't be taxed any further.

'There is a problem, however, with offshore services if you are a Singapore-based company performing services in Singapore for benefit of Indonesian company. Now, the Indonesian entity is supposed to withhold tax. Will Singapore then grant a foreign tax credit, because rightfully it is a Singapore-sourced income which will be taxed there? Foreign tax credits are only granted in Singapore if the income is actually a foreign-sourced income. If I perform services in Singapore then it is Singapore source not foreign source. So, technically you may not get the foreign tax credit. You'll have to be very careful in structuring your business as this is a grey area.'

The overall message, therefore, is that Indonesia has tightened control by increasing the provisions to cover all aspects of compliance and to ensure that all tax payers are covered. Before, a large percentage of residents did not pay tax. So Jakarta is trying to encourage compliance and provide for more stringent penalties, fines and imprisonment for non-compliance.

What does this mean for the Growth Triangle concept? Will it hinder or discourage companies from moving their factories from Singapore to Batam or Bintan? The tax expert is optimistic: 'In a way, it may not hinder. What it's trying to do is to set clearer rules and some companies may prefer that rather having it vague. If there is a rule that is sure to be enforced then in a way it facilitates planning. Because we used to say it's not very clear. You do what you think is right and hope. So it's a change for the better overall, although they are increasing the net as regards the tax base. Most MNCs would prefer such an environment so that rules are clearer like Singapore and it doesn't really hurt that much.'

WORKING IN JOHOR

There are several agencies which assist investors in Johor. The main one is the Johor State Economic Development Corporation (JSEDC), whose prime responsibility is to promote and undertake land development for industrial, agricultural, residential, mining and commercial purposes. The JSEDC is a one-stop centre, assisting investors to set up operation quickly and to get all approvals and necessary amenities. The JSEDC operates the Johor Investment Centre which is a permanent trade exhibits centre to provide visitors with general information on products, industrial development and manufacturing opportunities.

The South East Johor Regional Development Authority performs a similar function for that part of the state. The Malaysian Industrial Development Authority (MIDA) is the regulatory body for industrial development, issuance of manufacturing license, duty exemption investment incentives, expatriate employment and tariff protection.

Singapore and Johor have set up a Joint Committee on Business Cooperation to identify areas of mutual interest in trade and investments, comprising five businessmen and one government official from each side. The committee aims to resolve problems encountered by Singapore investors setting up factories in Johor, exchange information on economic opportunities and implement business cooperation programmes.

The Malaysian government allows foreign investors to hold up to 100 per cent share equity in a company that exports at least four-fifths of its production. It does not matter how much these products compete with local products. In other cases, the level of foreign equity participation varies according to the export level, technology level, spin-off effects, size of the investment, location, value-added and amount of local raw materials and components used.

For example, projects exporting between 51 and 79 per cent of their production, foreign equity up to 51 per cent will be allowed. But this percentage can be increased to 79 per cent depending on factors such as the level of technology, spin-off effects, size of investment, value-added, and utilisation of local raw materials and components. For projects exporting between 20 and 50 per cent of their production, foreign equity ownership of between 30 and 51 per cent will be allowed. For projects exporting less than 20 per cent of their production, foreign ownership up to 30 per cent will be allowed. But for projects producing high technology or priority products for the domestic market, the equity share can be as high as 51 per cent. Furthermore, a majority foreign equity ownership is permitted for companies involved in high-tech production or manufacturing priority products for the domestic market. Also, new hotel and tourist projects, subject to certain conditions may have up to 100 per cent foreign ownership for the first five years of operation. Lastly, up to 100 per cent foreign ownership is allowed for extraction/mining and processing of mineral ores.

Johor gives priority to investment projects which are export-oriented, support the State's resource development; substantially increase employment and carry out significant R & D activities.

Malaysia has set up a number of tax incentives to encourage foreign investment. The first general incentive is PIONEER STATUS, under which a tax holiday is given for five years commencing from the production date, extendible for a further five to 10 years for companies which fulfil certain criteria of the Ministry of Trade and Industry. An INVESTMENT TAX ALLOWANCE may be given to companies up to 100 per cent in respect to qualifying capital expenditures incurred within five years from the date of approval for the project.

The central bank, Bank Negara, has implemented an EXPORT CREDIT REFINANCING SCHEME which provides Malaysian exporters with credit at preferential rates of interest so they can compete effectively in the international market. A reduction of Adjusted Income for Exports to the amount of half of overseas sales to total sales and five per cent of the value of indigenous Malaysian materials which are incorporated in the manufacture of the products exported, is granted to manufacturing companies exporting directly or through agents. An EXPORT ALLOWANCE of five per cent based on the FOB value of export sales is given to trading companies which export products manufactured in Malaysia. Double deduction for promotional expenses incurred for the export of products manufactured in Malaysia are allowed for resident companies. These expenses allowed include those for overseas advertising, free samples, export market research, participation in exhibitions, overseas travel and accommodation and maintenance of an overseas sales office. An INDUSTRIAL BUILDING ALLOWANCE of an initial 10 per cent and then two per cent annually is given for buildings used as warehouses and bulk storage installations for export goods.

Incentives for expenses incurred for research activities approved by the Minister of Finance are eligible for double deduction; the

Industrial Building Allowance is also available for buildings used for the purpose of approved research; approved plant and machinery used for research are eligible for capital allowances, as well as those used for approved industrial training. A double deduction is granted to manufacturing companies for expenditure related to approved training.

There are also exemptions available on customs duty for direct raw materials and components, and excise duty on machinery and equipment. Companies within designated free trade zones pay no duties or taxes on the import of capital goods, raw materials and components. Companies can also apply for their operational area to be designated a LICENSED MANUFACTURING WAREHOUSE (LMW) when at least 80 per cent of their output is for export and when raw materials/components imported are not available locally. Companies with LMW facility can import raw materials and components without paying sales tax or duties.

MORE EXPORT INCENTIVES

The robust growth of the Malaysian economy since the late 1980s, with an annual GDP growth of eight per cent, was due mainly to the export-oriented industries whose capital was funded largely by foreign investments from Japan, Taiwan, United States, Britain and Singapore. To maintain sustainable growth, the Malaysian government has initiated measures to stimulate local reinvestment and to encourage Malaysian businessmen to invest in the manufacturing sector by providing attractive fiscal and tax incentives.

The Promotion of Investments (Amendment) Act of 1994 introduced new incentives and rules for investments located on the 'Eastern Corridor' (the states of Kelantan, Terennganu, parts of Pahang and the Mersing district of Johor), capital-intensive and high-technology industries, R & D companies and construction of infrastructural facilities. A company manufacturing a promoted product or engaging in a promoted activity in the Eastern Corridor, as well as Sabah and Sarawak, will be considered for the following incentives:

• Full exemption from payment of import duties on raw materials, components and parts used for the manufacturing process, if these are not available locally.

- Infrastructure allowance.
- Pioneer status or investment tax allowance.

Some of the promoted activities and products have been gazetted and include agricultural production, integrated agriculture such as cultivation and processing of coffee; processing of agricultural produce, manufacture of chemicals, petrochemicals and pharmaceuticals; all wooden products; manufacture of clay-based, sand-based and other non-metallic mineral products; manufacture of iron and steel and related products; manufacture of non-ferrous metals and their products; manufacture of transport equipment, components and accessories; supporting product services; manufacture of electrical and electronic products and components; manufacture of plastic products etc.

A company granted pioneer status will have 85 per cent of its statutory income exempt from tax for five years, with no possible extension unless its project is also considered of strategic and national importance. Any unutilized loss or capital allowance will not be available to be carried forward to the post-pioneer period except for capital expenditure incurred on providing plant used for the storage and treatment of disposal waste.

For a manufacturing facility within the promoted area, a company may apply for an INVESTMENT TAX ALLOWANCE (ITA) which may be granted retrospectively, subject to certain conditions. On approval, the company is given an ITA of 80 per cent of the capital expenditure incurred within the basis period and this lasts for five years from the date of approval. The ITA for each year, however, must not exceed 85 per cent of its statutory income for that year. Any unutilized ITA may be carried forward to be set off against future statutory income until the entire ITA is used. Effectively, a company granted ITA will given a 180 per cent deduction in the form of tax depreciation and ITA.

Similar concessions are available to an enterprise designated as a 'High technology Company' involving in new and emerging technologies, which currently encompasses automation, biotechnology, electronics, building materials, information technology and renewable energy. Aerospace is likely to join this list soon. A high technology company granted pioneer status enjoys a 100 per cent exemption from tax on statutory income for a five-year period, with no extension unless the project is of strategic or national importance. Alternatively, it can receive an ITA of 60 per cent for five years. Pioneer status and ITA is also available in certain categories of R & D.

A company which is resident for tax purposes and which has incurred capital expenditure on infrastructure facilities (construction, reconstruction or improvement of any permanent structure such as a bridge, jetty, port or road) for a business located in the promoted area will be given an allowance equal to the full amount of the expenditure. The allowance is for a five-year period which began on October 29,1993.

An Operational Headquarters (OHQ) incentive was first introduced for the manufacturing sector in the 1988 budget, and now all economic activities such as manufacturing, services, agriculture, construction and mining. The scope has been reviewed several times, with significant changes being made in 1993 and 1994 to further promote Malaysia as an international centre for providing research, management and financial services. It was originally intended for foreign wholly-owned companies or individuals, but from 1995 has been extended to local companies. Rationalization has also occurred to make the types of qualifying services more transparent by broadly classifying them into five categories – management and administrative services, treasury and fund management, other financial services, research and development and training and personnel management. An existing incentive for the procurement of raw materials and components for use overseas has been extended to procurement of finished products.

With the abolition of tax on offshore income remitted to Malaysia by resident companies from 1995, dividend income received by all OHQs, including companies set up before the incentive was introduced, will no longer be subject to income tax.[3]

MALAYSIAN RULES

In Malaysia, a business enterprise may take the form of a sole proprietorship, a partnership (two to 20 partners) or a locally incorporated company. A sole proprietorship and partnership must be registered with the Registrar of Business. A partnership may consist of individuals or companies. Corporations must be governed by the Companies Act 1965 and must be registered with the Registrar of Companies under the Ministry of Domestic Trade and Consumer Affairs. The Act recognises four types of companies: a company limited by shares; a company limited by guarantee; a company limited by both shares and guarantee; or an unlimited company. Each of these types can be either private or public. A private company is one which restricts share transfers, limits membership to 50 and prohibits public invitation or subscription to its shares or debentures or for loan of money to it. A public-listed company is essentially one whose shares are listed on the Kuala Lumpur Stock Exchange.

A foreign company may establish a presence in Malaysia either through a representative office or a regional office, setting up a branch of its own organization, and hence register as a branch of a foreign company in Malaysia, or incorporating a Malaysian company. A representative office is allowed to collect relevant information regarding investment opportunities in the country especially in the manufacturing sector, develop bilateral trade relations, promote export of Malaysian goods/products and to carry out research and development. The representative office is not allowed to have any business transactions and to derive income from its operation. A representative office when approved by the Ministry of International Trade and Industry (MITI) is allowed generally to exist within a certain period of time provided the conditions so specified for the setting up of such an office are complied with.

A regional office is that of a multinational corporation which serves as coordination centre for the corporate affiliates, subsidiaries or agents in Southeast Asia and Asia-Pacific. The office is not allowed to do any direct business transaction and derive income from its operation. An application is made to MITI, but for registration of a branch office, the approach must be, made to the Registrar of Companies. It is, however, difficult for a foreign corporation to register a branch office in Malaysia unless the branch is set up to undertake government or government agency projects. A branch office may employ local or foreign personnel to oversee the contract works and work permits would be granted to foreign personnel appropriate to the needs of the contract.

A locally incorporated company can be formed by following certain basic procedures. First, is obtaining approval of the proposed company name. Second, certain documents must be lodged with the Registrar of Companies, including the memor-andum and articles of association, statutory declaration by promoters and directors and particulars of directors. Registration fees are on a sliding scale and payable on incorporation. They are based on the authorised share capital of the company and range from a minimum of RM1000 to a maximum of RM70,000. The whole process of incorporation of a typical private company normally takes about six to eight weeks.

In addition to approvals from the Registrar of Companies and Registrar of Businesses, prior approval must also be obtain from other relevant authorities at national and local level for certain activities, including manufacturing, banking, finance and insur-ance, telecommunications, printing and publishing, shipping, hotels, restaurants and entertainment.

The government enforces import control through a system of import licensing. Imports from Israel are prohibited (Malaysia being a Muslim country). Import duties normally fall within a range of 15 to 25 per cent, but can rise as high as 300 per cent for certain luxury products. In addition, a surtax of five per cent is levied on all goods, but a rebate of up to four per cent may be given on all raw materials and machinery for new industries. Export control is done through licensing and licenses are only issued if supply to local customers are not affected. An export license may be imposed on a particular product to fulfil a bilateral contractual obligation with other countries (e.g. textiles where Malaysia has an export restraint agreement with some importing countries).

No permission is required from the Controller of Foreign Exchange for a non-resident to undertake direct and portfolio investment. Payments abroad can be made in any currency other than that of Israel. Payments within Malaysia must be made in the domestic currency, the ringgit. All payments to non-residents for any purpose, including repatriation of capital or profits, are freely permitted.

Non-Resident Controlled Companies (NRCC) in Malaysia may borrow up to RM10 million from all sources without permission from the Controller, provided it obtains at least 60 per cent of its credit facilities from financial institutions incorporated in Malaysia. Permission is required once the limit is exceeded. Residents may borrow in foreign currency from banks in Malaysia to supplement their financial requirements for businesses and productive purposes, but foreign borrowings over RM1 million require the prior approval of the Controller.[4]

CHAPTER NOTES

1. The information in this section is drawn from a wide range of published sources, mainly international financial and business conultancies, which are listed in the bibliography.
2. I am indebted to the Indonesian desk of Arthur Andersen Consulting in Singapore for its assistance in the preparation of this section.
3. Malaysian Budget 1995, Arthur Andersen Consulting.
4. *Guide To Doing Business In Malaysia*. Kassim Chan Tax Services Sdn.Bhd./Deloitte Touche Tohmatsu Tax Services Sdn.Bhd., Kuala Lumpur, 1993.

10 Singapore's Financial System

HISTORY OF BANKING

THE FIRST BANK in Singapore, a branch of the Union Bank of Calcutta, was established in 1840 but did not survive long. The Oriental Bank, owned and managed by the British, was set up in 1864. It was followed not many years later by the Asiatic Banking Corporation and the Commercial Bank of India, both of which collapsed in the mid-1860s. The Oriental Bank went bankrupt in 1884 when it speculated heavily in coffee and sugar whose price fell sharply. The period 1856-1883 saw the establishment of several other banks which proved to be successes. These were the

197

Mercantile Bank (1856), the Chartered Bank (1861), the Hong Kong and Shanghai Banking Corporation (1877) and the Nederlandsche Handel-Maatschappij N.V. (1883).

Their role was to finance Singapore's entrepot trading activities, mainly the export of tin and rubber and the import of manufactured goods. The three British banks formed an integral part of the colonial banking system with London as the headquarters. Until the Currency Board was established in 1899, they also issued currency notes.

With the expansion and growing prosperity of the Chinese business community, their need for banking services also became more apparent. Although the foreign banks could act as the middlemen, Chinese businessmen found the arrangement unsatisfactory, leading to the Kwong Yik Bank being established in 1903. However, in 1913 it faced financial difficulties due to excessive lending to its directors. Before its closure, some shareholders organized a new bank, Kwong Yik (Selangor) Banking Corporation, incorporated in Kuala Lumpur in July 1913. The Four Seas Corporation Bank was the second local bank to be set up in 1906. Three other local Chinese banks were established during this period – Chinese Commercial Bank (1912), Ho Hong Bank (1913) and Oversea-Chinese Bank (1919). They subsequently amalgamated in 1932 to form the Overseas-Chinese Banking Corporation (OCBC), which flourishes today.

By 1941, Singapore had a fairly large commercial banking sector. The British and Chinese banks had expanded, three Indian banks and several other foreign banks were set up in the 1930s. Twelve local Chinese banks were established during the period 1903-41. However, although the numbers grew, Singapore's financial system up to the Second World War could be described as rudimentary. There were no other types of reputable and sound financial institutions, nor was there a regulatory authority. There was no proper capital and money market. The local Chinese banks pursued their own credit policies.

The British banks played a role in the transfer of capital from Britain to Pan Malaya and acted as the intermediary between the Currency Board and the Crown Agents in London in the exchange of sterling for dollars and vice versa. The government also maintained accounts with them and the remittance of government funds to and from London was handled by the British banks.

During the post-war period up to the early 1950s, the banking network continued to expand, and finance companies began to emerge, mainly to undertake the smaller scale financing, hire purchase financing and other activities in which the commercial banks were less interested. Insurance companies were also established. The Central Provident Fund (CPF) was set up in 1955 but did not develop into a major financial institution until much later.

Financial activities were subject to closer regulation by the 1960s. The Banking Act and the Finance Companies Act were passed for the protection of depositors and for the proper control of the activities of the commercial banks and finance companies. The Insurance Act also came into effect in 1967. To encourage longer-term financing, the Government set up the Development Bank of Singapore (DBS) in 1968 and held a 49 per cent interest.

In the late 1960s, further change occurred when the Government announced its policy to develop a higher level of expertise in the financial sector to increase capital inflow and investment. One of the first steps taken in the development strategy was the abolition in 1968 of the withholding tax on interest paid to non-residents on deposits with banks in Singapore.

High priority was given to the creation of an active, sophisticated domestic and regional money market. Exchange control was liberalized on 1 June 1978, to remove the restrictions on the movement of funds. A non-resident is now exempted from tax on interest earned on deposits placed with approved banks in Singapore.

ASIAN DOLLAR MARKET

Offshore banking was developed in the mid-1980s through the creation of the Singapore-based Asian Dollar Market, using a separate book-keeping procedure known as an Asian Currency Unit (ACU) to accept foreign currency time and call deposits and make loans in foreign currencies. The Bank of America was the first to be given approval to set up an ACU, which have witnessed rapid growth, to a total of 198 units at the end of 1994. Assets have grown from US$155 billion in 1985 to US$386 billion.[1]

In order to boost the Asian Dollar Market, the MAS exempted the ACUs from the 18 per cent liquidity ratio normally required for commercial banks (see below). The government also abolished the stamp duties on Negotiable Certificates of Deposit (NCDs) and bills of exchange to encourage the growth of an acceptance market and secondary market in NCDs. To date, a number of banks have been given permission to issue NCDs denominated in Singapore dollars and various foreign currencies. As there is no exchange control, local corporations can borrow from the Asian Dollar Market.

The government also reduced the tax, from 40 to 10 per cent, on income derived by ACUs from offshore transactions and dividends distributed out of such profits, and abolished the stamp duty on ACU offshore loan documents and on Asian and Singapore dollar bonds. The concessionary tax rate of 10 per cent has also been introduced for income derived from offshore gold transactions by ACUs and Members of the Singapore International Monetary Exchange (SIMEX). Since 1980, non-resident banks have been allowed to is sue US$NCDs in the market.[2]

Qualifying activities of an ACU are: 1.Loans to persons outside Singapore to be used outside Singapore in currencies other than the Singapore dollar, where the interest on such loans is not borne directly or indirectly by a person resident in Singapore or a permanent establishment in Singapore;   2.Financing offshore trade transactions through bills of exchange or letters of credit;   3.Loans, deposits, bankers' acceptance of and transactions in bills relating to offshore trade, and transactions in negotiable certificates of deposits with other ACUs in Singapore and banks or branches outside Singapore;   4.Managing, underwriting, dealing, brokering, investing and transacting in Asian dollar bonds, other bonds, debentures and NCDs denominated in currencies other than the Singapore dollar;   5.Fees earned for providing fund management services to non-residents;   6.Transactions in gold or financial futures with persons outside Singapore, members of SIMEX and other ACUs in Singapore. 7.Providing financial advisory services to persons outside Singapore;   8.Income from providing offshore guarantees, performance bonds and standby letters of credit;   9.Commissions, custodian and nominee fees, handling and registration charges earned in respect of transactions undertaken on behalf of non-residents in foreign stocks and other securities denominated in foreign currencies and issued by foreign companies not incorporated in Singapore and Malaysia;   10.Commissions and other income earned in respect of offshore remittances;   11.Service income earned in respect of offshore transactions involving interest rate and currency swaps;   12.Foreign exchange transactions in currencies other than the Singapore dollar;   13.Income from trading in non-Singapore dollar securities with non-residents, other ACUs and approved securities companies;   14.Income from arranging, underwriting, managing and placing with non-residents international non-Singapore dollar securities issued from Singapore by non-resident companies.

Income from ACUs arising from syndicated offshore loans where the syndication work is carried out in Singapore is exempt from income tax. To qualify, the borrower must be a non-resident, the proceeds of the facility must be used outside Singapore, the lead manager must be an ACU, at least three participants must provide the credit, and the syndication work must be substantially carried out in Singapore. The exemption also covers income from other syndicated credit and underwriting facilities, including syndication of guarantee, performance bonds and certain underwriting facilities where the syndication work is carried out in Singapore.

Offshore income earned by investors from funds managed by ACUs, approved fund managers, approved operational headquarters companies and finance and treasury centres is exempt from tax provided the investors or beneficiaries of the funds are non-residents and the funds are invested in approved local and offshore securities. Fees earned by ACUs and approved fund managers for providing accepted fund management services are taxed at a concessionary rate of 10 per cent instead of the normal 27 per cent.

Income earned by approved securities companies from trading and transacting in foreign securities with or on behalf of non-residents, other ACUs and other approved securities firms is taxed at 10 per cent. Income from arranging, managing and placing with non-residents international non-Singapore dollar securities issued from Singapore by non-resident companies is also taxed at 10 per cent.

This same tax rate applies on income derived from insuring and reinsuring offshore general insurance risks, and on dividends and interest derived from the investment of the offshore insurance fund and capital funds used to support the offshore general business.

the reduced rate does not apply to Singapore dividends and interest other than ACU interest. But it is applicable to life insurance income attributable to policyholders, which includes premiums, investment income and profits on the sale of investments.[3]

KEY INSTITUTIONS

The financial system is relatively free of restrictions. The regulations which do exist are largely to ensure the financial institutions are prudent in their operations and their depositors are protected. There is a free flow of funds in and out of Singapore since exchange control was abolished in June 1978. Since 1970, the number of financial intermediaries has also increased. This led to a greater variety of financial instruments being available to those with surplus funds, as well as new sources of financing for those in need of funds.

In the public sector, the Monetary Authority of Singapore (MAS), CPF and the Post Office Savings Bank (POSBank) play a dominant role.

Prior to the formation of the MAS in January 1971, central banking functions were carried out by several government departments. But the desire to develop Singapore as a financial centre required a more focused approach. The MAS acts as banker, fiscal agent and financial adviser to the government. It has a duty to promote monetary stability, credit and exchange policies conducive to the growth of the economy, supervise and regulate the banking and financial sectors, develop the financial markets and introduce new instruments.

It administers various statutes: the Banking Act, Finance Companies Act, Exchange Control Act, Local Treasury Bills Act, Development Loans Act, Insurance Act, Money Changing and Remittance Business Act, Securities Industry Act and Futures Trading Act.

It not only provides current account and deposit facilities for the government but also manages the public debt. It is responsible for all transactions associated with the issue of government bonds, the servicing of these securities, including their redemption or conversion on maturity, and the flotation of government loans in overseas financial markets. Until June 1981, the MAS was also responsible for the investment and management of the official foreign exchange reserves, but this function was transferred to a newly-established Government of Singapore Investment Corporation (GIC). The MAS serves as an agent in official transactions with the International Monetary Fund, International Bank for Reconstruction and Development and the Asian Development Bank.

It is authorised to borrow, lend, to buy or sell, discount and rediscount securities, treasury bills, commercial bills and government securities. It has a rediscount window for import and export bills, the latter re-discounted at a promotional concessionary rate. Banks maintain a current account balance with the MAS in line with their obligation to maintain a minimum cash deposit with it – the money being used to control the money supply. The current accounts are necessary for the daily settlement of balances arising from the centralized clearing of cheques and remittances. The current accounts are also used for the settlement of balances between the banks and the MAS and the banks and government. The finance companies maintain accounts with the MAS to fulfil their statutory minimum reserve requirements. They make adjustments to their accounts, following changes in the size of their deposit liabilities, but they may not make any discretionary withdrawals from their accounts.

In its capacity as a supervisory authority, the MAS is authorised to inspect all financial institutions with the emphasis placed on capital adequacy, asset structure, soundness of control systems and management. It supervises by examining statistical returns and other information which the financial institutions are required to submit periodically. Institutions which deviate from statutory provisions or which are assessed as veering towards unsound business practices are informed of their weaknesses. These are rectified through consultations with the MAS, which has the mandate in the final analysis to withdrawal the licenses and operating approval of the offending institutions.

In consultation with the Ministry of Finance and Ministry of Trade and Industry, it also formulates policies and implements measures for Singapore's further development as a financial centre. It was the responsible for the establishment of the Asian dollar market and the introduction of new instruments such as the Singapore and US dollar negotiable certificates of deposit, already referred to. In the 1980s, the emphasis was on more advanced and efficient financial services, and the MAS worked closely with bo th local and foreign banks on the widespread introduction of automated teller machines and electronic funds transfer facilities. The range of borrowing instruments also expanded to include Note Issuance Facilities, Revolving Underwriting Facilities, Singapore dollar NCDs and Floating Rate Notes.

Going into the 1990s, the Authority identified three areas for strong development. The first was the further promotion of the capital markets. Second was risk management, promoting Singapore as the risk management centre where regional and global institutions can trade a full gamut of financial tools, including futures, options, foreign exchange and other money market instruments. The third area for development was identified as fund management, with tax incentives extended for this purpose.

The MAS also works closely with the Board of Commissioners of Currency, which is responsible for the issue and redemption of currency in Singapore. The local currency is 100 per cent backed by gold and official foreign reserves. The Board maintains a Currency Fund and a Currency Fund Income Account. US dollars received by the Currency Board in exchange for Singapore dollars are paid into the Currency Fund. At least 30 per cent of the resources of the Currency Fund is in liquid assets. The reserves of the Fund are invested abroad and the income and profits from such investments are transferred to the Income Account, from which any expenditure in the issue and redemption of currency is debited. Any surpluses are paid to the government, which also finances any deficits. The MAS is the intermediary between the Currency Board and commerci al banks in meeting the latter's currency requirements, with transactions being carried out through the Authority's clearing system.

The CPF is a social insurance scheme in which are employees and employers have a participate; the mandatory monthly contributions which they have to make add up to a vast sum and form a large proportion of domestic savings mobilised for the financing of public sector developments. Lately however, the government has allowed a percentage of the funds absorbed by the CPF to be recycled into the private sector through investment in the share market and property.[4]

The POSBank is a financial institution more akin to the commercial banks. It was established to encourage thrift and to mobilise savings also mainly for the public sector. The POSBank provides facilities for savings and the transfer of funds. With these resources at its disposal, the POSBank gives loans to government-owned enterprises and to statutory authorities, invests in government bonds, provides housing mortgages and redeposits some funds with commercial banks.

COMMERCIAL BANKS

These are licensed by the MAS, whose approval is also need for opening of a branch office or sub-branch. There are three types of license: full, restricted and offshore. Before 1971, there was only one. To develop Singapore as a financial centre, more banks obviously had to be admitted, but the size of the economy did not justify the admission of any more institutions simply to meet the needs of the domestic market. The future lay in offshore banking, and for this reason a new licensing system was introduced.

A full banking license allows a bank to engage in all types of activities permitted under the Banking Act, broadly the same as those undertaken by a commercial bank anywhere in the world. All 13 locally incorporated banks and 24 foreign banks admitted before 1971 qualify.

A restricted bank license enables the institution to undertake transactions similar to a full licensed bank, but it is not allowed open any branches, operate savings accounts or accept fixed deposits of less than S$250,000 per deposit. At the end of 1994, 14 foreign banks had received a restricted license.

An offshore bank license allows a bank to engage in wholesale banking with non-residents. In its dealings with residents, an offshore bank may extend credit and provide facilities such as opening of letters of credit, issuing trust receipts and giving overdrafts up to a total limit of S$100 million without the prior approval of the authorities. However, it may not accept fixed, savings or other interest-bearing deposits from residents. Nor may it open branches. At the end of 1994, there were 83 banks with offshore licenses.

Other than differences in the types of licenses, banks are distinguished by those with and without Asian Currency Units

(ACU). Of the 132 commercial banks, all but nine have approval to transact in the Asian Dollar Market. As already mentioned, the MAS requires them to set up a separate book-keeping unit where all transactions in the ADM are recorded. The purpose of this is to isolate the movement of funds in and out of the market in order to minimise any disruptive effects on the domestic monetary system. All restricted and offshore banks have ACUs, along with all but nine of the full banks. ACUs can also transact business with each other, as well as undertake brokerage business, invest in foreign currency securities, open letters of credit, discount bills, issue and renew guarantees.

For commercial banks, the main provisions of the Banking Act are:

• A bank, incorporated in Singapore, is required to have a minimum paid-up capital plus published reserves of S$800 million net of any debit balances in its profit and loss account. The minimum paid-up capital for a bank whose head office is outside Singapore is the equivalent of S$200, net of any debit balance in its profit and loss account. In addition, foreign banks with branches here are also required net head office funds of not less than S$10 million in respect of its business in Singapore, of which not less than S$5 million must be in the form of assets approved by the MAS.

• A minimum cash balance has to be maintained with the MAS. Since July 1975, banks have kept six per cent of their deposits in cash reserves. However, the minimum cash reserves of banks varies within a band of one per cent of the required six per cent on a day-to-day basis. The variation in the minimum cash balance is one of the instruments used by the MAS to implement its monetary policy.

• Banks also have to maintain a liquid asset ratio of not less than 18 per cent of its liabilities base each day. Liquid assets may comprise government securities held by banks under Overnight Repos (Repurchase Agreement), subject to a maximum of five per cent of their liabilities base; a balance held by the Authority which is excess of the minimum cash balance of six per cent; notes and coins which are legal tender in Singapore; securities issued by the Singapore government subject to a minimum of 10 per cent of the liabilities base; bills of exchange in Singapore dollars, accepted or endorsed by banks in Singapore, which are from genuine trade

transactions and are payable within three months, subject to a maximum of four per cent of the liabilities base.
• The total credit a bank may extend to a single customer or a group of related companies with respect to the bank's facilities including guarantees is limited to 25% of the bank's capital funds. However, with approval from the Monetary Authority, this may be raised to 100 per cent. This limit does not apply to transactions with the government, transactions between banks nor facilities granted against documentary credit in respect of imports into or exports from Singapore.
• A bank is not allowed to grant substantial loans to a single customer or a group of related companies which, in aggregate, exceeds 50 per cent of its total credit facilities. The term 'substantial loan' is defined as 15 per cent of the bank's capital funds. This is applicable only where the total Singapore dollar credit facilities exceeds S$100 million.
• The amount a bank may invest is subject to a limit of 40 per cent of its capital funds. The value of immovable property which it may own is also limited to 40 per cent of its capital funds.
• A bank is not allowed to engage in commercial trading activities including import and export whether on its own account or on a commission basis. Although it is not prohibited by the Banking Act from establishing a subsidiary company to carry out commercial trading activities, such moves will not be well received by the MAS.
• A bank is required to maintain a reserve fund. The fund can be transferred from the net profits after providing for tax. So long as the size of the reserve fund forms less than 50 per cent of the bank's paid-up capital, it has to transfer at least 50 per cent of its net profits to the fund. If the percentage of reserve fund to paid-up capital is between 50 per cent to 100 per cent, it will have to transfer at least 25 per cent of its net profits to the fund. If the reserve fund exceeds the paid-up capital, the bank only needs to transfer a maximum of five per cent of its profits to the reserve fund. Foreign banks may apply the exemption from this provision.
• A bank has to submit regular statistical returns to the Monetary Authority. Income and expenditure statements have to be submitted annually. The books of the bank may be inspected by the MAS at any time.

FINANCE COMPANIES

They accept deposits and extend credit, like the commercial banks, but differ in many other respects. Most were set up in the 1950s, but a license to operate was needed only from 1967 with the passing of the Finance Companies Act. Legislation was introduced as the mushrooming of finance companies led to growing concern over the lack of proper control and protection of depositors' money.

Unlike commercial banks, there is a uniform license for finance companies. All 27 currently registered are locally incorporated, of which 14 are affiliated to banks. The latter set up wholly-owned subsidiaries to provide financing services mainly for consumer durables and home mortgages, but later ventured into lease and accounts receivable financing. The finance companies of some banks serve as substitutes for additional bank branches and sources for deposit collection, some of which may be channelled to the parent company.

Finance companies may accept fixed and savings deposits, but not demand deposits and therefore do not provide cheque facilities. They do not finance international trade directly, but can do so indirectly through the opening of letters of credit for a local importer through inventory financing in which they provide funds against the storage of goods in warehouses. Some companies concentrate on housing mortgages, while others specialize in hire purchase arrangements for items such as motor vehicles and machinery.

They are are licensed by the MAS and must comply with the Finance Companies Act and any other applicable MAS regulations, the main provisions being:

• Companies are required to maintain a minimum cash balance with the MAS amounting to six per cent of its liabilities base, along with a liquid assets ratio of 10 per cent.

• A company with paid-up capital exceeding S$2 million has to transfer part of its annual net profits to a reserve fund depending on the size of the latter. If it is less than half the paid-up capital at least 30 per cent has to be transferred; if more, at least 15 per cent must be transferred. If the reserve fund is larger than the paid-up capital, only five per cent of net profits needs to be transferred. The MAS has been considering a more stringent arrangement

setting the capital requirement for companies at $80 million. Most of the independent financial companies are capitalized at between $5 million and $25 million, so it is likely they would have to seek a merger with each other or a bigger house if they are to survive.
• The investment by a finance company in one enterprise may not exceed 25 per cent of its paid-up capital and reserves. However, this ceiling may be increased to 50 per cent with MAS approval.
• Investments of finance companies in immovable property may not exceed 25 per cent of their paid-up capital and reserves.
• A company's books may be inspected by the MAS at any time. The activities of finance companies are supervised by the Authority through field inspections and the review of the regular reports they are required to submit.

Finance companies cannot operate in the Asian Dollar market or issue negotiable certificates of deposit, nor can they deal in gold or handle foreign exchange transactions.

MERCHANT BANKS

The first approved merchant bank was set up only in 1970. By March 1994, there were 76, some of them branches of overseas institutions and others joint ventures between local and foreign partners. The predominant activity is offshore banking, with 75 institutions operating ACUs, which account for 85 per cent of their assets. The merchant banks generally are less homogenous that the commercial banks or finance companies. There is a certain degree of specialization, depending on the shareholders and the expertise available.

There is no specific legislation governing merchant banking activities, although they need MAS recognition to operate. Merchant banks are registered under the Companies Act. Those with ACUs are indirectly regulated under the Banking Act. In their offshore banking activities, they have to observe the relevant MAS guidelines. For domestic transactions, the MAS sets the following guidelines:
• Merchant banks are not permitted to accept Singapore dollar deposits or borrow from individuals, or issue promissory notes or other commercial paper. They are also not allowed to offer cheque facilities.

- They may accept deposits or borrow from banks and other financial institutions.
- They are not allowed to open branches.
- Merchant banks are allowed to make loans to any single or group borrower up to value of 30 per cent of it's capital fund. The limit may be increased to 100 per cent if the facilities in excess of 30 per cent are guaranteed by the bank's head office or shareholders or if there are subordinated loans from its head office or shareholders to cover the excess.
- Capital fund provisions of the guidelines only apply to domestic currency financing. Asian Currency Unit operations do not have the same restrictions and are covered under the Banking Act and certain general banking guidelines. A number of restrictions have been introduced in respect of credit facilities, in particular to related companies, directors of the bank and staff, as well as certain types of securities.
- On the investment side, merchant banks may not acquire more than a 20 per cent share of any company. However, the directive will not apply if the acquisition comes in the way of enforcing security to satisfy debts to the bank, or in fulfilling an underwriting agreement. Consultation with and approval must also be obtained from the MAS for the appointment or re-appointment of an external auditor.
- Merchant banks must observe the MAS policy of discouraging the internationalisation of the Singapore dollar. The MAS must be consulted in writing before credit facilities exceeding $5 million are extended to non-residents or for use outside Singapore. This also applies to syndicated loans, bond issues or other financial papers denominated in local dollars.

OTHER FINANCIAL INSTITUTIONS

The insurance industry comes under the MAS, to which which both local and foreign-incorporated companies need to apply for a license to carry on life and general insurance business. At the end of 1993, there were 141 registered insurers, but the government would like to attract more as it seeks to develop Singapore as the regional centre for insurance and reinsurance. In the three years to 1993, both the life and general insurance businesses registered double digit growth.

International money brokers, who facilitate foreign exchange transactions by providing a link between banks in major financial centres, were introduced into the Singapore financial system only in 1971, when the first international broking firm was granted MAS approval. The establishment of this firm, a joint venture between a local bank and a London broking firm, as followed by three others, all wholly-owned subsidiaries of London houses. By the end of 1993, this number had risen to 10.

About 50 commercial and merchant banks have established representative offices, some with the intention of eventually gaining full recognition to operate in Singapore. No MAS licence is needed, but the authorities' approval is still needed before a representative office can be opened.

Finance leasing, first developed in the United States in the 1950s as a means of enabling expensive equipment to be used without the need to tie up capital purchasing it, began to take roots in Singapore two decades later. Many companies now operate, mostly through joint ventures, with the Japanese dominating, and they offer a wide range of equipment, ships, aircraft construction machinery etc. for lease. The MAS does not regulate these activities, although it is normally consulted before a company is set up. Leasing firms, however, are governed by the Companies Act.[5]

INTERNATIONAL FINANCE CENTRE

In the 1980s, much of the focus was to develop Singapore as an international finance centre. As a result, the emphasis in the financial sector shifted towards capital market instruments and related activities such as risk and investment management. The domestic financial market was considerably broadened and offshore activities were actively promoted. New financial instruments and papers have become available. Negotiable certificates of deposit, both in Singapore and US dollars, are issued by several banks. Commercial paper and government securities of a wide range of maturities are also available. Gold certificates have been introduced to investors.

Following the establishment of the ACU, depositors have the opportunity to place funds in foreign currencies with these institutions. With the entry of foreign banks, many of which are licensed to undertake offshore banking, the system became more international and the financial markets more complex.

In the early 1970s the money market, which hitherto had been a market for inter-bank funds, was expanded to include the discount market following the establishment of four discount houses. The discount market facilitated the flow of short-term funds among the financial institutions, with the Monetary Authority standing ready to provide 'lender of last resort' facilities and to assist the discount houses to square their positions at the end of the day. These discount houses have now closed.

The securities market was revitalised in 1987. In the new market structure, there are primary and registered dealers. Primary dealers, who underwrite auctions of treasury bills, notes and bonds, ensure the liquidity of the market. Registered dealers are also market makers but they do not have the privilege and obligation of bidding directly in auctions of new issues. As banks are now able to invest directly in government securities in the range of maturities and at competitive market yields, the attraction of placing funds with discount houses diminished significantly.

The discount houses have been converted to take on the role of market makers in government securities. The foreign exchange market saw changes in terms of the large expansion in the volume of transactions, increased third-currency trading and arbitrage activities. The bullion market too expanded, following the liberalization of gold dealings by residents. In September 1984, Singapore took another step forward in its growth as a financial centre with the introduction of the Singapore International Monetary Exchange (SIMEX). It has its origins in the Gold Exchange of Singapore which was established in November 1978. In May 1987, the Singapore Government Securities Market started operations, providing a liquid market in fixed income securities and serving as a benchmark for future corporate bond issues.

Banks continue to shift towards automated banking services. These allow for the increasing use of cashless payments at retail shopping outlets, and for electronic transfers of salaries and bill payments and electronic applications for shares.

STOCK EXCHANGE

The stockbroking industry was strengthened by a series of

measures initiated in 1986 in the wake of the shock recession. Chief among these were the passing of a new Securities Industry Act and the opening up of local stockbroking firms to ownership by local and foreign financial institutions. Brokerage rates were shaved as brokerage houses adopted a graduated commission scale with a view to moving towards freely negotiable rates. A settlement system based on the American five-day rolling settlement system was adopted for great trading efficiency.

The result has been a stockbroking industry that is better capitalized and more competitive, and that offers a better range and quality of services and better investor protection. Also, to enhance settlement efficiency, main board stocks are currently undergoing conversion to a computerized book-entry settlement system, doing away with the inconvenience of a physical delivery system.

The Stock Exchange of Singapore is reputed to be the third largest in Asia in terms of volume of transactions after Tokyo and Hong Kong. A joint stock exchange with Malaysia existed from 1939 to 1973. But in June of that year, following the termination of the currency interchangeability agreement with Malaysia, a separate stock exchange was established. Listed Singapore and Malaysian companies continued their dual listing on both the exchanges until 1989.

Then, Malaysian-listed companies were prohibited by the Kuala Lumpur Stock Exchange from maintaining a dual listing with the SES and all Malaysian incorporated companies were delisted on 31 December. Two days later, the SES introduced an over-the-counter market known as CLOB International to allow investors to trade in international securities listed on the respective foreign stock exchanges. In January 1995, there were 130 counters listed, comprising 116 Malaysian stocks, 10 from Hong Kong, 10 from Hong Kong, and one each from the Australia, Europe, Indonesia and the Philippines. Trading of selected US over-the-counter stocks is also encouraged. The. SES and the National Association of Securities Dealers Inc. (NASD) in the United States have started a link to provide for the exchange of quotations and other financial trading information on a selected 35 companies traded on NASDAQ. The NASD-SES link gives the investor, while in the Asian time zone, opportunities to invest in selected US and European stocks, thus facilitating portfolio investment and diversification, but the facility has not been too active so far, according to local analysts.

The domestic capital market was further diversified by the launching of the Stock Exchange of Singapore Dealing and Automated Quotation Market (SESDAQ) in February 1987 to give an opportunity to raise funds through a public listing to promising young companies lacking the track record required for listing on the main board. At the time of writing, there were 238 shares listed on the SES main board, and 43 on SESDAQ.

The SES has 33 member companies with a combined paid-up capital of $600 million. The Exchange is self-regulated by means of a nine-member committee comprising four elected stockbroking members and five appointed members from outside the stock-broking industry. There are several sub-committees to deal with specific functions such as disciplinary and listing matters. SES member companies must meet certain financial conditions including the maintenance of an adjusted net capital of at least $5 million, limits on gearing ratio, limits on the exposure to a single client and a single security, and maintenance of a reserve fund into which a prescribed percentage of the member's annual profit must be transferred.

Since 1986, wholly-owned subsidiaries of local banks have been admitted to the SES as member companies. From 1987, foreign brokerage houses and foreign financial institutions were permitted to own up to 49 per cent of a limited number of local broking firms-allowed to rise to 70 per cent after three years if at least half of the business transacted is from overseas. One of the goals of this is to introduce more foreign investors and listed companies to the Singapore exchange. In 1992, foreign brokers were also admitted to the exchange as 'International Members', permitted to deal in SES securities with non-residents.

In a further relaxation from February 1995, any approved foreign broker was allowed to trade directly in stocks listed or quoted in foreign currencies on the SES instead of having to deal through SES members. 'With the new scheme, foreign brokers can deal directly for their clients with contracts exceeding $5 million or its equivalent in foreign currency. Once implemented, this scheme will give foreign brokers access to 38 listed and 14 foreign-currency stocks on the SES. ''This scheme should lead to increased liquidity in the trading of foreign shares and improve the exchange's competitiveness in trading such securities," said SES Deputy Chairman George Teo. He added that deals put through these approved foreign brokers would attract the same commission rate as those charged by SES member brokers. Since foreign brokers are non-clearing members of the SES, the exchange will maintain a fund to be established with deposits to be placed by each of the brokers.'[6]

The requirements for seeking a listing on the SES are:
• Locally incorporated firms must have a minimum issued and paid-up capital of $15 million, of which at least 25 per cent should be owned by not fewer than 500 shareholders; a minimum track record of five years with profits in each of the last three years for listing on the main board; possess adequate working capital; show continuity in management.
• Companies seeking quotation of debt security must have at least $750,000 of debt securities of the class to be quoted, and which must be owned by least 100 holders; the securities must be created and issued in accordance with the Trust Deed.
• Foreign companies must be already quoted on their home exchange; have net tangible assets of at least $50 million; have had a cumulative pre-tax income of not less than $50 million for the last three years and a minimum of at least $20 million for any one of the three years; have 2,000 shareholders; have two million shares publicly held.
• Investment funds denominated in foreign currency must be managed by a reputable and established management company with at least a five-year track record; a minimum size of $30 million; at least 20 per cent of its share capital must be held by members of the public.

Admission requirements for the second board, SESDAQ, are less stringent. There is no minimum capital requirement, but at least 500,000 shares or 15 per cent of the company's paid-up capital must normally be in public hands when dealing commences. Companies should normally have been operating for at least three years although they are not required to be profitable before they can gain admission.

The venture capital industry, after a slow start, is beginning to take off. Temasek Capital investments, a local venture capital fund, was set up to '... help young technology companies to internationalise their activities in the Far East'. The company has forged alliances with reputable venture capital firms in the United States. American and Japanese funds have also been established.

The Singapore Government securities market was restructured in May 1987. Since then, taxable book-entry (scripless) government securities, ranging in maturity from three months to seven years, have been issued regularly by auction at market determined interest rates. The objectives of developing this market are to provide investors with an additional avenue for investment and the capital market with a relatively risk-free benchmark for pricing long-term issues, and to develop skills in the fixed income markets necessary to complement Singapore's role as an international financial centre. Currently, seven primary dealers provide liquidity by making two-way prices in all market conditions. Applications for new government securities offered at auction must be submitted through these primary dealers. Among dealers, prices are quoted in standard lots of $3 million for current issues and $1 million for off-the-run issues. The spread between the bid and offer prices is as fine as five cents.

The government issues 91-day treasury bills weekly. The 182-day and 364-day treasury bills, two-, five- and seven-year bonds are issued according to an annual calendar. A market committee comprising representatives from each primary dealer provides feedback on conditions in the market to the MAS.

To foster the growth of Singapore as a leading international financial centre, the Singapore Foreign Exchange Market Committee was established in March 1986 to succeed the Foreign Exchange and Money Market Practices Committee. The committee monitors the developments in the treasury markets and recommends appropriate measures for their continued growth and development. It also serves as a channel for information and dialogue between market participants and the MAS and aims to promote and maintain the highest standard of technical knowledge and professional conduct among market participants. The committee works closely with the Association of Banks, the Singapore Merchant Bankers' Association, the Singapore Foreign Exchange and Money Brokers Association and the Forex Association of Singapore.[7]

INVESTMENT INCENTIVES

The concessions given to ACUs, in order to develop the Asian Dollar Market, were discussed earlier in this chapter. But there are also other incentives on offer for foreign companies who want to participate in the financial sector. They are administered by the MAS – including the OPERATIONAL HEADQUARTERS INCENTIVE, normally handled by the Economic Development Board (EDB), where the application is made by a bank or an insurance company.

To encourage companies to set up their regional bases in Singapore, an approved operational headquarters company that provides management, technical or support services to its affiliates outside Singapore is granted tax exemption on dividends received from foreign affiliates. Other approved offshore income, such as management fees, interest, royalties, and trading in foreign exchange and offshore investments is taxed at a reduced rate of 10 per cent. To qualify for this incentive, the holding company must have a minimum paid-up capital of $500,000 and its role cannot be merely that of a passive holding company that does not provide any services from Singapore.

Dividends paid out of exempt income are also tax free to the shareholder. The incentive is granted for a period of up to 10 years with provision for extensions. Other non-qualifying income of an operational headquarters is taxed at 27 per cent. There are no restrictions placed on other activities of the operational head-quarters company.

The FINANCE AND TREASURY CENTRE SCHEME is aimed at encouraging reputable multinational institutions to centralise their international or regional financing and treasury operations in Singapore. The scheme offers a reduced tax rate of 10 per cent in income derived by a FTC from providing services such as regional and international treasury and fund management, corporate finance and advisory services, economic and investment research and analysis, and credit control and administration.

To attract the establishment of 'pure' insurance captives by large, reputable and financially sound multinational companies, a 10 per cent concessionary tax rate is granted to profits from the offshore business of the captive. Captive insurers are not allowed to operate as commercial insurers. They are allowed only to write risks of their parents and related companies.

Members of SIMEX and ACUs pay a reduced 10 per cent rate on income derived from their gold bullion or gold futures transactions with persons outside Singapore, another SIMEX member or an ICU, and this also applies to financial and energy futures. Corporate members of SIMEX receive this treatment also on profits derived from spot transactions in designated currencies.

A special incentive is offered to encourage financial institutions to develop new and more sophisticated financial services such as financial engineering and financial research and development. A double tax deduction is given for expenses relating to the establishment and development of approved financial activities. The incentive is given on a highly selective basis for a period of five years, which could later be extended.

Finally, to encourage the trading of stock options on securities traded on the SES, no stamp duty is levied on these transactions. There is also no stamp duty on contract notes and instruments of transfers relating to share warrants, rights in shares and units in unit trusts. Contract notes and transfer instruments for transactions in stocks and shares are subject to stamp duty, however.[8]

SIMEX

SIMEX began offering financial futures as additional risk management tools to corporations and individual investors in September 1984. The Exchange is designed along the lines of the Chicago Mercantile Exchange (CME) and incorporates many of the latter's well-tried and tested systems which are aimed at safeguarding the financial integrity of the Exchange and protecting customer interests. These include an open outcry system of trading, daily mark-to-market of positions, gross margining, the common bond system and segregation of customer monies. SIMEX, which comes under the purview of the MAS, is self-regulating with a sound audit, market surveillance and compliance system in place to safeguard the integrity of the market.

SIMEX currently offers the following contracts in Futures and Options – three-month Eurodollar, three-month Euroyen, Nikkei Stock average, Japanese Yen, Deutschmark – and the following Futures – three-month Euromark, British Pound, gold, high sulphur fuel oil, gasoil, MSCI Hong Kong Stock Index, Japanese Government Bond and deferred spot currency. Four contracts – Eurodollar, Deutschmark, Japanese Yen and British Pound futures – are traded on the SIMEX-CME Mutual Offset System, an innovative system straddling two time zones which allows trades initiated in either exchange to be liquidated or transferred to the other, giving market participants such benefits as extended trading hours, more effective management of overnight risk and price movements in different time zones, greater liquidity, reduced transaction costs and single margin structure.

Following an understanding reached with the International Petroleum Exchange (IPE) in London, a mutual offset system for trading in Brent crude oil contracts in Singapore was launched in June 1995. 'Energy derivatives contributed less than three per cent of SIMEX's total volume last year. But there is no reason to believe that this cannot be expanded significantly and rapidly,' a senior official said, adding that this was possible given Singapore's position as the main oil trading centre in Asia outside Japan and the rapidly increasing energy demands of the growing Asian economies.[9]

SIMEX presently has three categories of membership – corporate clearing, corporate non-clearing and individual non-clearing. The corporate clearing members of the Exchange guarantee its obligations. They have to guarantee the transactions which they clear for non-clearing members and for this they receive compensation in the form of a clearing fee. Thus, they have to be institutions of strong financial integrity. The corporate non-clearing category covers those institutions which are likely to have significant trading or broking business but do not shoulder the financial obligations of being a clearing member. The third category of members are individuals or 'Locals' who trade for their own account. As at the end of 1993, there were 38 corporate clearing, 31 corporate non-clearing and 516 individual members.

There is a special category of membership called commercial associate members specifically for reputable companies to trade only in oil futures for their own accounts or for accounts of their related companies. Their trading rights are limited to oil futures contracts, with all trades to be qualified by and cleared through a clearing house member. At the end of 1993, there were 12 such members.

Special trading permits are also issued to individuals. From November 1993, the exchange extended its Trading Permit scheme to include new Deferred Spot Currency contracts. A Trading Permit allows the holder, who pays a fee of $250 a month, to trade on the SIMEX floor in deferred spot currency contracts, as well as energy gold, currency futures and the MSCI Hong Kong Index contracts. These individuals are not required to own or lease a SIMEX seat as the other individual non-clearing members, who may trade in any Simex contract.[10]

FUTURES AND COMMODITY TRADING

While encouraging the development of Singapore as a futures and commodity training centre for the region, the government has shown itself well aware of the potential for abuse, which could damage the city-state's carefully built-up reputation for financial probity. Any loopholes detected are quickly sealed up. Thus, in January 1995, the government tabled a bill to expand the scope of the Futures Trading Act to include the regulation of leveraged foreign exchange trading.

The Futures Trading (Amendment) Bill sought among other things to prohibit futures brokers from trading against a customer without his consent. It would also empower the MAS to approve the listing of any futures contract on an exchange. The amendments proposed included extending the defition of a 'futures broker' to cover people who deal in forex trading on a margin basis (or leveraged terms). Under the Bill, the definition of 'futures brokers' representative' would be modified to include the company's directors, officers and salaried employees. They would all have to be licensed first before being able to perform the functions of a futures broking firm.

Leveraged forex trading means trading in foreign exchange in the over-the-counter market on a margin basis. It includes the provision of any advance, credit facility or loan, or the discretionary management of customer's funds for forex dealing. According to a local report: 'These amendments will bring a group of forex traders in investment houses not previously governed by any set of regulations except for the Companies Act, under the Futures Trading Act. While the Bill gives these traders a grace period in which to be licensed, it also provides for the winding down of businesses which are not granted licences. The grounds for the refusal of an application for a licence is widened to include among other criteria "inability to perform the functions efficiently, honestly, and fairly, inadequate educational and other qualifications and unsatisfactory track record". The MAS will also be allowed to prescibe minimum financial requirements for a futures trading adviser – defined as any corporation which manages funds, whether on a discretionary or non discretionary basis, for futures and forex investments.

'The Bill also seeks to prohibit a number of activities which run against the interests of the client. These include front-running – when a broker trades ahead of a customer for his own account after he has received the order, trading against the customer without his consent, and crossing a customer's trade in-house without exposing his order on the trading floor of the exchange. Besides regulating leveraged forex trading, the Bill also seeks to protect the small investor. It requires the setting up of a "fidelity fund" to compensate "non-accredited investors" (those who are not of a certain minimum net worth) who suffer a loss because of a defalcation committed in the course or in connection with trading a futures contract by a member of the futures exchange.'[11]

Another area of concern was so-called 'forex bucket shops' offering an allegedly fast track to riches for unsophisticated amateur investors. Again in January 1995, the Government announced it was looking at possible legislation to regulate foreign exchange trading for the first time. Bankers and investors were quoted by a local newspaper as urging the authorities to permit only bona fide investment companies to operate, because the lack of control had enabled many unscrupulous brokers to get away with 'get-rich-quick' schemes promising naive investors attractive returns. There is no official figure on how much small-time investors have lost to bucket shops. Apart from complaining to the Monetary Authority of Singapore, these investors have little legal recourse because forex trading is not governed by any legislation at the moment. A Peregrine Futures director Lim Yok said it was important the new legislation on forex trading be as precise as possible. Calling on the authorities to stipulate a minimum margin requirement for forex trading, he said most of the unregulated forex traders currently require their clients to place a margin of only one per cent to start trading. So, with a deposit of US$1,000 they can trade up a US$100,000 contract. 'It's ridiculous to think that with so little money, you can trade this sort of volume.'

'Mr Lim said forex traders should charge their clients a margin of about 2–3 per cent – the same as that levied by SIMEX corporate members for their contracts on currency futures. "This is to ensure that their clients have enough money in their accounts to buffer against the volatilities of forex trading, so that investors do not trade beyond their abilities," he added. Housewife Madam Alice Lee, 45, who lost about $30,000 trading with bucket shops last year, said the introduction of legislation would educate investors. She said dealers and sales staff of such investment houses should obtain professional qualifications before they were allowed to handle client's accounts.'[12]

Commodities trading is another lucrative area for Singapore which it is eager to expand. In 1994, the sector contributed $9 billion to the country's total trade last year, but Ms Tan Seok Lee, the Trade Development Board's Deputy Director (Commodities) insists the actual volume and value of the commodities trade is likely to be much larger as offshore and transshipment trade if not included. The three top commodities traded in 1994 were metals ($2.5 billion), chemicals ($1.2 billion) and timber ($885 million).

To further develop the trading infrastructure, the TDB provided $18 million to develop the Singapore Commodity Exchange (SICOM) into a fully-fledged institution. 'The TDB and SICOM aim to launch one new commodity futures contract per year. Products such as options and indices are being studied. The TDB is encouraging companies to develop "value-added" projects to enhance the quality of commodities traded by Singapore. Some examples are spice and seed sterilization plants. The board also aims to increase the number of "locals" from 36 to 50 by next month to allow more individuals to trade on Sicom. It wants to groom local companies to become world players by playing a more active role in identifying investment projects in resource–rich areas such as Indochina, China, Eastern Europe and Russia.'[13]

SIMEX AND BARINGS

After Chinese New Year, at the beginning of February 1995, SIMEX introduced the Nikkei 300 futures contract based on the movements of stocks that make up the Nikkei (Nihon Keizai

Shimbun) average in Japan.The Nikkei 300 was launched on the Osaka Stock Exchange at the beginning of 1994, designed as a hedging tool for investors worried about volatility within the the Japanese stock market because it covered a much wider basket of stocks than the existing Nikkei 225 contract (of which some 30,000 were traded on SIMEX in 1994). The Nikkei 300 had limited success on the Osaka exchange, being less liquid as its more established rival. In Singapore, however, there was optimism that it would be more successful, with dealers attracted by the fact that SIMEX fees were lower than those in Osaka as well as the fact that contracts would be traded on the open outcry system of pit trading (the Japanese now preferring to do everything via a computer screen). And this seemed justified in the opening days when considerable business was attracted from Japan itself.

No one could have imagined then, however, how quickly the futures option would be at the centre of a global controversy which would lead to the collapse of one of the most venerable banking institutions in Britain. The Barings disaster occurred while this book was being written. It cannot be ignored in any consideration of the Singapore financial system, but with the likelihood of legal proceedings, perhaps dragging on for some time, it would not be wise to comment too much.

Nevertheless, the case did raise issues for a financial centre with world-class aspirations. The demise of Barings as a British banking institution (it having been saved from bankruptcy by the intervention of the Dutch Bank ING) stems from the actions of a Barings trader in Singapore who bought up unprecedented numbers of Nikkei futures contracts in the hope of making a financial killing on the assumption that the Nikkei average would recover from a prolonged slump. Alas, it did not – slumping even more – leaving Barings with huge losses that it simply did not have the capacity to meet. Among the victims were a number of Japanese banks who had extended loans to Barings on the assumption that it was running a fiscally tight and unsinkable ship.

Mention has already been made of how Singapore moved aggressively into the financial derivatives market to boost its international role. SIMEX – the world's fourth largest foreign exchange market – was the first in the region to trade in futures, and was the first overseas to offer Japanese stock index futures.

The exchange believed it had carved out an important and growing niche in the financial markets. Only weeks before the Barings' debacle, SIMEX Chairman Ms Elizabeth Sam had noted that banks, faced with shrinking returns in many traditional activities, were turning increasingly to derivatives. 'Banks will find more and more, that helping their clients to manage their risks is going to be just as rewarding, if not more so, than lending money.'[14]

In November 1994, Finance Minister Richard Hu was congratulating himself in public that Singapore had escaped the welter of losses in 'derivatives' markets suffered by international investors. 'While we encourage a thriving and innovative foreign exchange market, I also stress that it is our position to ensure a high level of integrity and soundness in the market.' Two months later, he returned to the theme in adding to numerous earlier warnings from the authorities that institutions dealing in the high-risk derivatives had to conduct their business according to the highest standards of professionalism and prudence. "In order to avoid unanticipated losses, both financial institutions and their customers must exercise diligence in evaluating and understanding the risks." Institutions had to employ robust internal checks to monitor [the risks]. There must be proper review and audit systems in place.' At the same time, the MAS, in its annual report, had reiterated the need for adequate in-house supervision and risk management of derivatives.[15]

Unfortunately, self-regulation proved inadequate. In fact, experts say that with derivatives trading becoming ever more complex, regulation whether internal or external becomes ever more difficult.

This fact notwithstanding, within days of Barings' collapse commentators were writing: 'Singapore's reputation for tough regulatory control has been called into doubt amid questions why [SIMEX] failed to detect the looming problem at Barings.'[16] To be fair, it does seem that officials of the exchange were aware of unusually heavy trading by the dealer at the centre of the storm and on several occasions made inquiries to Barings, only to be assured that the bank was in a position to meet all its outstanding obligations.

And once the scale of the disaster was clear, the Singapore authorities moved quickly, announcing tighter rules, notably in areas where Barings made itself vulnerable. SIMEX will have to ensure that dealers will not take charge of settlements[17] and that proprietory traders, who deal on the firm's own account, do not handle customer business. Traders will also have to be licensed annually and need character references. One immediate consequence for the colleagues of the dealer under investigation, according to market sources, was that they were blacklisted by the Singapore authorities, thus becoming unemployable by any other company in the republic.[18]

Bankers in Singapore were impressed at the speed at which the authorities moved to contain the crisis with minimum disruption to the markets, serving to restore confidence and even strengthen their reputation for tough single-mindedness. The essence of Singapore's response to any critics demonstrated its ability to maintain the integrity of its markets in dire, adverse circumstances. The atmosphere was certainly far different than that during the 1985 crisis caused by the failure of the Pan-Electric Group to honour forward share contracts. That crisis led to five brokerage firms going under and the stock exchange being closed for three days. This time, everything remained up and running.

Nevertheless, it was a sobering experience for the Singapore authorities. If nothing else, it demonstrated that, despite all its success and its ambitions, SIMEX for the moment is still a backwater compared with the vast international markets such as Tokyo and Osaka. As big as Barings was in Singapore – and it seems that its deals had generated most of the momentum in futures trading there – it could never hope to influence the Japanese market. Trading is likely to be far more subdued for some time.

CHAPTER NOTES

1. Although over 20 foreign currencies are accepted and dealt with by the ACUs, the US dollar predominates.
2. *The Investors Guide to Singapore*. 1994 Edition. Singapore International Chamber of Commerce.
3. *Doing Business in Singapore*. Price Waterhouse 1992.
4. The workings of the CPF are discussed in Chapter Eleven.
5. Information drawn from several official sources, plus 'Financial Institutions in Singapore'. Ernst & Young, Singapore, 1994, pp 15-32.
6. 'SES to allow some foreign brokers to deal directly for clients'. *Straits Times* 10/1/95.
7. *The Investors Guide to Singapore*.
8. *Doing Business in Singapore*.
9. *Straits Times* 10/1/95.
10. *The Investors Guide to Singapore*.

11. *Straits Times* 24/1/95.
12. 'Industry hails plan to rein in bucket shops', *Straits Times* 10/1/95.
13. 'TDB outlines commodities trading strategy', *Straits Times* 26/1/95.
14. 'Pride in integrity takes a blow', by Kieran Cooke and Gordon Cramb. *Financial Times*, 27/2/95.
15. Ibid.
16. 'Prompt treatment for futures shock', by Peter Montagnon and Kieran Cooke. *Financial Times* 3/3/95.
17. One of the biggest problems in the Barings' case allegedly was that the trader who handled all the contracts also dealt with their settlement so that there was no independent supervision of his activities and, in particular, no one to raise the alarm as the losses mounted into the hundreds of millions of pounds.
18. London *Times* 10/3/95.

11 Labour issues

ESTABLISHING LABOUR PEACE

IN THE 1950S and early 1960s, Singapore had a politically active and radical, confrontational labour movement with left-wing leadership. The PAP came to power in 1959 as the moderate wing of a coalition based on grass-roots support of this labour movement, but it quickly achieved dominance by suppressing the left-wing within and without its own ranks. In particular, left-wing unions were deregistered and their leaders and sympathetic politicians arrested and placed under political detention without trial in 1963. The National Trades Union Congress (NTUC), supported by the PAP, became the national umbrella organization of a newly pacified and moderate labour movement.

After Singapore's separation from Malaysia in 1965, the government's strategy of industrial development and employment generation hinged on attracting foreign investment in labour-intensive, export-oriented manufacturing. This, it believed, required low wages and labour discipline, which were ensured by administrative regulations governing the registration and deregistration of unions, compulsory arbitration procedures to limit strikes and new labour laws in 1968.

The Employment Act standardized terms and conditions of employment, defining the maximum and minimum limits of fringe benefits. The Industrial Relations Amendment Act removed such issues as recruitment, retrenchment, dismissal etc., from collective negotiations and defined the framework and procedures for labour negotiations and conflict resolution.

These political and legal moves achieved their aims. They depoliticized the labour movement, established *de facto* government control over unions, transferred bargaining power from workers to employers, and ushered in an era of labour peace that persists to this day. Between 1968 and 1978, man-days lost through strikes and other labour action were negligible. After 1978, there were no industrial stoppages, although these remain legally permissible.

The industrial relations system is based on cooperation rather than confrontation among workers, employers and government. Union membership reached a peak of nearly 250,000 or about a quarter of the workforce in 1979, but since then has fallen despite employment growth. More than 90 per cent of total union membership is affiliated with the NTUC, which has itself become involved in many cooperative ventures, including profit-making consumer enterprises such as supermarkets, taxis, insurance, workers education and welfare programmes including child-care centres.

In 1972, the tripartite National Wages Council (NWC) was formed with representatives from the Government, the NTUC and employers' associations. Its main function so far has been to formulate annual wage guidelines for the economy. Until 1979 wage increases were modest (less than 10 per cent a year in nominal terms) with the exception of a large 20 per cent increase in 1974 to compensate for the previous year's high inflation and declining real wages.

In 1979, as part of the restructuring strategy, the government through the mechanism of the NWC introduced a three-year corrective wage policy to 'restore wages to market levels'. Labour costs increased by an average of 20 per cent in each of the first two years and 28 per cent in the third year. In 1982 and 1983 nominal wage increases returned to the pre-1979 level of seven to eight per cent a year.

As Singapore's economy went into recession in 1985, the NWC recommended wage restraint to help companies regain their cost competitiveness and the unions accepted the freeze. With the economic recovery in 1988, companies were urged to pay as much of the wage increases as possible in the variable component to maintain flexibility. It also emphasized that built-in wage increases should lag behind productivity growth.

NWC recommendations are guidelines only and are intended to serve as a general basis for negotiations between management and labour. 'But the Council has been an important institution in Singapore. It has brought about real wage increases for workers without undermining Singapore's international competitiveness, and it provided a useful forum for the government, employers and unions/workers to understand one another's problems and expectations on wages and related matters. It has provided an opportunity for the three parties to work together with goodwill and good sense, with the aim of seeking acceptable solutions in an area vital to Singapore's well being'[1]

Since self-government in 1959 the union movement has come increasingly under the dominance of the ruling party and government bureaucrats. Government bureaucrats have been involved in the running of the umbrella NTUC through its Labour Research Unit.[2] Until the late 1960s, NTUC leaders were mostly men with trade union experience. In the late 1970s the ruling party began appointing scholars and bureaucrats without union experience to key positions in the NTUC as part of its effort to make the labour movement more responsive to national priorities. In 1978 a non-unionist MP, Lim Chee On, was appointed as its secretary-general and then made a cabinet minister without portfolio two years later. But in 1983, Lim lost his job because, it was said, his leadership style had apparently antagonized grass roots union leaders. Ong Teng Cheong, then the Minister of Communications and also a man without previous union experience then replaced him. In 1995, the organization was headed by Lim Boon Heng, who also has a political background.

In the late 1970s, a group of non-union MPs were appointed as 'advisers' to individual unions and in 1981 it was announced that advisory councils of MPs, government officials and other ruling party members would be formed to exert tighter control over unions at a time when government policy was to break up the large industrial unions like the Singapore Industrial Labour Organization and Pioneer Industries Employees' Union, first into industry-based unions and then into individual house or company unions.[3]

In the 1990s, a primary role for unions is seen as mobilizing workers for increased productivity. Singapore has followed the lead of the Japanese industrial relations system in encouraging company or house unions where workers can identify their interests more closely with those of the employers, who responds relieving the state of some of the burden of providing social and welfare benefits.

Labour unions in Singapore have contributed to the development process by helping to ensure the labour peace necessary to attract private investment, especially foreign investment, and by ensuring a stable, productive workforce. Apart from the NWC, union representatives also sit with government and employers' representatives on policy-making bodies like the EDB and Jurong Town Corporation.

FOREIGN WORKERS

Since the first appearance of full employment in the early 1970s the Singapore economy has increasingly relied on the importation of unskilled and skilled foreign labour to make up the shortfall in the domestic labour supply. Exact numbers are hard to come by, but there are possibly around 450,000 foreign workers in the country. The construction, shipbuilding and ship repair and even the electronics industry would be in deep trouble without them. In addition, many Singaporean women are able to continue their careers after childbirth because of the presence of large numbers of domestic maids, primarily from the Philippines and Sri Lanka.

Anyone who is not a Singapore citizen or a permanent resident who enters Singapore for employment purposes needs permission from the Controller of Immigration under the Immigration Act. Those who earn more than $1,500 a month or hold a recognized qualification need an employment pass or a professional visit pass; others need a work permit. Under the work permit scheme, employers pay a monthly levy per worker which varies from sector to sector: in construction it is $250 for skilled, $400 for skilled; marine: $250 for skilled and $350 for unskilled; manufacturing – $300 for first 35 per cent of company's work force and $450 after that; for a foreign maid the levy is $300.[4]

As a general rule-of-thumb, the higher the skill level the easier it is to get into the country. There is usually little difficulty in obtaining employment passes where the applicants are senior executives of large foreign corporations or well-qualified specialists or persons required to start up new industrial, financial or service undertakings. Investors should talk to the EDB or MAS about their need to employ non-citizens. Employment passes are normally issued for a period of one to three years and may be renewed. Professional visit passes are issued to persons intending to work in Singapore on short assignments (eg., consultants and installation personnel). The spouse and dependent children (under 21) may be issued a dependent or social visit pass for the duration of the pass-holder's employment. They need permission to take paid work.

To control the dependence on imported labour, as well as meeting concerns over the social and economic repercussions of having so many foreign workers in Singapore, there are some restrictions on their employment. Excluding those on an employment pass or a three-year work permit, foreign workers may not exceed 75 per cent of a company's workforce in the construction industry, two-thirds in the marine industry and 45 per cent in manufacturing and 20 per cent in services. The difficulty in obtaining Singaporean workers, or foreign substitutes, is often the trigger, along with rising costs, for a manufacturing operation deciding to move elsewhere – hence the emergence, for a start, of the Growth Triangle.

EMPLOYMENT ACT

Part IV of the Employment Act regulates the conditions of employment applicable to workmen and other employees whose monthly salaries do not exceed $1,500. It fixes the standard working week at 44 hours but allows employers the flexibility to alternate working schedules which involve less than 44 hours in one week and up to 48 hours in the next. The average hours per week over any continuous period of three weeks must not exceed 44, however.

Employees are entitled to one-and-a-half times the hourly rate of pay for overtime work and two days' pay for work on weekly rest days. Rest days may be scheduled on different days in the week. For holiday work, an employee is entitled to a day's pay in addition to the normal pay for that day. Overtime is limited to 72 hours a month unless prior approval has been obtained from the Commissioner for Labour. An employee is entitled to paid sick leave of 14 days a year if no hospitalization is necessary. If hospitalization is required, the number of days inclusive of the out-patient sick leave may be extended to 60 a year.

Employees are entitled to seven days' annual leave for their first year of service and an extra day's leave for every subsequent year of service up to a maximum of 14 days a year. The Act also provides for 11 paid public holidays. Annual vacation for executive personnel is not covered by legislation and varies according to the contract of employment. Local executive personnel are usually given three to four weeks annually and expatriates four to six weeks.

Retrenchment benefits may be payable after three years' service. The provisions in the Employment Act relating to payment of bonuses, annual wage supplement and annual wage increases were amended in 1988 to provide greater flexibility for companies to pay wage increases and variable bonuses that are more closely linked to corporate and individual performance.

The Act distinguishes between termination of contract and dismissal for misconduct, which contravenes the conditions of employment. In the latter case, an employee may refer his case to the Minister for Labour if he feels he has been wrongfully dismissed. If considered justified, the Minister may order reinstatement or direct the employer to pay compensation. Anyone employed under a contract of service must be given one of the following minimum termination notices: 1.One day's notice if employed less than 26 weeks; 2.One week's notice if employed for 26 weeks to under two years; 3.Two weeks' notice if employed for two to under five years; 4.Four weeks' notice if employed for five years or more.[5]

In 1993, 305 companies retrenched 6,487 workers while preliminary figures for 1994 suggested at least 7,743 workers were retrenched by about 230 companies, Labour Minister Lee Boon Yang told parliament while this book was being researched.

Based on feedback, many of those retrenched had no difficulty finding a job, he added. Several hundred employees were retrenched when Dynasty Hotel closed in 1994, for example, '. . . but due to the tight labour market many were snapped up by other hotels'.[7]

Confirming this, NTUC chief Lim Boon Heng said the job losses were more than offset by the fact that at least 46,000 new positions were created in the first nine months of the year alone. He said most of the retrenchments were due to corporate restructuring, which would be good if workers became more skilled and competitive as a result. But one worrying aspect of economic restructuring from a union viewpoint was the widening wage gap

'The wage gap will widen on account of skill and ability. Top talent is in short supply and commands world-class wages. The unskilled are plentiful and wages are pulled down by countries with plenty of cheap labour. But we cannot solve the lower income earners' problems by negotiating for higher wages for them. Raising wages faster than productivity. We raise earning capacity through retraining and upgrading. In this way we do not chase away jobs by paying uncompetitive wages.'[8]

To facilitate part-time employment, the Ministry of Labour issued guidelines in 1990 adopting the principle of pro-rating the benefits as stipulated in the Employment Act and form the basis for employers and their part-time employees to mutually work out terms and conditions of employment that best suit their needs. There are no equal opportunity regulations in Singapore.

The duration of collective agreements should not be less than two years or more than three years. A collective agreement becomes operative upon certification by the Industrial Arbitration Court. On issues relating to wage increase, the Court would take into account recommendations made by NWC. Any dispute arising from the implementation of the NWC guidelines may be referred by either party (employer or employee) to the Industrial Arbitration Court. For other industrial disputes, a joint application must be made to the Court.

If disputes arise of any issue and disagreements cannot be solved by direct negotiations, the dispute can be referred by either party to the Labour Relations Department, Ministry of Labour, for conciliation. Failing settlement, the dispute may be referred to the

Industrial Arbitration Court. In 1992, eight cases were referred to the Court. Once the Court has taken cognisance of a trade dispute, a strike or lock-out action is prohibited under the Trade Disputes Act.

Companies are encouraged to adopt a flexible wage system in which increases are paid in two parts – a moderate built-in increment and a variable component . Such a system enables companies to adjust more quickly to changing economic conditions and provides greater job security to workers. More than 70 per cent of companies in Singapore have implemented the system.[9]

It is customary for the employer to provide medical benefits to all employees. Some union agreements provide transportation for employees where the place of work is distant from their homes. A few companies provide child day care centres.[10]

Factories are regularly inspected by the Department of Industrial Safety. Industrial accidents that result in more than three days' absence from work or one day's hospitalization are required to be reported. The Department of Industrial Health undertakes the prevention and control of occupational diseases and monitors industrial hygiene in the workplace.

Tougher safety measures were introduced in January 1995 when parliament passed the bill. Its original scope was widened to include more workplaces where workers may be exposed to hazards such as warehouses and industrial testing laboratories. Some safety provisions of the bill were also extended to cover small factories with fewer than 10 employees, and where no mechanical power or dangerous substances are used.

'Labour Minister Lee Boon Yang noted that the number of accidents at workplaces dropped from 4,257 to 4,003 [in 1994]. The number of accidents resulting in deaths also dropped from 77 to 53 last year. But he said any death was one death too many and that despite safety measures "totally preventable" accidents were still occurring. The amendments to the bill aimed to minimize these accidents, he said. Among other things, it includes new internationally-recognized ventilation standards to make sure workers do not work in a polluted environment. It also requires chemical processes that generate toxic dust, fumes or other contaminants to be carried out in isolated areas or in closed vessels or systems.

'It exempts machinery or plant that is part of an aircraft or belongs to an aircraft owner from being bound by the safety requirements under the Bill. This is because civil aviation authorities already regulated these parts and it was impracticable to require these parts to be modified to comply with the bill; but workers who make use of structures or fixtures put up for them to gain access to work on these equipment will be protected, Dr Lee said. He added that similar exemptions from safety rules applied to machinery and plant on board ships, and explained these provisions were to prevent ships and aircraft calling at Singapore's port and aircraft from having to make unnecessary modifications.

'The bill also raises the penalties for those who flout its rules to a maximum fine of $300,000 if contravention results in the death of two or more workers and a maximum fine of $50,000 if one worker dies. Maximum jail term for an offence remains at one year. Inspections of premises which reveal unsafe conditions can lead to an instant fine of $1000 to encourage swift rectification.'[12]

SOCIAL SECURITY

The main feature of the statutory social security system is the national pensions scheme, the Central Provident Fund (CPF). This provides for a lump sum at the normal retirement age of 55, comprising past contributions at prescribed rates, by the employee and his employer and interest thereon. A CPF member may withdraw the funds in his account upon leaving Singapore and West Malaysia permanently. All Singaporean employees are required to contribute to the CPF. Foreign employees of Singapore companies previously were also required to make CPF contributions, but for contracts signed since 1 August 1995, this requirement has been abandoned.

Pension contributions may be made to approved private provident funds set up in Singapore, provided the benefits are no less favourable than those of the CPF and the major part of the funds is invested in Singapore government and other approved securities. In practice, it is difficult to obtain approval for new pension funds. Foreign workers who are work-permit holders do not fall within the scheme.

Contributions are withheld from the wage payment and the employer accounts monthly to the CPF Board for both the employer and employees' contributions. These are wholly deductible by the employer for tax purposes and are tax allowable for the employee up to a certain limit.

Although the CPF is basically a pension scheme, employees may use the funds in their account for the purchase of property and approved investments up to prescribed limits and also to pay tertiary education expenses.

Up to the mid-1980s, the two sides contributed 25 per cent each, but in the wake of mid-1980s recession – identified in part as due to Singapore becoming prohibitively expensive for foreign companies in regard to labour costs – the employer's contribution was reduced to 15 per cent, but the employee's levy remained unchanged. From the start of the current decade, the two rates have gradually be nudging closer together again, although at a lower combined figure of 40 per cent .

A CPF member has three separate accounts known as Ordinary, Medisave and Special. The middle one is obvious – a stand-by for unusual medical expenses. The Special is for old age and 'contingencies' and normally cannot be touched until retirement. The Ordinary can be used in ways similar to a bank savings account – money can be withdrawn to buy selected stocks, for example – within limitations. At the age of 55, a member can withdraw his CPF, after setting aside a minimum sum, which was $34,000 in 1994, in a Retirement account.

With effect from 5 January 1995, cash savings in the CPF Retirement and Special accounts received 1.25 percentage points above the CPF normal interest rate, which is based on the average of the month-end 12-month deposit rates of the Big Four local banks over the previous six months, or a minimum rate of 2.5 per cent as guaranteed by the CPF Act. The minimum sum will be gradually increased to $80,000 over the next 10 years, reflecting the need to meet the expected rising standard of living of future retirees as well as ensuring that the elderly will not be a burden on the working population. Members are allowed to deduct contributions from assessable income for income tax purposes. In the 1995 fiscal year, the ceiling for individuals was $13,320 and for self-employed persons $12,290.[13]

INDONESIAN LABOUR RULES

The Indonesian Government is currently hoping to secure better working conditions for its workers by setting minimum wage rates to be used as a guide for employers. It has been proposed that when an investor applies for an investment license, the BKPM (Investment Coordinating Board) should recommend the payment of the minimum wages set by the government before approval is granted for the project.

From April 1,1995, the government raised the daily minimum wages in 19 provinces by between 10 and 35 per cent. The measure did not cover the remaining eight provinces and Batam as the government was still waiting for proposals from these areas. The wage increases are in line with government plans to raise minimum wage levels from the current 97 per cent to 107 of the worker's minimum physical needs. These are set by provincial wage councils based on their calculations of living costs taking into account local prices of goods services. As a result, wages in Riau, excluding Batam, were raised 34 per cent from 3,100 to 4,150 Rupiah a day. Wages on Batam are usually higher than the national average. The Department of Manpower set minimum wages on the island at 100,000 Rupiah per month for unskilled workers and 150,000 Rupiah for skilled workers. But, as noted in Chapter Three, most of the workers in Riau are trans-migrants from the more populated neighbouring provinces of Sumatra and Java and employers are forced to pay above average wages in an effort to retain them beyond the initial contract period.

A government decree announcing the wage changes in early January 1995 stipulated that the new minimum rates should apply for a seven-hour working day or 40 hours per week. It was announced as the only officially sanctioned labour union, SPSI, reported that there were 1,130 strikes in 1994 – three times the level of the previous year – mostly over pay and working conditions as many companies refused to meet the government-set wage levels.[14]

Usually, the hours of work are either eight hours per day from Monday to Friday or seven hours per day during the week and five hours on Saturday. Increasingly, a five-day working week is becoming popular. Employers are expected to grant their employees the following paid leave benefits: annual leave of at least fourteen days per year, sick leave for a period of up to twelve months, maternity leave of three months: and leave of absence to attend to government and recognized religious duties (Indonesia being primarily a Muslim country).

Companies are required to join the ASTEK programme if they employ more than 25 persons or have a payroll in excess of RP1 million per month. ASTEK, a Workers Social Insurance Programme, has three separate components. The employee must contribute a percentage of their wage to only one programme, the retirement benefit fund (one per cent). The employer must contribute a percentage of the employee's wage to all three programmes: workers compensation insurance (0.24-3.6 per cent), retirement benefit fund (1.5 per cent) and life insurance 0.5 per cent).

New employees are normally placed under a three-month trial; the employee may be dismissed if found unsatisfactory within that period. Thereafter, dismissal can prove difficult and may require approval from the Department of Manpower. With the exception of serious offences, it is necessary to give the employee three written warnings prior to termination. The employee is entitled to one or two months wages for each year of service up to four years, plus one to two months wages for each subsequent five years of service, upon termination of employment. Some negotiations over severance pay is not uncommon.[15]

WORKING IN JOHOR

Currently, there is no national minimum wage law covering the manufacturing sector in Johor. Generally, wages are determined by market forces, but in many establishments, wages are negotiated through the collective bargaining process. The Employees' Social Security Act 1969 provides for the administration of the Employment Injury Insurance Scheme and the Invalidity Pensions Scheme by the Social Security Organisation. For employees earning under M$1,000, a minimum contribution of 1% is required. The Workers Compensation Act of 1952 provides for employers who are not required to contribute under the Social Security Act to insure with a locally registered insurance company in respect of any liability which they may incur. This Act covers all manual workers irrespective of their wages and on manual workers whose earnings do not exceed M$500 a month.

The Employees Provident Fund Ordinance 1952 provides for a provident fund for employees and covers all those employed under a contract of service. Both employers and employees are required to make a monthly contribution towards the Fund. The present rate is 11 per cent for employers and nine per cent for employees.

Under the Employment Act, all workers are entitled to at least one complete rest day per week, at least eight paid days of annual leave, at least 60 days of maternity leave and allowance for female employees, at least 14 days of paid sick leave annually, at least one month's notice for termination of service; not more than 48 hours of work per week; and at least ten days wages as lay-off benefits if the employee has worked for the same company for more than one year.

If an employee is absent from work for more than two days without prior leave, or a valid excuse, the employee may, after a fair inquiry has been held, be dismissed on the grounds of misconduct. The Arbitration Tribunal will only interfere in cases involving unfair labour practices. The Employment Act requires that all employees must be given one month's notice before termination of their services. If the employee has worked for the same employer for more than a year, this employee is entitled to at least 10 day's wages as lay off benefits.[16]

CHAPTER NOTES

1. Trade, Employment and Industrialisation in Singapore. Lim, L. and Rang, E.F. International Labour Organization, 1986, Printworld Services Pte. Ltd., Singapore, 1987, pp11-12.
2. There has also been movement in the other direction – for example, C.V.Devan Nair, an early secretary-general of the NTUC, who became the country's president in the 1980s, and the current president Ong Teng Cheong.

3. Trade, Employment and Industrialization in Singapore. p72.
4. *The Investor's Guide to Singapore*. 1994 Edition. Singapore International Chamber of Commerce.
5. Ibid.
6. *Doing Business in Singapore*. Price Waterhouse.
7. *Straits Times* 24/1/95.
8. Commentary written in NTUC Weekly News 30/1/95.
9. *Investors Guide to Singapore*.
10. *Doing Business in Singapore*. Price Waterhouse.
11. 'Safety and health rules for workers tightened.' *Straits Times* 24/1/95.
12. Ibid.
13. *Straits Times* January 5,1995.
14. *Strategic Business Opportunities in the Growth Triangle*, by Goh.M, et al. Longman Singapore, 1992.
15. Ibid.
16. Ibid.

12 The Cultural Dimension

KEY POINTS

- Singaporeans – a goal-driven people
- *Kiasu*, or the fear of losing
- Singaporean humour – or lack of
- Co-existence of high-tech and old traditions
- Views of Westerners
- Changing, contradictory social values
- The importance of face
- Practical tips for doing business with Singaporeans

THE PEOPLE

SINGAPORE, not unlike the United States, has been a melting pot for different ethnic groups, and has put a great deal of emphasis into creating a uniquely Singaporean culture. At the same time, each of the main racial groups has retained a specific identity, with its own traditions and languages carried over from the homelands of the original arrivals. The Malays are the only ones who can claim to have always called Singapore home, being the indigenous people of the island. But the bulk of the present community of Chinese, Indians, Eurasians, Sinhalese, Europeans, as well the Malays, have prospered largely because of the imperative that existed in the nineteenth century and remains as true today: work, thrift and survival (although the definitions may have changed to some extent). More than one writer has commented that Singaporeans live with the view that earning a living, and a good one at that, is what life is all about. Some critics refer to this as an obsessive preoccupation with social climbing; but to most Singaporeans, this means mobility as a measure of success.

241

This attitude is in no small measure helped along by frequent and foreboding reminders from the government that Singapore is a tiny nation whose survival depends on the efforts of every citizen; that, in a nation of three million, every economic head counts and there can be no shirkers; that, in a neighbourhood of giants, everyone has to remain economically vigilant 24 hours a day, 365 days a year; that lack of land and natural resources means dependence on the goodwill of other countries for national survival.

Like it or not, consciously or not, most Singaporeans appear to have internalized this message, with the result that they are noticeably goal-driven, willing to work relentlessly to achieve their aims. Unfortunately, given human nature the world over, there is a tendency sometimes for this to be carried to excessive lengths. Singaporeans can be terribly afraid of failure, which can make them ultra-cautious in everything they do. For many, planning a party or a vacation can take the same kind of effort as that going into planning a business venture. The hunger for social acceptance and the need for status that haunted the earliest 'Singaporeans', coming as they had from economic and political hardship, still exists today – although, again the definitions have changed.

The word most often used to describe Singaporeans is *kiasu*, a Chinese Hokkien dialect word that roughly translates into 'being afraid to lose' but in recent years has taken on a far broader local connotation of 'always wanting to be number one' and 'always wanting bargains'. Kiasu-ism is a topic for discussion and laughter in local literature, television and theatre, in comedy clubs and cartoon strips, and even in schools. Much has been said about this quality which manifests itself in everything from the oft-mourned lack of local entrepreneurial spirit, to the much-publicized tendency of Singaporeans at buffets to stack their plates with the most expensive food on offer, far beyond their ability to truly enjoy, so that they can obtain 'value for money'.

The fact that Singaporeans can laugh at this seemingly unattractive side of their character is evidenced by the success of Johnny Lau's comic books published since 1989 featuring Mr Kiasu – a wide-eyed, short-haired, bespectacled character with a permanent toothy grin, his girlfriend Ai Swee and other locally recognizable characters. The titles, drawing on the Singapore slang known as Singlish, include 'Everything Also Must Grab' and

'Everything Also Want Extra', which gives the flavour of what *kiasu* is all about. The international market is now to face Kiasu-ism with a whole range of spin-off products from the cartoon character initially aimed at the region, but with Japan, the United States and Europe to be targeted later.

But set against this, and preventing it from becoming a sweeping generalization about all people, is the pleasing contradiction to be experienced on a daily basis in Singapore: stop by the scene of a traffic accident, eavesdrop on fans at a soccer match, or listen in to a bird-singing contest, and you will find an unmatched eagerness to gamble – on the license-plate number of the crashed vehicle, on the team that is going to score (although this may now be something of a no-go area since a soccer gambling scandal erupted in Malaysia), and the sweetest feathered crooner.

On the subject of paradoxes, foreigners often see Singaporeans, and Singapore in general, as being almost humourless in the drive for symmetry, control and results that can be quantified. Combined with the fact that Singaporeans in general appear to be less than immediately and openly friendly, and noticeably reserved about showing emotion and sharing opinions, and the impression is sealed. But to counter this is the rising popularity of comedy in writing, on stage and television, that pokes fun at and even celebrates peculiarly Singaporean attitudes and behaviour. It may come as a surprise to learn that the most watched television show at the time of writing is a local spinoff of Britain's *Candid Camera* and *Beadle's About* shows, which highlights the absurd and the funny. Add to that, another increasingly popular television show that invites Singaporeans to take part in look-alike-sound-alike contests; here, to the amazement and delight of local audiences, are to be found senior army men, bank managers and teachers dressing up and thoroughly enjoying themselves doing passable, and less-than-passable, imitations of Elvis Presley, Tom Jones and the Bee Gees. What does all this add up to? Yet another paradox about the so-called typical Singaporean behaviour.

The last seeming 'contradiction' that may be worth noting is one in which a serious belief in astrology and other forms of soothsaying inherited from the 'old country' sits comfortably alongside the likes of systems science and biotechnology. In fact, a number of politically and socially prominent Singaporeans are known, but no less respected, for heeding the forecasts of traditional Chinese and Indian astrologers. There is a healthy respect for the inexplicables, such as numerology and *fengshui* or geomancy. And foreign companies and foreigners operating in Singapore over the years have come to show the same respect. Whether it is genuine understanding or only a gesture, American and European MNCs have been known to consult a geomancer on just where the new office should be sited, at which side should the entrance door be located, and where the chief executive's desk should face in order to reap the full benefits of the right convergence of elemental forces.

And yet, Singaporeans can be almost unbearably 'quantitative', with a keenness to judge merit according to tangible and countable results.

DEALING WITH WESTERNERS

Foreign residents at first are often taken aback by the high degree of religious and racial tolerance that exists in multi-ethnic Singapore. This has been set in stone, almost by legislation, as well as by the fact that Singapore was set up to make money for everyone. As long as lifestyles continue to improve, then a comfortable level of tolerance is likely to prevail, although not everyone will agree with this.

But if there is an easy familiarity between Singaporeans, who can identify each other without words in the corner of a remote London restaurant, for example, the same familiarity does not yet exist with foreigners, especially those of Caucasian origin who are still seen as separate entities, and something of a curiosity. Although is is slowly changing as more expatriates come to Singapore on 'local terms', living among the masses in government housing, the old stereotype is difficult to shake off: namely, the foreigner who comes in on a fat salary, insists on living in the elite and highly expensive postal District 10, and enjoys the ministrations of a chauffeur and a well-trained maid or two.

The simple difference in appearance, and media portrayal of the West, have also helped keep foreigners at a psychological distance from Singaporeans, even though they may live next door and buy their vegetables from the same 'wet market'. More often than not, the West is portrayed via the Western media itself as being ridden with violent crime, unemployment, drugs, random shootings, and individualism. By the same token, Singapore to many Westerners stands for such things as caning for even 'petty' crimes (the 1994 decision to apply three strokes of the cane to the backside of American teenager Michael Fay, a convicted vandal, being the most frequently-cited case), the banning of chewing gum, hefty fines for littering and not flushing public toilets, the lack of press freedom and the controls over the free flow of information (already discussed in Chapter Eight).

But, as is true for a lot of people, Singaporeans feel that it is o.k. to laugh at themselves, but it is not necessarily acceptable for a foreigner to do the same, unless you have proven by word, deed or gesture that your laughter is genuine and not simply the laughter of the patronizing. Similarly, Singaporeans are fond of complaining about their lot, but their patriotic passions are aroused when an outsider does the same. Which is certainly not to say that Singaporeans generally are breast-beating patriots; they are not. It tends to be a quiet, undemonstrative kind of patriotism, but no less deep for that. The same goes for personal relationships. The feelings may be there, but you are unlikely to see any obvious display of it in public.

CHANGING SOCIETY

Traditional society is changing as more outside influences intrude. Singaporeans are among the most well-travelled people in the world, with no less than 75 per cent of the population falling into the middle-class category (earning them a label as leading purveyors of a consumerist culture in which money talks and money rules). Where before, the family might consider it a major expedition to go down town to see the latest movie, they now tend to fly off with boring regularity to Perth, Sydney or Phuket for a weekend of golf or a shopping expedition.

'Traditional' Singapore society is becoming more and more Westernized – a source of concern to some elder statesmen who like to promote 'Asian core values' – more liberal in attitude, and less rooted in the ideas of antiquity. This is creating new tensions. The present young generation is straddling both worlds, sometimes showing behaviour that is extremely liberal and at other times extremely conservative. This is seen, for example, in a willingness of many young Singaporeans to study overseas, coupled with an unwillingness to marry out of their race; or the pursuit of higher and higher levels of education to challenge existing intellectual frontiers, along with a willingness to enter into a traditional arranged marriage.

Time and technology create tensions. Singaporeans are moving away from their immigrant beginnings; and further away, too, from the hardships suffered by their ancestors first under British colonial rule, then Japanese occupation, and then the sudden shock of independence. This generates concern that the early ethics of hard work, thrift and filial piety will be eroded. A generation that has not had to struggle, it is felt, will have little incentive to work hard except for personal gain. And a generation that is being raised in a world of cashless payments and credit cards will have little incentive for thrift. Filial piety, too, goes missing in a situation where individualism is increasingly important.

A psychologist who works in a leading executive recruitment firm laments that these days – as opposed to as recently as five years ago – new entrants into the job market want to know right off what their prospects are, what their title is going to be, and what the potential employer can do for them. 'It seems that they interview us, instead of the other way round. There is scant premium placed on the working environment, loyalty, camaraderie. These new entrants want to make it and make it fast. They don't want to be like their fathers, who may have been content to work for 10 to 15 years before being made a manager.'

Technology, in such forms as Internet, causes some concern. Seen as a necessary tool in today's imperative to manage information, it is also giving to previously-sheltered Singaporeans access to sources and kinds of information they would never otherwise have enjoyed. There is some fear that this access will change, for the worse, the tastes and attitudes of the young and impressionable who have to form the backbone in carrying Singapore safely into the twenty-first century.

DOING BUSINESS WITH SINGAPOREANS

• **Kiasu-ism**. 'You have to talk about this, especially in business,' said a local management consultant when asked about his experiences in dealing with foreigners. 'And, of course, we are *kiasu* – that's why Singapore has been so successful.' But there is a downside to this, in that 'Singaporeans are totally afraid of failure, of making a mistake or failing in some way that could be career-damaging. And this is directly at odds with Westerners, who, in general, believe it's acceptable to take ri sks and make mistakes from which valuable lessons can be learnt for the future. This can be something of a problem for the Western employer of Singaporeans to deal with.'

• **Face**. This is important in any Asian society. The word is a short form for showing respect, not placing your partner in a humiliating or embarrassing way. A well-travelled Chinese Singaporean businessman observes: 'Face is very important in Asia, and the foreigner must never forget that. It is not a difficult concept; it's just difficult for people coming from a very liberal, let's be-honest and let's-thrash-it-out culture to adopt this style. But he must or risk failure.' The philosophy also applies at all levels – superiors, equals and subordinates. 'We are not confrontational people by nature, so we appreciate it if problems or reprimands are carried out minus an audience,' said the management consultant quoted above.

Foreigners can also have difficulties dealing with a further dimension of face. To the Asian, it is 'giving face', but to the outsider it is being two-faced. In the words of one foreign journalist who has seen it at work: 'It's hypocritical. You feel one thing, but show another. You are angry, but you show a neutral face. To me this is dishonest.' Singaporeans would argue that, no, not dishonest, merely a cultural difference to be understood and coped with.

• **Business cards and titles**. The designation on your business card is very important and carries a great deal of weigfht, as in Japan. 'To us, that job title is an indication of the person's status and we're very conscious of this,' said a local businessman.

• **The little gestures**. This same businessman describes himself as 'very traditional and still somewhat suspicious of foreigners'. This latter aspect is still very strong, the management consultant agrees: 'The average Chinese businessman, who has only worked for himself, as opposed to an MNC, still feels this way. An Asian non-Singaporean has a better chance of success with this man, than a Westerner.' Given this attitude, it is often important for the foreigner to make some little gestures that show an effort to understand and fit – the sprinkling of Mandarin or Malay words in the conversation, the understanding of face. But a word of caution is required. As one local businesswoman observed: 'I appreciate these gestures, but not when I sense the foreigner is doing it strictly to "score points" with me, or because he thinks some of our speech patterns are laughable. If this is the motivation, I'd rather he didn't make the effort.'

• **Non-verbal cues**. In a meeting with a third party – important now that Singapore is trying to play the role of facilitator between two different business partners – a foreign may hear the word 'yes' and thinks the deal is set. The Singaporean middleman notes the lack of enthusiasm in the third party's eyes, the non-commital tone of voice and sees a slim chance of the deal coming through. 'It's completely intangible, non-verbal and almost impossible to pick up unless you're from a similar culture. This goes beyond language,' explains the management consultant. Furthermore, the styles of doing business in many parts of Asia are such that, for instance, it can take six months to get a telephone in country A if you go through the proper channels, but with the right 'incentive' to the right person the job can be done in three weeks. 'I know this from the way the guy is speaking and the little hints he's dropping, like the irrelevant mention of his four children. We may not practise this in Singapore, but I connect with him because we know we understand each other. The foreigner, unfortunately, does not usually realize what's happening. Many foreign companies are not willing to do business in this way, and that's their prerogative. But they must at least be aware of this subtle level of communication that takes place so often.' The consultant adds that it can be very demoralizing and disappointing for the foreigner when he does not get the deal or the job done because of factors beyond his control, or that he is unaware of.

• **First impressions**. Because the Singapore system is so result-oriented, there is a premium placed on facts and figures. Little priority is given to flashy presentations and the 'gift of the gab'. According to a public relations executive: 'We go for substance, Westerners go for first impressions. If you can talk, they think you're great.' What this means is that Western executives need to get used to local colleagues who may not be exactly Toastmasters material, but who manage to deliver the goods anyway. Those coming from cultures in which everyone has an opinion have often voiced frustration at not being able to interact in this manner with most Singaporeans.

• **Acceptance/passivity**. Another source of frustration for those who hail from relatively liberal climes is the fact that Singaporeans in general appear to passively accept certain situations which would be deemed unacceptable elsewhere. We are talking here, of course, of the list of restrictions that apply to those living in Singapore. But increasingly, as business people travel further and further afield, it is being recognized that to sustain the kind of order and safety that has made Singapore such a choice place in which to do business, there must be some controls. As one British businessman who has operated out of Singapore for more than a decade put it: 'You can't have your cake and eat it. Some foreigners may not be too comfortable or happy with the way some things are done here, but at the end of the day, we're here to do business and it works just fine.' Author Michael Chiang sums this up as follows: 'You call it clean, they call it sterile. You call it safe, they call it boring. You call it order, they call it repression.'[2]

It might be added that a number of management consultants and executive search firms report than an increasing number of expatriates who live here for three to five years ask to stay on after their initial term is over. One consultant observed that apart from the fact thaty the business environment is good and things work, there is also a considerable allure to the 'Club Med' lifestyle that is available in Singapore which is attractive not only to the executive but also to the rest of the family.

The rules for success in Singapore are not difficult to learn and a bonus is that they mostly apply to the rest of Asia. The best advice is: feel your way, keep an open mind, ensure your attitudes and views are always presented in the appropriate context, and be willing to be transparent in all your dealings. On a personel level, be willing to probe below the surface and you will find a wide range of human personality and behaviour that will enrich your life considerably.

CHAPTER NOTES

1. For example, *Living in Singapore: An expatriates Guide*. American Association of Singapore 1993.
2. *Singapore: Island City State*. by Michael Chiang. Times Editions 1990.

13 Summing Up

KEY POINTS

- Constant battle against rising costs
- Concerns about 'over-dependence' on key products, key markets
- Drawbacks of regionalization
- Maintaining social cohesion
- Dangers of the meritocratic approach
- Keeping up with rising public expectations
- Fear of losing
- Government's need to maintain a tight grip

RISING COSTS AND OTHER PROBLEMS

THE FAST-TRACK Singapore economy is today coping with the problems of its own success. Given the rapid rise in the foreign exchange reserves to around US$60 billion, it is not surprising that the Singapore dollar has become one of the world's strongest currencies – rising 10 per cent against its US counterpart in 1994 and five per cent against a basket of other currencies. This is both a source of pride and a source of concern.

So far, the export performance has shown no sign of being damaged, but other sectors, such as tourism and retail, are likely to suffer if the Singapore dollar strengthens further, as it may very well do given the positive mid-term economic indicators showing up on the computer screens of the government's economic planners. Strenuous efforts are being made to try and keep the exchange rate on a level where it will not have an adverse affect on economic performance. But, given the fact that Singapore operates an open system, it is hard to stop large amounts of foreign funds parking in the local currency.

The exchange rate has been the traditional tool of economic management, used to curb inflation and costs. But coping with liquidity in the system has proved difficult. 'Asset inflation' has become a big problem. Property prices went up about 40 per cent in 1994, for example (although, as will be discussed shortly, they then went into something of a decline at the beginning of 1995). To control the number of cars on the roads, the government operates a quota system – with documents obtained through monthly bidding. A Certificate Of Entitlement, the vital official piece of paper that allows one to purchase a car, has driven the price of even the cheapest new model to more than $90,000, placing it out of reach of an increasing number of Singaporeans – which may well be the government's objective, but which generates growing resentment (see below).

Reacting to this, the MAS, in February 1995, introduced measures which included restrictions on unsecured credit to those with annual incomes of less than $30,000. Officials said the aim was to stop Singaporeans borrowing beyond their means. According to one senior financial official, retail banks were being 'too lax in their loans', and the concern was that Singaporeans were shedding their thrifty habits and borrowing beyond their means. Worse, they were doing so to fund consumption rather than fixed investments. Bank lending to individuals, now the biggest single market, shot up in 1994, while loans to the construction sector were flat and funds provided to manufacturing just nudged higher. All very good reasons for the tightening of the screws – except that the perception among lower income groups is likely to be that, once again, they are being penalized in the name of the general economic well-being of Singapore.

Deputy Prime Minister Lee Hsieng Loong, in his February 1995 speech at Nanyang Technological University referred to in the opening chapter, noted that government surveys showed more than half the people polled felt their lives had not become better over the past five years, which he found 'amazing'. But there are those in Singapore who are not surprised, arguing that it is becoming a more unequal society with an increasingly wealthy elite presiding over a lower class than finds the cost of everyday life ever harder to bear, especially as the government eschews welfarism as a disease that saps initiative and threatens economic decline.

On the business front, however, the concerns are more with the rising costs of production and low profit margins, due to the strong dollar, which could erode the ability of Singapore companies to meet the increased competition coming from other rising Asian economies such as Malaysia and Taiwan. An annual survey[1] by Singapore Manufacturers Association of its members found that production costs rose 7.66 per cent in 1993 and slightly more in 1994. Yearly wage increases are running at over nine per cent on average. But companies have not only had to cut their costs, but also been forced to reduce their prices to stay competitive.

A report from the National Trade Unions Congress in June 1995 warned that wage rates for both bosses and workers were rising so fast that the country's competitiveness would inevitably be eroded with devastating consequences. Increased productivity managed to offset this in 1993 and 1994, but there is no guarantee that this can continue to be the case year in, year out. The NTUC was particularly concerned at the rises given to management personnel – in line with the government's emphasis on attracting top quality people with high moral standards (i.e. being paid so well they will not be tempted into corruption). Management gross salaries, it pointed out, were 11 per cent higher than those in Paris, 50 per cent above London rates and 66 per cent above those prevailing in Sydney.

Urging restraint at the top, it said: 'If our total wage packets rise to the same level as in the West, it will make us less attractive as a local base for multinational companies to invest and push up our unemployment rate.' Singapore used to be top choice for Japanese companies relocating to Southeast Asia, for example, because of the strength of the Yen. 'But of late, some Japanese companies have decided to skip Singapore for other newly-emerging economies where wage costs are lower. If these countries have workers with required skills, they are preferred.' It said that near full employment, and thus a tight labour market, had contributed to the present situation. 'But will our labour market remain tight as more industries are relocated?'

This, in fact, highlights one of the problems of the regionalization drive much discussed in this book. As more and more employees are being posted abroad, some analysts suggest, companies are being forced into attractive pay increases in order to hire and retain qualified staff. Many of these concerns are equally felt by foreign as well as domestic companies. A survey of American businessmen by the Economic/Political Section of the US Embassy, for example, observed that: 'Contributing to Singapore's growing reputation as an expensive business environment are the high cost of land and rentals, and the rising cost of living for expatriates.'[2]

The survey also found a chronic labour shortage at many skill and educational levels. 'Numerous American companies cite the difficulty in finding and keeping clerical, systems, technical and skilled personnel. There is also the phenomenon of "job hopping". Reflecting the tight labour market, they feel that some Singaporean workers harbour unrealistic expectations about promotions and pay/benefits increases. Several US firms surveyed by the embassy also feel a little squeezed by the aurhority's tight control on the importation of foreign labour.'

So, can Singapore keep its position as one of the world's fastest-growing economies? Sceptics point to recent signs to the contrary, such as a fall in productivity. Chronic labour shortages are bound to continue to force up wages, which will encourage some firms to move out. The SMA survey already mentioned found that, faced with a shortage of skilled workers, 65.9 per cent of the respondents said they would try and stick it out in Singapore while trying to further raise labour productivity through skills upgrading and training, while almost half would automate their operations and only slightly less shift into higher value-added products. But around 40 per cent planned to relocate part of their business in neighbouring countries (although only a handful thought it was necessary to move their entire operation abroad). These ranged from a low of 22.6 per cent for the pharmaceutical and chemical sector to 62.5 per cent for textiles and garments. Total relocation was highest (10.5 per cent) for food and beverages.

As discussed in Chapter Four, this is certainly in line with government policy to shift the labour-intensive operations offshore, while concentrating on capital-intensive, high-tech at home. But despite the millions invested in R & D and other facilities, Singapore still does not have a broad ability to create its own technology base. One analyst has suggested that this is due to the fact that, while its people are skilled, they have had 'the creativity and enterprise squeezed out by an over-protective, over-

intrusive government'.[3] Singapore, therefore, will remain dependent on MNCs for some time to come and be prey to adverse
developments in the region and in the global business
environment.

PARALLELS WITH 1985

Returning to Singapore in 1995, one is reminded of the situtation
that existed in the mid-1980s when a long period of rapid
economic expansion pushed up business operational as well as
individual living costs, and ended in a unprecedented recession.
Graham Hayward, Executive Director of the Singapore International Chamber of Commerce,[4] agrees that there are some
similarities between 1995 and 1985, although these should not be
overstressed. 'In the 1984-85 scenario, costs went up so high, so
fast that we were definitely non-competitive. There was also an
economic downturn in the United States and that really hit us.
Nobody realized it because we had had ten boom years and
nobody realized that anything could go wrong; so, we were too
slow in spotting it.

'It's like a heavy farm cart. If the brakes fail and the cart starts
rolling down the hill, you realize pretty quickly that the brakes
have failed but it takes some time to stop it rolling down the hill.
That's exactly what happened in 1984-5. It takes time to reverse
the slide. I'm sure the government is monitoring it carefully, but
there is still a time-lag between the statistics coming out and the
trend being spotted. I think the job cuts announced by companies
like AT&T, Thomson, Mitsubishi [see Chapter Seven] at the end of
1994 should be a warning signal that costs are beginning to bite
again and they must look at them very carefully on a regular basis.
For a company to move offshore it doesn't happen at a committee
meeting on Friday morning. It's a long, considered process over
one or two years, with the head office involved, so I'm sure that
redundancies announced in November and December were
probably decided a year or more ago, because they had to build
the facility in the other country.'

According to Hayward, the government's reaction was
outstanding, once the trend was spotted back in 1985. The
employer's CPF contribution rate as well as property tax were
slashed, and a great deal of buying power was pumped into the

economy in a short time to ensure the recession was a short one and Singapore came bouncing back quickly.

In a speech to the Singapore Rotary Club at the beginning of January 1995, the SICC head voiced some of his concerns about what he perceived as 'extreme fragility' in a number of key areas, with parallels to the situation that existed 10 years earlier. He predicted, for example, a decline of 15 per cent in property prices and was vindicated 10 days later when the government held its first property auction of the year and the prices were, indeed, 15 per cent off the previous year's figures.

'Why I believe it's fragile is that 90 per cent of the stock of housing is built by and, in theory, owned by government. Only 10 to 12 per cent is in the free market – the landed property and private condominiums etc. Any increase of supply in that area is geometric rather than arithmetic, because it is such a small number. The supply coming on stream in the last two years is three times annual uptake. We know people are upgrading from government to private flats, but even so it's a lot of units to take up. Most of the people buying these are doing so on loans, and they are only able to pay back the loans because, in many instances, they are investment properties through having a tenant. The expatriate population is not expanding fast enough to fill all those new flats.

'Bank loans in the past two years increased tremendously to private people. And that was for three things: COEs for cars, share transactions and property. What is happening now is that all three are collapsing together. The COE values have dropped so the car you paid $250,000 for last year may only be worth $200,000 this year, because its COE value dropped. Secondly, the share market has dropped quite significantly and could go further; thirdly, property is already starting to dip and we have seen rental levels for expatriates and richer Singaporeans already fall and that usually prefaces a capital decline. We are in rather a delicate situation. If there was a slowdown in the economy and a sharp jump in interest rates, we could see a major collapse quite quickly in several key elements in the economy – more for individual rather than corporate. There are people who borrowed to play the stock market and lost heavily. There are people who bought a second house who now cannot afford to pay back the loans for various reasons and cannot get rid of it at the price they bought it at. The key factor is whether you can get a tenant. What happened in 1985 was that the property market collapsed by 50 per cent because a lot of people could not maintain payments. I would say we could have a smaller recession this time around in the economy, but that could produce a bigger collapse in the property market because I think it is very highly geared.'

Another key factor in the 1985 recession was the decline of the American economy on which Singapore was heavily dependent – about 45 per cent of its exports went to the US, for example. This aspect has been partly corrected by a greater divergence in export markets. The United States now takes only about 21 per cent of the island's exports. Yet, Singapore remains vulnerable because it is still dependent on a few vital elements, including a heavy concentration on the highly volatile electronics industry. Once again, the United States is the key. It has invested some $30 billion. American companies employ 91,000 out of a total workforce of 1.4 million and pay $1.3 billion per year in wages. Trade with the US is worth $27 billion, of which Singapore's exports accounted for a lopsided $22 billion.

To sum up: the island relies heavily on export-led growth; its domestic companies, which are mainly small infrastructural support-oriented concerns, rely heavily on MNC customers, particularly in the dominant electronics industry, where investment continues to grow in 'top-end' manufacturing. Many of these giants are American. Thus, Singapore is clearly still very dependent on the financial health of the US, as it was in 1985.

REGIONALIZATION CONCERNS

To offset its domestic disadvantages, such as labour and land shortages and the high costs for both thus generated, the government has tried to create a Greater Singapore encompassing first adjacent territory in Indonesia and Malaysia through the Growth Triangle concept, and then further afield – China, India, Myanmar, Vietnam – through the ambitious regionalization programme.

Many companies, both foreign and Singaporean, have taken advantage of the Growth Triangle arrangement to move some or all of their manufacturing operations to areas where land is freely available and cheap, and there is abundant cheap labour. But, there have been some problems. The Batam and Bintan projects suffer to some extent because they are artificial – in that the labour has to be imported from outside, along with virtually everything else for the support of the growing po pulation for the time being. A transient population creates problems for entrepreneurs trying to plan their future based on a stable labour force.

Singapore has also sold the idea abroad based on the one-stop shopping idea of handling all the administrative details of any investment, particularly in Indonesia. This is based on a less than subtle message that: we'll take care of everything because you know we are efficient and trustworthy. This is not necessarily the sort of message that the Indonesians or Malaysians would like to see put across. Thus, investors moving into Batam or Bintan assuming that everything had been settled in Singapore are quickly brought down to earth by local officials who rightly point out that 'you're on Indonesian territory now, so you'll deal with us and do it our way'. This has led to the occasional complaint from foreign businessmen of being 'abandoned' by the Singapore authorities when problems occur.

At the same time, the continued wellbeing of the Growth Triangle cannot just depend on Singaporean enthusiasm for it, but requires an equal commitment from Jakarta and Kuala Lumpur. This cannot be taken for granted, and certainly not if there is any change of government in either capital.

The same 'trust us, we're Singaporean' salesmanship is now going into the regionalization programme, which is the subject of great enthusiasm within the Economic Development Board and the other statutory bodies and ministries involved. It is too early to say if this will work, although the preliminary indications look good. Nevertheless, the concept is not without its difficulties.

Despite all financial incentives to Singaporean companies to move overseas, there is still evidence of some reluctance to do so. One key aspect, identified by government officials, is that life has become so comfortable – 'cushy' – at home, that Singaporeans are loathe to move abroad to take risk or to live in a less comfortable environment. One could argue that this is inevitable, particularly for a generation that has been raised on total government paternalism, with everything laid on the plate for the man or woman willing to conform. Being a pioneer in those circumstances requires a difficult psychological transition. Equally, for the government, there is the concern that Singaporeans who do heed the call to strike out into fresh fields abroad might return some day contaminated with ideas that are not too welcome at home.

Graham Hayward of the SICC notes another downside of the regionalization policy: 'Our members are becoming very concerned about the difficulty they are experiencing in reaching senior government officials and Singapore managers, who are travelling constantly in connection with regional investment projects. While there has been much talk of a "hollowing out of manufacturing" through these policies, the relocation of some of Singapore's top managers overseas also contributed to a "hollowing out" of Singapore management.'[5]

SOCIAL ISSUES

Singapore has taken great pains to provide the right environment for the foreign investment it feels it needs for survival. The infrastructure is certainly there – good port, good telecommunications, good transportation links with surrounding countries, sound financial base etc. But it is the social infrastructure that now concerns Singapore's leaders more than anything else. Society is changing. A new generation has grown up or is growing up with no knowledge of anything else but national success and growing affluence. The government's social engineers worry whether this new generation can be honed to the task of keeping the country ahead of the pack; whether, in fact, it will prove to be 'lean and mean' enough to face the inevitable difficulties ahead.

Lee Hsien Loong considered this issue in the February 1995 speech from which much has been quoted already. He took up the two pivotal concerns – social cohesion and rising social expectations. Singapore, in many respects, takes Japan as its role model and its yardstick. Mr Lee observed that, being an homogenous nation, Japan had been able to achieve great social cohesion which had been crucial in times of difficulty. He went on:

'Unlike Japan, Singapore is not a country of one race and one language. But social cohesion is as important to us as to the Japanese. In a crisis, will we pull together like the Japanese? Singapore runs a meritocratic system, which gives individuals every incentive to do well for themselves and to compete against each other. This is the right way to release the drive and energy of our people and the fair way to distribute the fruits of Singapore's success. The more you contribute, the more you succeed, the more you benefit.

'But at the same time, this element of individual competition must be balanced by a strong sense of social cohesion. When education and advancement is by merit, successful parents will tend to have successful children. Over time, this trend will cause our society to become more stratified. This happens in all societies as they mature, unless they undergo a major upheaval or a revolution. We cannot prevent this from happening to us, but we must slow down the process wherever possible. We must emphasize and broaden the common ground between the well-off and the less well-off. Singapore is a different society from Hong Kong [where] it is socially acceptable to display one's wealth, in fine clothes, fine dining, Rolls Royce. But if affluent Singaporeans flaunt their success and deliberately distinguish themselves from others less well-off by the way they dress, the lifestyle they lead, the overseas holidays they take, this will lead to unhappiness and resentment.'[6]

One concern, and again one that has been created by Singapore's great economic success, is that of the rising expectations of its people. Because everything has gone so well for so long – with only that slight blip in the mid-1980s – young Singaporeans want, and expect, instant gratification of their dreams. No-one, it seems, is prepared to wait and work hard for a steady improvement in lifestyle and living conditions. It has got to a BMW or Mercedes parked outside on graduation or the system has failed.

As Lee Hsien Loong observed: 'We have created a broad middle class, and equipped a majority of Singaporeans with the skills and training to pursue rewarding professional careers. Unfortunately, graduates and diploma-holders tend to compare themselves with graduates and diploma-holders who are five or 10 years older. Several young people have lamented to me that they should have been born a few years earlier. They think that if only they had [. . .] they would by now have bought the car and house, which instead they can only dream of. But they forget that the older group of graduates formed a much smaller share of their cohort. If they really had been born five or 10 years earlier, they might never have had the opportunity to go to the polytechnic or the university at all. I told them that; they were not consoled.

'In dollar terms, most fresh graduates today earn more than their counterparts five or 10 years ago, even adjusted for inflation. Unfortunately, prices of houses and cars have gone up even more, as a result of limited supply and strong demand. The government could double and quadruple the university and polytechnic intakes. But to double or quadruple the supply of land for housing or road space for cars is beyond our powers. We just don't know how to do that.'

But it is not just the younger generation's concern for the material things of life that is an issue. What if it also demands more freedom of thought, speech and action than a traditionally paternalistic government is willing to give, out of concern for Singapore's perceived vulnerabilities? The PAP believes it alone has the expertise and altruistic commitment to keep Singapore on the right track. It may well be right – as no-one else has had any opportunity to prove otherwise since Singapore became independent. And no-one has ever argued that PAP rule has not achieved a great deal. One could perhaps put up an argument, as Lee Kuan Yew has done on a number of occasions, that without the stern paternalistic hand on the tiller Singapore would not be here today as an economc role model for aspiring developing nations.

Paranoia – if one can use that word in a non-perjorative sense – is part of the Singapore psyche – and is reflected in the use of the Chinese word *Kiasu* ('afraid to lose'). Thus, at government level, there is a constant fretting about falling behind in the economic race; a constant fretting about what is considered to be the coroding influence of many Western ideas; and an incessant worry about losing political control. But although its popular vote has been steadily eroded, the PAP, at the time of writing, holds 77 of the 81 seats in parliament, and its influence stretches into every facet of Singaporean life. There would not appear, therefore, to be much to worry about.

But let us look at the case of the respected and highly experienced local journalist Catherine Lim who, in late 1994, wrote an article gently criticizing the government, and hinting that Prime Minister Goh Chok Tong was overshadowed by his predecessor Lee Kuan Yew. Earlier promises made by Mr Goh of a more open, consultative style of government had been abandoned, said Ms Lim, and the old 'authoritarian' style of Mr

Lee had returned. The reaction that Ms Lim's article provoked seemed to belie the PAP's position as one of the world's most enduring political machines.

'When my authority is being undermined by wrong observations, I have to correct them, or the view will prevail that I am indeed not in charge,' said Mr Goh. 'Singapore is not America,' said his press secretary in a lengthy letter to the *Straits Times*. 'It is small and fragile and needs a strong and fair government to survive. If its government is continually criticized, vilified and ridiculed in the media and pressured by lobbyists as in America, then the government will lose control. The result will not be more freedom, but confusion, conflict and decline.'

Faced with such arguments, Dr Chee Soon Juan, a member of the small opposition Singapore Democratic Party, says that while the PAP has done many good things, it is caught in a time-warp and is out of touch. 'People are tired of paternalism and elitism,' he says. And PAP veteran Tony Tan says the party risks 'political schlerosis', its thinking and policies in danger of becoming fossilized. 'If we are not alert to this danger we will wake up one day to find that we have been left behind by a younger electorat e whose aspirations and aims are different than those of the party,' he warned.[7]

Thus, there is the prospect of a different type of society emerging than the one which helped create the Singapore economic miracle, bringing with it the possibility of social tension.

CONCLUSION

For the foreign visitor, none of this seems evident on the surface in Singapore, today. Here is a country that really 'works'. The buses and trains run on time. The telephones always work. You can get business done quickly and well. The streets are spotless and are safe at nights. You can jet off to business appointments in surrounding countries for weeks on end knowing that the family is going to be safe and well on your return (the biggest tragedy likely to be that the maid has broken one of madam's best china dishes). Shopping is a joy (if a somewhat expensive one) and the plethora of indoor and outdoor restaurants offer a global menu for every taste and budget that should satisfy the most demanding gourmand.

Most businessmen living and working in Singapore, love it. As this book, hopefully, has demonstrated, it still makes a lot of sense to do business there. And any criticisms, for the moment, would have to be low on the Richter scale. Hopefully, they will remain so.

CHAPTER NOTES

1. Published December 1994.
2. *Directions*, January/February 1995.
3. 'The view from the cockpit,' by Kieran Cooke. *Financial Times* supplement on Singapore 24/2/95.
4. Interview in Singapore 16/1/95.
5. *Straits Times* 5/1/95.
6. *Straits Times* 14/2/95.
7. 'The fear of losing political control,' by Kieran Cooke, *Financial Times* 24/2/95.

Appendix A: KEY ORGANIZATIONS IN SINGAPORE

ECONOMIC DEVELOPMENT BOARD was set up in 1961 as the statutory board responsible for the planning and promotion of industrial development in the manufacturing and services sector. Besides dealing with enquiries and evaluating applications for tax and other incentives, the EDB through its one-stop service, assists investors to obtain land and factory space, long-term financing, skilled manpower and other services, and to locate suppliers, subcontractors and joint-venture partners. The EDB has various operational divisions dealing with a wide range of business sectors. It also has **Strategic Business Units (SBU)** which have been set up to undertake special projects which required enhanced focus and attention. Currently, these are biotechnology, international business development and China. EDB, 250 North Bridge Road, #24-00 Raffles City Tower, Singapore 0617. Tel: 65-336-2288. Fax: 339-6077. The EDB also has offices in the United States (Boston, Chicago, Los Angeles, New York, San Francisco and Washington DC), Europe (Frankfurt, London, Milan, Paris and Stockholm) and Asia-Pacific (Hong Kong, Jakarta, Osaka, Taipei and Tokyo).

INTERNAL REVENUE AUTHORITY OF SINGAPORE. Fullerton Building, Singapore 0104. Tel: 65-535-4244. Fax: 535-5393.

JURONG TOWN CORPORATION was established as a statutory board in 1968 and is responsible for the development and management of industrial estates, including the allocation of prepared industrial land sites with infrastructural facilities on lease terms of 30 years or more; construction and leasing of ready-made standard and flatted factory buildings; provision of port and bulk cargo handling facilities at the Jurong Industrial Port; provision of engineering and logistics back-up for the Asia-Pacific offshore oil industry at the Jurong Marine Base. JTC has under its direct management 30 industrial estates. It has drawn up several development programmes to promote new investments by high technology and skill-intensive industries. One of these is the **Singapore Science Park** located next to the National University of Singapore and designed to stimulate research, development and innovation in the manufacturing sector. JTC is also developing business parks to enhance Singapore's position as a total business centre and placing the emphasis on a high quality life and working environment. The first site, the **International Business Park**, is located near the Jurong East MRT Station and the first building was due to be ready for occupation in mid-

1995. Besides building up local business, JTC has also developed an external strategy to tap industrial develop ment opportunities in east Asia for Singaporean foreign companies. It has already entered into several industrial township and infrastructural projects in China, Indonesia and Thailand. Jurong Town Corporation, 301 Jurong Town Hall Road, Singapore 2260. Tel : 65-560-0056. Fax: 568-8646.

MONETARY AUTHORITY OF SINGAPORE, which operates as the central bank, has already been described in detail in Chapter Ten. MAS Building, 10 Shenton Way, Singapore 0207. Tel: 65-225-5577. Fax: 229-9491.

NATIONAL COMPUTER BOARD is the government agency responsible for promoting information technology in Singapore. It has an applied R & D arm known as the **Information Technology Institute**. NCB, 71 Science Park Drive, Singapore 0511. Tel: 65-778-2211. Fax: 778-9641.

NATIONAL PRODUCTIVITY BOARD was established in 1972 with a slogan of 'developing a world-class quality workforce with a rewarding worklife' in Singapore. In September 1981, its work was supplemented by the creation of the **National Productivity Council**. Quality is the theme for the 1990s. This is done at both national and company level. At national level, November is designated Productivity Month with specific campaign themes related to quality linked to in-house activities, including the developing of quality control circles. The NPB provides considerable assistance to companies through training and management consultancy programmes. NPB, 2 Bukit Merah Central, NPB Building, Singapore 0315. Tel: 65-278-6666. Fax: 278-6667.

SINGAPORE INSTITUTE OF STANDARDS AND INDUSTRIAL RESEARCH (SISIR) is the statutory board set up to lead local industries towards greater international competitiveness through quality and industrial technology. With about 500 employees, a high percentage of them qualified scientific personnel, the institute offers an integrated package of services covering contract R & D, design and development technological consultancy and training, testing, failure analysis, calibration and other technical services. Its other role is that of Singapore's national standards authority. Its main divisions cover Standards and Quality, Materials Technology, Products and Process Technology, Technology Transfer and Electronics and Computer

Applications. Local manufacturing companies can get help from the Materials technology Division, for example in the selection, evaluation of materials such as metals, plastics and chemicals. The Products and Process Technology Division provides basic infrastructural support in product and process development, promoting and disseminating technology in design and development, food technology and food biotechnology and electronics testing There is no doubt that SISIR is one of the most important organizations in Singapore's economic and i ndustrial development. SISIR, 1 Science Park Drive, Singapore Science Park, Singapore 0511. Tel: 65-778-7777. Fax: 778-0086/3798.

SKILLS DEVELOPMENT FUND was established in October 1979 with the primary objective of encouraging employers to train persons in employment and retrain retrenched workers. It does this by providing financial incentives to employers through a number of training grant schemes. These incentives are financed by collections from the Skills Development Levy imposed on employers with workers earning $750 or more a month, and currently standing at one per cent of the basic pay. There are a large number of industrial training schemes, some of them in collaboration with other statutory bodies but many involving a tie-up with local and multinational corporations such as Singapore Airlines, AT & T Motorola, Philips and Seiko. The SDF operates as part of the National Productivity Board (NPB), whose details are given above. A separate body is the **Institute of Technical Education (ITE),** which was established in April 1992 as a post-secondary educational establishment succeeding the former Vocational and Industrial Training Board. It provides training opportunities for school leavers and workers. For school leavers, full-time training and apprenticeship are offered at 11 technical institutes, while for workers, skills training and further education are offered under Continuing Education and Training programmes. ITE's mission is described as 'maximizing the human potential of Singaporeans to develop the quality of the workforce and enhance Singapore's global competitiveness'.

SINGAPORE TRADE DEVELOPMENT BOARD was established in 1983 with the twin mission of elevating Singapore's position in the international trading arena to a hub for all forms of international trading activities and promote Singapore's export of goods and services as well as develop new markets by organizing the participation of Singapore companies at international exhibitions and in trade missions. STDB provides assistance to both local and foreign companies to use Singapore as a base of operations for all types of trading activities, including third-country trade, entrepot trade, countertrade and regional warehousing and distribution. It has 28 offices in major cities around the world. It also disseminates a wide range of current trade investment and market information through an on-line computer system, newsletters, talks and seminars. Among these, the most important are Singapore Trade Connection CD-ROM, with several comprehensive databases including Singapore external trade statistics, and the regular Economic Survey of Singapore, with statistics on industrial production, retail sales, business expectations, and forecasts; an on-line retrieval service with link-up to international databases for current information on products, industries, markets, changes in trade regulations etc.; Trade and Investment Enquiry Service, providing information on general and technical trade, including import regulations of overseas markets, import licensing and control, import and export documentation and general investment; a Trade and Investment Guide Series, which are resource books on selected countries for entrepreneurs venturing overseas and a Market Information Series providing comprehensive reports on specific markets. STDB, 1 Maritime Square #10-40, World Trade Centre , Singapore 0409. Tel: 65-271-9388. Fax: 274-0770 or 278-2518.

TELECOMMUNICATIONS AUTHORITY OF SINGAPORE
regulates and implements the government's telecommunications policies. TAS, Comcentre #05-00, 31 Exeter Road, Singapore 0923. Tel: 65-738-7788. Fax: 733-0073.

URBAN REDEVELOPMENT AUTHORITY was set up to resettle
persons affected by public development projects, undertake land reclamation and provide infrastructure for future development, as well as manage and maintain state property. URA Building, 45 Maxwell Road, Singapore 0106 or P.O.Box 1393, Robinson Road, 0106. Tel: 65-221-6666. Fax: 224-8572.

Other useful addresses (Singapore):
Civil Aviation Authority of Singapore. Changi Airport, P.O. Box 1. Singapore 9181. Tel: 65-542-112?. Fax: 542-1231.
Customs and Excise Department. 1 Maritime Square, #03-01/#10-01 World Trade Centre. Singapore 0409. Tel: 65-272-8222. Fax: 277-9090.
Immigration Department, 95 South Bridge Road, 7/8th Stories, Pidemco Centre, Singapore 0105. Tel: 65-530-1801. Fax: 530-1840.

Ministry of Finance. Treasury Building, 8 Shenton Way, Singapore 0106. Tel: 65-225-9911. Fax: 320-9435.

Ministry of Labour. 18 Havelock Road, #07-01, Singapore 0105. Tel: 65-534-1511. Fax: 534-4840.

Ministry of Law. 250 North Bridge Road, #21-00 Raffles City Tower, Singapore 0617. Tel: 65-336-1177. Fax: 330-5887.

Ministry of National Development, 5 Maxwell Road, #21-00 and 22-00 Tower Block MND Complex, Singapore 0106. Tel: 65-222-1211. Fax: 322-6254.

Ministry of Trade and Industry. 8 Shenton Way, #48-01 Treasury Building, Singapore 0106. Tel: 65-225-9911. Fax: 320-9260.

Port of Singapore Authority. 460 Alexandra Road, PSA Building, Singapore 0511. Tel: 65-274-7111. Fax: 279-5711.

Public Utilities Board, which handles gas, water and electricity supplies to domestic and industrial users. 111 Somerset Road, #16-05 PUB Building, Singapore 0923. Tel: 65-235-8888. Fax: 731-3020.

Singapore Chinese Chamber of Commerce and Industry. #03-01 Chinese Chamber of Commerce Building, 47 Hill Street, Singapore 0617. Tel: 65-337-8381. Fax: 339-0605.

Singapore Indian Chamber of Commerce. #32-01/04 Tong Eng Building, 101 Cecil Street, Singapore 0106. Tel: 65-222-2855. Fax: 223-1707.

Singapore Institute of Management, SIM Management House, 41 Namly Road, Singapore 1026. Tel: 65-468-8866. Fax: 468-0779.

Singapore Manufacturers Association, SMA House, 20 Orchard Road, Singapore 0923. Tel: 338-8787. Fax: 338-3358/336-5385.

Singapore Tourist Promotion Board. 250 North Bridge Road, #36-04 Raffles City Tower, Singapore 0617. Tel: 65-339-6622. Fax: 339-9423.

Registry of Companies and Business. 10 Anson Road, #05-01/15 International Plaza, Singapore 0207. Tel: 65-227-8551. Fax: 225-1676.

Registry of Trade Marks and Patents. 51 Bras Basah Road, Plaza by the Park, Singapore 0718. Tel: 65-330-2700. Fax: 339-0252.

Other useful addresses (Foreign):

American Chamber of Commerce, #16-7 Shaw Centre, 1 Scotts Road, Singapore 0922. Tel: 65-235-0077. Fax: 732-5917.

British Business Association, 41 Duxton Road, Sinjgapore 0928. Tel: 65-227-7861. Fax: 227-7021.

Japanese Chamber of Commerce and Industry. #12-04 MAS Building, 10 Shenton Way, Singapore 0207. Tel: 65-221-0541. FaxL: 225-6197.

New Zealand Business Association, #15-02 Ngee Ann City, 319A Orchard Road, Singapore 0923. Tel: 65-738-7453. Fax: 732-5595.

Singapore-Australian Business Council, #11-02A Golden Mile Tower, 6001 Beach Road, Singapore 0719. Tel: 65-298-6117. Fax: 293-3780. *Singapore International Chamber of Commerce.* 6 Raffles Quay, #10-01 John Nancock Tower, Singapore 0104. Tel: 65-224-1255. Fax: 224-2785.

Appendix B: KEY PROVISIONS OF RECENT BUDGETS

1995

Contrary to the hopes of the business community, Finance Minister Richard Hu provided little of substance, especially in not succumbing to widespread demands to cut the corporate tax rate by at least one per cent. For fund managers, there were two main provisions: a five per cent concessionary tax rate for incremental profits from high value-added financial activities involving companies handling at least $5 billion worth of business annually, and no tax on distributions to non-resident unit-trust holders. In the area of stock trading, stamp duty on all transactions was cut from 0.1 to 0.05 per cent, with the duty waived on loan agreements for SES listed stocks. For individual Singaporeans, the government returned $1 billion from its $7 billion 1994 budget surplus in various forms, including a one-off 10 per cent rebate on personal income tax, and a $500 pay-in for everyone's CPF accounts.

Dr Hu explained his cautious approach by saying that the Singapore economy was entering the third year of very strong growth, but care was needed to avoid over-heating. He reiterated his goal to bring the corporate tax rate down to 25 per cent, but added: 'There is no need to lower the rate again this year to further stimulate an already vibrant economy so soon after the three per cent cut in 1994.' Instead, he chose to 'fine tune' the tax system by offering specifically targeted incentives aimed primarily at fund managers performing high-value activities and at companies venturing abroad. For instance, for firms who feel it necessary to form consortiums or holding companies in order to venture overseas, he removed the constraints on onward payment of tax-exempt dividends out of foreign income.

1994

The 1994 Singapore budget was an important one because a Goods and Service Tax (GST) of three per cent came into effect on 1 April 1994. Several incentives and rebates for individuals and households were introduced (business incentives had been introduced in the 1993 budget – see below).

There was no change in the corporate tax rate which remained at 27% – having reduced it from 30 per cent in 1993 – although the government has pledged a reduction to 25% in the 'medium term'. By comparison, Malaysia's rate is 30%, while Indonesia's is 35% .

An idea of a 'consumption tax' – out of which the GST emerged – was first raised by the 1986 Economic Committee Report which recommended that the government should switch from direct to indirect taxes as its main source of income. While acknowledging it was hard to administer a consumption tax, the committee argued that it would allow the government to lower personal and corporate income tax which would make the economy more competitive. But the timing was not right. In the second half of the decade, the government had to introduce a number of measures to help the economy out of recession and it was considered unwise to introduce a new tax at that time. But, with the economy back on track in the early 1990s, the government began consulting the public concerning the shape of the proposed GST.

As a result, from 1 April 1994, all goods and services supplied by GST-registered businesses include a three per cent GST. With overall prices rising slightly, however, the government took steps to ensure that consumers were not disadvantaged, including reductions in income tax and other rebates and concessions to help with the adjustment. The measures removed an estimated three-quarters of potential income-tax payers from the grasp of the Inland Revenue Authority of Singapore, while the remainder paid less than before – resulting in an estimated net loss in government revenue for the first year of operation of about S$240 million. With effect from 1 April 1994, motor vehicle import duties and the duty on petrol and diesel fuel were also reduced to offset GST, while restaurant and hotel 'cess' charges were cut from four to one per cent and the five per cent charge on telephone calls was dropped.

The government emphasized the fact that the Singapore GST was the lowest in the world – compared to, say, Britain (17.5%) and Germany (15%) – and pledged to hold the rate at three per cent for five years.

1993

In the 1993 budget, the government announced several initiatives to help Singaporean companies venture abroad as well as attract offshore activities to Singapore.

From 1986, a unilateral tax credit was given for specific services income repatriated from some countries without a tax treaty with Singapore. From fiscal 1994, the scheme was extended to services including management consultancy and financial advice. The territories covered were extended to Fiji, Kampuchea, Laos, Myanmar (Burma) and Vietnam. The existing double tax deduction scheme for promoting the export of goods was expanded to cover the export of services, and the list of qualifying activities was extended to include feasibility studies, product certification and packaging for export. Double deduction was also allowed for approved expenses incurred in exploring and developing overseas investment opportunities.

From fiscal 1994, a 10 per cent concessionary tax rate is on offer for approved art and antique dealers on income gained from transactions on behalf of non-residents with approved auction houses. The concession intially is for five years with the prospect of further extension. Well-established auction houses which conduct substantial activities in Singapore as well as private museum operators can qualify for a tax exemption on their income under the pioneer services incentive. The initial exemption is for five years, with a similar extension possible.

The income of SIMEX (the Singapore futures market) has been exempted from tax since it was established in 1984. This tax holiday was extended for a further five years in 1993 to allow the exchange to sustain its rapid growth and maintain investor confidence by strengthening its capital base.

The income of approved warehousing or servicing companies was given a similar relief in 1993, with the exemption being for five years maximum on each occasion. This continues an incentive first offered in 1978. In 1983, meanwhile, a tax exemption scheme was introduced to promote the development of loan syndication activities covering income from approved offshore credit and underwriting activities. When the tax holiday expired in 1993, however, the government approved a further five-year extension in line with Singapore's desires to be the leading syndication centre in Asia.

Appendix C: SINGAPORE TAX REGULATIONS

Corporate income tax is imposed on a territorial basis, taxing all income which arises in Singapore and offshore income which is remitted there. Tax could thus be minimized for offshore income by not remitting there.

Companies pay a single base rate of income tax on their annual profits. These are determined from the annual audited financial statements adjusted to take account of the tax laws. There are no extra taxes and no capital gains tax. However, the Inland Revenue is likely to investigate transactions producing large gains in an attempt to attribute income characteristics which can then be taxed. Care is needed, therefore, in categorizing capital gains.

Companies can pay dividends out of their taxed profits to shareholders without additional withholding tax, subject to the availability of accounting reserves.

Taxable income is arrived at after allowable business deductions, the main ones being:

(i)Expenditure wholly and exclusively incurred in the production of the income being assessed.

(ii)Capital allowances (tax depreciation) for assets owned and used for the purpose of producing income.

(iii)Tax losses and unabsorbed capital allowances from prior periods.

(iv)Interest on money borrowed and employed in producing income provided that, where the interest is paid to a non-resident, withholding tax has been deducted and accounted for to the Inland Revenue Authority.

(v)Royalties if they are wholly and exclusively incurred in producing the income being assessed. Royalties paid to non-residents may be deemed to be sourced in Singapore and subject to withholding tax at 27 per cent.

(vi)Provisions for doubtful debts provided they are reasonably expected to be bad and the debt has previously been included as revenue of the company.

However, some expenses incurred in the production of income cannot be deducted, the major ones being:

(i)Commercial depreciation charged on fixed assets.

(ii)Capital expenditure, even if treated as revenue expenditure for accounting purposes. Capital allowances may nonetheless be available on such expenditure.

273

(iii)Income taxes paid or payable in Singapore or overseas.

(iv)Payments to provident funds or societies which are not approved by the Minister of Finance. Generally, only Singapore provident funds are approved by the Minister. Consequently, contributions to foreign company pension schemes or to foreign national security schemes are not allowable.

(v)Expenses incurred on certain catagories of private motor vehicles.

Investment income which arises in Singapore is fully taxable there with the notable exception of interest on deposits with the Post office Savings Bank. Interest arising on deposits with an approved bank in Singapore is also exempt from tax where it is received by a non resident individual or a company which does not have business connections with the country. Investment income arising offshore is not taxable unless received in Singapore. Tax residents are charged at the same graduated rates as employment in come (see below). Companies and non-resident individuals are are taxed at the basic rate.

Personal Income Tax

Employments based in Singapore are considered to produce Singapore sourced income, the whole of which will be tuxable in Singapore regardless of where it is paid. The one exception is for area representative status, where an employee travels widely throughout the region and whose pay is not charged to a Singapore business. Such individuals only pay tax on a pro-rated basis for the time spent in the republic.

The personal rates begin at 2.5 per cent for an annual chargeable income of $5,000 up to a top rate for $400,000. There is no P.A.Y.E. and as tax can mount up fairly quickly, individuals are recommended to organize an efficient system for setting aside money to meet the bill.

Income tax is imposed on virtually all cash rumuneration and benefits including educational allowances and per diem expenses. The only major exception is accommodation provided by the employer, the taxable benefit of which is deemed to be one-tenth of the other remuneration. The actual cost of the accommodation, if less, is disregarded.

An individual can claim personal reliefs and reduced rates of tax. Compulsory contributions to the Central Provident Fund are fully deductible, and life insurance and other provident schemes can bring relief up to a maximum of $5000.The other main reliefs are a personal one of $3,000, plus $1,500 for an unemployed spouse, and $1,500 each for up to three school-age children, and $300 each for the fourth and fifth child, delivery and hospitalization expenses up to a maximum of $3,000 and up to $2,000 towards any approved educational fees.

[Information drawn from guides published by the British Business Association and the Singapore International Chamber of Commerce].

INVESTMENT COMMITMENTS 1994

Industry Group	FAI S$m	% of total
Aerospace and defence	195.4	3.4
Chemicals	2,728.8	47.3
Electronic components	1,131.7	19.6
Electronic systems	425.5	7.4
Engineering systems	398.4	6.9
Light industries	305.7	5.3
Manufacturing systems	579.4	10.1
Total	5,764.7	100

SOURCE: Economic Development Board

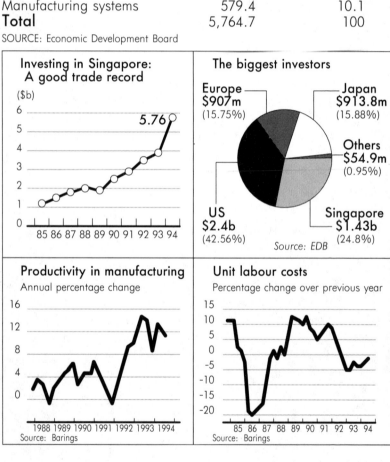

Investing in Singapore: A good trade record

($b)

5.76

85 86 87 88 89 90 91 92 93 94

The biggest investors

Europe $907m (15.75%)

Japan $913.8m (15.88%)

Others $54.9m (0.95%)

US $2.4b (42.56%)

Singapore $1.43b (24.8%)

Source: EDB

Productivity in manufacturing
Annual percentage change

1988 1989 1990 1991 1992 1993 1994
Source: Barings

Unit labour costs
Percentage change over previous year

85 86 87 88 89 90 91 92 93 94
Source: Barings

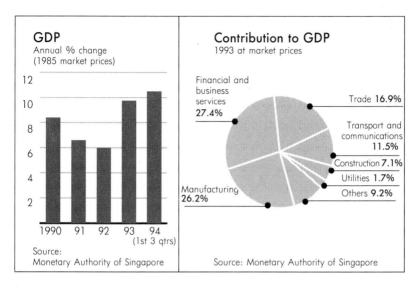

GDP
Annual % change
(1985 market prices)

Source:
Monetary Authority of Singapore

Contribution to GDP
1993 at market prices

Financial and business services **27.4%**

Trade **16.9%**

Transport and communications **11.5%**

Construction **7.1%**

Utilities **1.7%**

Others **9.2%**

Manufacturing **26.2%**

Source: Monetary Authority of Singapore

BIBLIOGRAPHY

Books

American Association of Singapore. *Living in Singapore: An Expatriate's Guide.* 1993.

Arthur Andersen & Co., Singapore. *The Growth Triangle – A Guide to Business.* 1991.

Arthur Andersen HRM (Tax Services) Sdn Bhd., Kuala Lumpur. '95 Malaysian Budget.1994.

Chan, K.B. and Chiang, S.N., Centre for Advanced Studies, National University of Singapore. *Stepping Out. The Making Of Chinese Entrepreneurs.* New York, Prentice Hall. 1994.

Chiang, M. *Singapore Island City State.* Times Editions, 1990.

Chong, A. *Singapore's New Premier Goh Chok Tong.* Palenduk Publications (M) Sdn. Bhd., Malaysia. 1991.

Coopers and Lybrand Foreign nationals working in Singapore: Tax and other matters. Global Tax Services to Executives Abroad Series.1994.

Devan-Nair, C.V. (ed). *Towards Tomorrow. Essays on the Development and Social Transformation in Singapore.* NTUC Singapore, 1973.

Economic Development Board. Growing With Enterprise, A National Effort. 1993.

Economic Development Board Yearbook 1994.

Ernst & Young, Singapore. Doing Business in Singapore. 1991.

Ernst & Young, Singapore. Doing Business in Riau. 1992

Ernst & Young, Singapore. Financial Institutions in Singapore. 1994.

Ernst & Young, Singapore. Taxation of Companies in Singapore.1994.

Ernst & Young, Singapore. Taxation of Individuals in Singapore. 1994.

Evans, A.(ed.). *Business Singapore. An A to Z Guide.* British Business Association of Singapore, 1995.

Goh, M and others. *Strategic Business Opportunities in the Growth Triangle.* Longman, Singapore, 1992.

Institute of Southeast Asian Studies, Singapore. *Growth Triangle: The Johor-Singapore-Riau Experience.* 1991.

Kassim Chan Tax Services Sdn. Bhd./Deloittte Touche Tohmatsu Tax Services Sdn. Bhd.Kuala Lumpur. Guide To Doing Business In Malaysia. SNP Publishers Pte Ltd. 1993.

Lee, T.S. Overseas Investment: Experience of Singapore Manufacturing Companies. Institute of Policy Studies/McGraw-Hill Book Co. 1993.

Lim, Y.C. and Pang, E.F. *Foreign Direct Investment and Industrialization in Malaysia, Singapore, Taiwan and Thailand.* Development Centre of the OECD. 1991.

Lim, L and Pang, E.F. Trade, *Employment and Industrialization in Singapore.* International Labour Organization, 1986. Printworld Services Pte Ltd., Singapore. 1987.

Lim, C.Y. and others, National University of Singapore. *Policy Options for the Singapore Economy.* McGraw-Hill Book Co. 1988.

Ministry of Finance. Final Report of the Committee To Promote Enterprise Overseas. Singapore National Printers Pte Ltd. 1993.

Ministry of Trade and Industry (Economic Planning Committee). The Strategic Economic Plan: Towards A Developed Nation. Singapore National Printers Pte Ltd. 1991.

Natarajan, S. and Tan, J.M. *The Impact of MNC Investments in Malaysia, Singapore & Thailand.* Institute of Southeast Asian Studies, Singapore, 1992.

National Computer Board, Singapore. A Vision Of An Intelligent Island: The IT2000 Report. 1992.

Price Waterhouse World Firm Ltd. Doing Business in Singapore.1992. Supplement to this edition 1993.

Quah, S.T. (ed.). *In Search of Singapore's National Values.* The Insitute of Policy Studies and Times Academic Press, Singapore, 1990.

R. Ian Lloyd Productions. Singapore. 1994.

Registry of Companies and Business. A Good Start: RCB's guide to setting up business in Singapore. Singapore National Printers Pte Ltd. 1993.

Singapore International Chamber of Commerce. *The Investor's Guide to Singapore.* 1994 Edition.

Singapore International Chamber of Commerce. *Expatriate Living Costs in Singapore.* 1994/5 Edition.

Tan, C.H. *Strategic Policies and Business in Singapore: A Manager's Reference.* McGraw-Hill Book Co., 1995.

Trade Development Board/Arthur Andersen & Co.Trade & Investment Guide: Indonesia. 1993

U.S.Foreign and Commercial Service, U.S. Embassy, Singapore. *Doing Business in Singapore: 1994 Guide for US Exporters.*

Woon, G.K. *Fengshui: the Geomancy and Economy of Singapore.* Shinglee Publishers Pte Ltd., Singapore, 1991.

Other sources:

ASEAN Handbook 1992/3. ASEAN Chambers of Commerce & Industry, 1993

Borneo Review, Journal of the Institute for Development Studies (Sabah).

Business Times.

Directions, The Business Magazine, Singapore.

Economic Bulletin published by the Singapore International Chamber of Commerce.

Far East Economic Review Yearbook 1995.

Financial Times, London.

Singapore Investment News, published by the Economic Development Board.

Singapore Enterprise, jointly published by the EDB and seven other government organisations.

Singapore Oil Report.

Straits Times.

SINGAPORE AT A GLANCE

- SPACE – 641.4 sq km
  Built-up – 316.5 sq km
  Non-built-up – about 300 sq km
- PEOPLE – 2.87 million
  Workforce – 1.6 million
  Tertiary educated – 95,000
  Primary 6 or lower – 850,000
  Foreign workers – 300,000
- ECONOMY – $90.2 billion
  Gross National Product
  Manufacturing – 27.5 per cent
  Financial and business services – 28.8 per cent
  Commerce – 17.8 per cent
  Transport and Communications – 12.1 per cent
  Construction – 7.4 per cent
- EXPORTS – $119 billion
  To USA – 20.3 per cent
  To Malaysia – 14.2 per cent
  To Hongkong – 8.6 per cent
  Main exports:
  Machinery and equipment, mineral fuels,
  manufactured goods, chemicals
- INVESTMENTS – $28.16 billion invested abroad
  In Malaysia – $4.7 billion (22 per cent)
  In Hongkong/China – $4 billion (19 per cent)
  In USA – $1.8 billion
  In New Zealand – $1.5 billion
  In Indonesia – $0.5 billion.
- RESERVES – $69.6 billion
  Per person – $24,252.

Sources: Economist Intelligence Unit 1994; Department of Statistics 1994

INDEX